SEEING CLEARLY

GUIDES TO THE GOOD LIFE

Stephen Grimm, series editor

Seeing Clearly: A Buddhist Guide to Life
Nicolas Bommarito

SEEING CLEARLY

A Buddhist Guide to Life

Nicolas Bommarito

OXFORD
UNIVERSITY PRESS

OXFORD

UNIVERSITY PRESS

Oxford University Press is a department of the University of Oxford. It furthers
the University's objective of excellence in research, scholarship, and education
by publishing worldwide. Oxford is a registered trade mark of Oxford University
Press in the UK and certain other countries.

Published in the United States of America by Oxford University Press
198 Madison Avenue, New York, NY 10016, United States of America.

Library of Congress Cataloging-in-Publication Data
Names: Bommarito, Nicolas, author.
Title: Seeing clearly : a Buddhist guide to life / Nicolas Bommarito.
Description: New York : Oxford University Press, 2020. |
Includes bibliographical references.
Identifiers: LCCN 2019044760 (print) | LCCN 2019044761 (ebook) |
ISBN 9780190887506 (hardback) | ISBN 9780190887520 (epub) |
ISBN 9780190092559 (online)
Subjects: LCSH: Buddhist philosophy.
Classification: LCC B162 .B66 2020 (print) | LCC B162 (ebook) |
DDC 294.3/444—dc23
LC record available at https://lccn.loc.gov/2019044760
LC ebook record available at https://lccn.loc.gov/2019044761

9 8 7 6 5 4 3 2

Printed by Integrated Books International, United States of America

For my parents

CONTENTS

Contents 12

SERIES EDITOR FOREWORD

Several ancient philosophers held that the point of studying ethics was not just to learn about ethics—as one might learn about chemistry, astronomy, or history—but to become a better human being. They also recognized that this was not easy to do. In order for thinking about ethics to make a difference in our lives, they argued that our habits and inclinations needed to be educated right alongside our minds. They therefore claimed that what mattered to living well was not just what we thought but *how* we thought, and not just how we thought but how we emotionally responded to the world and to other people.

The books in this series highlight some of the transformative ideas that philosophers have had about these topics—about the good life, and the practices and ways of life that help us to pursue it. They tell us what various philosophers and traditions have taken to be most important in life, and what they have taken to be less important. They offer philosophical guidance about how to approach broad questions, such as how to structure our days, how to train our attention, and how to die with dignity. They also offer guidance about how to deal with the sort of everyday questions that are often neglected by scholars, but that make of the texture of our lives, such as how to deal with relationships gone wrong, family disruptions, unexpected success, persistent anxiety, and an environment at risk.

Because the books are written by philosophers, they draw attention to the reasons and arguments that underlie these various claims—the particular visions of the world and of human nature that are at the root of these stances. The claims made in these books can therefore be contested, argued with, and found to be more or less plausible. While some answers will clearly compete with one another, other views will likely appear complementary. Thus a Confucian might well find that a particular practice or insight of say, Nietzsche's, helps to shed light on his or her way of living in the world, and vice versa. On the whole, the idea is that these great philosophers and traditions all have something to teach us about how to be more fully human, and more fully happy.

Above all, the series is dedicated to the idea that philosophy can be more than just an academic discipline—that is it can be, as it was for hundreds of years in the ancient world, a way of life. The hope is also that philosophy can enhance the ways of life we already feel pulled towards, and help us to engage with them more authentically and fully.

Stephen R. Grimm
Professor of Philosophy
Fordham University
September 2019

PREFACE

Buddhism is about you, your life, and how to get through it. It's about the problems you face and where they come from. It's about taking a long, hard look at the world and finding that it's *very* different from how it first seemed. The fundamental source of these problems, Buddhists say, is that the world is very different from how our ordinary experiences make it seem. You fix it by changing your outlook so it better matches the way things really are.

That's all pretty lofty. This book will discuss some pretty lofty ideas, but it will do so because they're important for understanding the practical guidance Buddhism offers about how to live a better life. In presenting these ideas, my aim isn't to sell you on a particular form of Buddhism or to convert you into a Buddhist. The important thing is for you to think over these ideas for yourself. If it makes sense, then accept it. If it doesn't, at least you'll have thought about new ideas about how to live and understand why you don't think they're right.

I'm also not here to hold up a particular flavor of Buddhism as "real" or "authentic." Cards on the table, I'm deeply skeptical of such judgments. I'm not promoting a particular teacher, sect, or community. Buddhism means very different things to different people around the world. It's more accurate to think of various

Buddhisms, different people in different times and places, who, despite a shared outlook, would still have plenty to disagree about.

Some of these agendas run deep and are impossible to avoid—for example, Buddhist texts often contain fantastical and supernatural aspects. Some Buddhists take these at face value. Others reinterpret or de-emphasize them. Personally, I'm not a fan of the supernatural and favor other ways of understanding such strands. At the same time, my aim here is to present a window into Buddhism *as a whole*, not merely a secularized, modernized, and sanitized version of it.

I want you to better understand Buddhism, to understand what sorts of things Buddhists do, what they think, and most importantly, *why*. Understanding here doesn't just mean knowing facts. It's okay to be curious about Buddhism because it's strange and different from what you're used to. But understanding it means that, eventually, it won't seem as strange anymore. So when you have contact with Buddhist ideas or practices, even if you don't accept them yourself, you can think, "Yeah, that's something a normal person would do. I get why they're doing that."

You can think of this book as a zoomed-out map of the Buddhist world and what it has to offer. It's a *big* world, so it'll cover a lot of territory. This means the landmarks in some neighborhoods won't appear and there won't be as much detail as on more localized maps. But, especially if you've never been there or if you've only visited a small part of it, it will get you familiar with the lay of the land and help you to find neighborhoods that you'll feel more at home in, or at least that you'd like to visit.

In introducing you to this world, I'll be speaking with two voices: I'll be both your guide and a fellow traveler. I will point out important landmarks, even the ones I'm not personally fond of. I'll also explain how I've made sense of this world, my way of navigating it, and how I've made it meaningful.

In doing so, I speak as a philosophy professor who has spent much of his life studying Buddhist thought and practice in many places around the world. I'm not a lama, guru, roshi, or any other formal Buddhist master. My interpretation of Buddhism is one that I think makes sense, but it does not have the authority of any particular Buddhist institution. Everyone who writes about Buddhism presents their own take on it, and I'm no different. My take aims to be one that is not only philosophically and historically informed, but also beneficial for your life.

Buddhism in the West has a long history of people, often educated white guys like me, projecting all their hopes and dreams into it. This typically ends with some combination of disappointment, anger, denial, and cynicism. Some people feel that there simply *must* be completely pure and good versions of all their hopes and dreams *somewhere* in the world. And since the people and institutions in their neighborhood don't seem to fit the bill, their dreams must live in Japan or Tibet.

Buddhism is something that's been immensely beneficial and meaningful to people all over the world for thousands of years. It has been personally very important to me and my life. When someone is important to us, there's a temptation to overlook flaws ("Well, that's not who they *really* are!") and feel hostile to criticism ("How dare you say that about him!"). But people and institutions everywhere have the flaws that people and institutions always have. Just as idealizing a person is an unhealthy and unsustainable attitude, so is doing it for a culture or tradition. This isn't to say that there's nothing wonderful or true or insightful in Buddhism, but you need to be careful of projecting what you're looking for as it can obscure the reality and variety of what's actually there.

What's there is a rich and interesting vision of what the world is like—the philosophy—and a wide range of tools and techniques to better navigate it—the practices. These aren't separate worlds but work together to help you better navigate and understand your life.

ACKNOWLEDGMENTS

Thanks to my family: Charles, Laura, and John Bommarito—You've always been there for me, and the time spent writing this book has been no different. Thanks also to all my friends who encouraged me throughout the writing process, especially Nomy Arpaly, Lowell Cook, Thomas Doctor, Itsuki Hayashi, Bhaskar Neog, R. Rajendran, Jakob Reckenrich, Hagop Sarkissian, and Minako Takeuchi.

My editors deserve special thanks: Hannah Doyle, you worked so hard to make everything happen smoothly. Stephen Grimm, you believed in the idea of the book from the very start and, more than that, believed in me. Lucy Randall, you did so much of the hard and tedious work of shaping it that I can't imagine having done it without you.

I was very lucky to have many people give me thoughtful comments on earlier drafts of the book: Myisha Cherry, Shina Chua, David DiValerio, Owen Flanagan, Jay Garfield, Bhavya Sharma, and Louise Williams all helped to make this book far better than it otherwise would have been.

I also need to thank those who not only gave me insightful comments but also encouragement that got me through the rough and discouraging parts of writing a book: Laura Bommarito, Kerry Lucinda Brown, Jonardon Ganeri, Russell Guilbault, Mike Kicey, Tanya Kostochka, Emily McRae, and Pierce Salguero all helped me both to improve the book greatly and to actually write it. Your support means a lot to me.

In this respect two people deserve special gratitude. Both talked me through endless doubts, questions, frustrations, and details from start to finish. Michael Connolly, you always gave me some much needed perspective on things. I'm lucky to have you as a friend. Alex King, you were in the trenches with me as I wrote the book because you're *always* in the trenches with me. You're an amazing partner in philosophy and in life.

Part I

Philosophy

Philosophy

| THE PROBLEM

You wake up every morning and you have to deal with what comes next. You interact with other people; some are great and others are complete assholes. Most can be both, depending on the day. You try to do things, big and small; sometimes it works out and sometimes it doesn't. Mostly it's mundane. Brush your teeth, catch up with an old friend, wait in line—regular stuff.

Some people happen to be lucky and, at their particular time and place, they have only the regular stuff, and dealing with it is easy. We should all be so lucky, but such luck doesn't often last. We start to lose things: our health, our status, our loved ones. Gradually or suddenly, these things vanish in the end, and when they do, no book anywhere can adequately describe the pain. It's usually such a loss that prompts reflection on this part of life. We only notice it when we lose a job or a friend, but it's the precarious situation we're in all of the time.

This is true in the good times too, but it's easier to ignore. You achieve a goal or have some good luck. But there's still a slight buzz just underneath the sound of celebration—a kind of anxiety that the success, whatever it is, is fleeting. You now have to protect against losing what you've won. People will expect you to replicate or even better it. For some achievements, you feel a target on your back—people now have the goal of taking you down, of bettering you. Though it's not always apparent, each success brings with it new problems and new goals that pop up like weeds.

This isn't to say life is all bad, but even for the happiest of us, life always has these troubling aspects. One way of dealing with this fact is to ignore it. Leave the funeral thoughts for funerals. This is what most of us do most of the time. And it works too, except when it doesn't. But facing these facts doesn't have to lead to pessimism or despair. The person you love most in the world will die someday. This is a painful thought, but there are benefits to facing it rather than ignoring or denying it. Internalizing this fact can make you value each moment you spend with them, even the mundane moments spent waiting in line or having lunch. It can help you to enjoy the time you have together in full knowledge of how things are, without that faint buzz ringing in your ears.

Buddhism is about taking a long, hard look at the way things are. When we do this, some of what we find is harsh: People get sick. People die. People cheat, steal, and lie. We look out for our own. Things that we put together will, eventually, come apart. Rather than pretending things aren't that way or wishing and hoping that somehow things might be different, Buddhism offers a way to live at ease in full view of such facts. The world is the way it is, and we'd be better off examining it closely and living accordingly.

The basic insight of Buddhism is that the source of this fundamental problem is a mismatch between our most basic feeling about the world and how it really is. The painful experiences, the faint buzz of anxiety, they happen because our outlook on life has certain assumptions built into it that are out of step with reality. Think of someone who is paranoid and thinks everyone else is out to get him. This outlook leads him to misconstrue kind words as threats and prevents him from becoming close to anyone. His outlook doesn't match up with reality, and so it causes a lot of anxiety and isolation. According to Buddhists, we're in a similar position except that the flaw in our outlook runs much deeper. Rather than making a mistake about other people and their motives, we make a mistake about the fundamental nature of ourselves and the world, a mistake that infects our entire outlook on life.

Buddhism is a method for dealing with what happens day in and day out. It's a strategy for dealing with the stuff that we're confronted with in life, both dramatic and ordinary. This isn't just a matter of changing what you *think* or *believe*, but also how you perceive, feel, and experience life. On the ground, how we respond to people and situations is not simply a matter of what we think (or what we *think* that we think). Our responses are a result of a more fundamental outlook we have on life that involves our deepest feelings about the world and how it works.

This is also true of the more ordinary outlooks people have. Lawyers don't just *know* a lot about what the laws are and how the courts work, but also experience things in legal terms. When the rest of us just see a set of icy stairs, they see a potential lawsuit. What will seem to many like just harsh words, they hear as slander or libel. Or think about someone you know who is optimistic. An optimistic person doesn't just believe that good things will happen but also perceives people and situations in a certain way. They *see* the glass as half full; they have fond *feelings* for a stranger they just met. Having an outlook means you carve up life in certain ways and relate to the world on certain terms.

You might think to yourself, why bother having an outlook at all? Seems like a hassle. But you already have one, whether you know it or not. Someone who thinks reflecting on life is a waste of time *has* an outlook on life, one that says not to reflect on things. We all have ways of responding to what life confronts us with. Saying, "I don't like whining about anxiety. I just put my head down and power through," *is* a way of responding to life and its problems. Given that you have one anyway, it's worth spending some time considering alternatives and trying to pick a good one.

Since the source of the problem is that our way of experiencing things is misaligned with the world, it is important to think and examine both our outlook and the world very carefully. Doctors have to closely examine a patient's body and some pretty disgusting symptoms to figure out what disease someone has, what caused it, and how to treat it. In the same way, we have to look closely at the world and some ugly features of it to figure out the source of the problem and how to solve it. In both cases, this involves a lot of trial and error, but luckily we don't have to start from scratch. Just as doctors today build on years of medical research and attempts to cure different ailments, Buddhists can draw on thousands of years of philosophy, psychology, and practical experience to help solve the problem.

2 | THE SOLUTION

The fundamental problem, our deep anxiety and insecurity, comes from a mismatch. The way we relate to the world is fundamentally misaligned with how it really is. Realigning our way of relating to the world is no simple task. It has two complementary aspects: philosophy and practice. As we'll see, this distinction isn't so clear-cut, but for now it's helpful to think of these two general strands in Buddhism.

Philosophy involves understanding the nature of the world and our minds. It involves careful examination, reasoning, and analysis of the world in general and ourselves in particular. It's the intellectual task of figuring out what there is, what it's like, and what to do about it.

Practice involves specific techniques to bring about a change in how we respond to the world. It aims at changing our mental habits and ways of experiencing life. Suppose you learned with complete certainty exactly how the world is, a flash of insight into the nature of all things. Following this revelation, you'd still be faced with the very difficult task of changing your old beliefs, feelings, and habits. Old habits die hard, and it's often not enough to simply *know* how the world is. Buddhist practice involves specific techniques, concrete steps you can take that, over time, will help you to change not just your intellectual beliefs, but your entire outlook on life.

These two aspects can, and often are, discussed separately. This is no surprise given how monumental each task is; people sometimes devote their entire lives to only *one* philosophical question or Buddhist practice. Many people take up Buddhist practices without having thought much at all about the philosophical underpinnings. Others study Buddhist philosophy in detail without ever doing any Buddhist practices.

Nevertheless, these two aspects do inform each other. Philosophy helps to establish the aim of practice. Changing your responses to match how reality is means figuring out the nature of reality and your mental habits. Practice, on the other hand, can help you to have certain experiences which can, in turn, inform your ideas about how the world works. There are some things that only a skilled person can see. When a skilled mechanic looks at an engine or a skilled computer programmer looks at source code, they are able to see how things work precisely because they have practiced their craft for a long time. In the same way, Buddhist practices can help you to see things about the world that you couldn't before.

Suppose you decided that you want to live a healthier lifestyle. That would require knowing some facts, particularly facts about food and the human body. You'd also need to know what to do in light of those facts—what sorts of activities to do and how often, what kinds of foods to eat and how much. But knowing these facts is not enough. Just reading health journals and physiology textbooks won't make you a healthy person. You also have to change your habitual ways of living. You have to actually eat the salads and get off the couch.

The more serious problem that Buddhism aims to solve is a bit like this. Solving it requires knowing some facts, fundamental facts about how the world is and how our minds work. This is the role of philosophy—to uncover how the world really is. But as with getting healthy, this isn't enough to eliminate the underlying problem. You have to take steps that change your usual way of relating to the world. This is the role of Buddhist practice. This is why Buddhist teachings, both philosophical and practical, are often likened to a lamp—they're supposed to illuminate things you couldn't see before and so help you to navigate the world better.

Unlike getting healthy, your current habits and ways of relating to the world that have to be reoriented are much deeper and more fundamental than changing how often you run or how many carbohydrates you eat each day. This realignment involves a more radical change in how you feel about yourself and your place in the world. Something like this happens when people have a crisis of identity. Some people who for years thought of themselves as a doctor or a punk or a loner come to realize that they can't stand seeing patients or hearing noisy rock bands or staying home on Friday nights. Sometimes this comes after years of unhappiness, or at least not feeling quite right. A mistaken feeling about who you are can cause a lot of misery and can take years to finally come around to. The kind of misconception Buddhism aims to fix is like this, except the mistake is not that you've had the wrong identity but that you have an identity at all.

The solution is radical in that it does not primarily aim to fix things *within* our misconceptions about reality but to attack such misconceptions at their source. Think of someone having a night-mare. Things and events in an awful dream aren't real, but they are still incredibly upsetting. Rather than trying to comfort someone by accepting the reality of the dream ("So you showed up to the regional meeting naked and unprepared; at least it'll make for a good story!"), it is better to point out that the feelings are based on illusions ("Don't feel bad—there were no people laughing at you. None of that really happened!"). In the same way, Buddhism aims to cut off the thoughts and feelings that misrepresent the world at the roots.

This doesn't mean that you never have pleasant or unpleasant thoughts or feelings. It does mean that you recognize these for what they are and see clearly the ways they misrepresent reality. Even if you realize that you are dreaming, your dreams can still be pleasant or unpleasant. But once you get that it's only a dream, the experiences aren't quite the same because you know that the world they conjure up isn't real. Buddhism doesn't deny our experiences entirely, but it does point out that our everyday waking experiences trick us in important ways. The aim of Buddhist philosophy and practice is to change our minds so that we no longer fall for the trick.

"Why should *I* change?" you might find yourself thinking. Why not change the *world*? Consider a famous analogy by the Indian Buddhist philosopher Shantideva (pronounced *Shahn-tee-day-vuh*): It's really painful to walk around barefoot. The ground is hard and sharp and it cuts up your feet. One solution is to cover the entire earth in leather. Even if you managed to gather the leather, acquire all the land, and summon the manpower, it would be a massive undertaking. No more concrete roads, craggy mountains, pebbly beaches. Sure your feet would be okay, but where would the food grow? Who's going to repair the leather when it's damaged? Where do you grow the grass to feed the cows for more leather? The problems multiply. And yet, with just the tiny amount of leather for a pair of sandals, you can walk anywhere. As grandmothers around the world have told us for centuries: You can't change the weather. Put on a sweater.

To be sure, we can change the world. But changing it in ways that get at the root of the problem, that eliminate the *source* of that faint buzz of anxiety that hovers around life—we can't do that. It's important to make the world better, but it's incredibly difficult. And some facts about reality we just can't change. Two and two make four. Water is wet. People die. These things aren't up to us, so the best method is to change our minds, not in ways that deny these truths but in ways that allow us to accept them and navigate through our lives accordingly.

This can all sound pretty difficult, and it is. And yet, there are reasons to be optimistic. If you're reading this you're already pretty fortunate. You were born as a human and didn't die from illness as an infant. Somebody, somewhere in your life, taught you how to look at a bunch of symbols and derive meaning from them. And you were smart enough to catch on! You're either wealthy enough to afford this book, fortunate enough to borrow it from a library or a friend, or clever enough to steal it without getting caught. You've been able to get enough food and water to survive up to this point. All this suggests that you're smart enough to reflect on your own thoughts, opinions, and feelings and motivated to do so in a way that makes life better. There's work to be done, but a lot of things have lined up to enable you to do it.

Of course, being in a position to do something is not the same as having done it. We're all in a position to make at least some progress in correcting the mismatch between our experience of the world and how it is. But there's a name for those who have actually done it: buddhas.

3 | THE BUDDHA

Buddha is not someone's name. It's a title, like president or doctor. This particular title refers to someone who has solved the problem and successfully changed their orientation to the world on a fundamental level. It literally means someone who has woken up. Someone who is dreaming mistakes their dream for reality, while a buddha is awake and sees things clearly.

There have been many buddhas. When we talk about *the* Buddha, we're referring to the historical Buddha, the one who lived in India and started what we call Buddhism. His name was Siddhartha Gautama (pronounced *Syd-har-thah Gow-tuh-muh*) and, being from the Shakya clan, he's often known as Shakyamuni Buddha. He's not the jolly fat man some people picture. That's a different figure (called Budai in Chinese or Hotei in Japanese) seen as granting good luck and often associated with the *next* buddha. (Yes, there will be buddhas in the future.)

The life of the historical Buddha is worth learning about for a few reasons. It is, of course, an important part of Buddhism and known by Buddhists all over the world. But it also serves as an example, a vision not only of someone who has solved the problem, but what the *process* of solving it looks like. As with many stories of important people, it is both biography and guidance—the story is especially important because of the lessons contained within it.

Where you begin telling the story of the Buddha's life depends a lot on your worldview. A traditional approach starts eons ago: A popular collection of stories in Asia called the *Jataka Tales* tells fables of the Buddha's lifetimes *before* he became the Buddha. They describe how he behaved when he was born as a rabbit, a king, an elephant, or a merchant. These stories typically involve him doing things of astounding selflessness—when he was an elephant, for example, he ran off a cliff so that a group of starving travelers could eat. There are hundreds of these stories, which draw on previously existing moral fables with various lessons; taken together they emphasize what an incredibly long and difficult road it is to become a buddha.

The story of the final life of the Buddha is one of the most told and retold stories in the world. It's the subject of countless works of art and literature and has numerous variants. The broad strokes, however, are fairly straightforward. He was born around 500 BCE to a rich and moderately powerful family in what is now Nepal. As the warrior son of a powerful man, his parents had very high hopes for him. He was predicted to become either a person with deep spiritual insight or a very powerful king. His parents preferred the latter so, to keep his life on track, they kept him secluded in the palace in relative luxury. But that would work for only so long. One day when he was in his late twenties, curiosity got the best of him and he decided to venture into the outside world. What he saw hit him hard and changed the course of his life.

It was a stark confrontation with the harsh realities that he had been sheltered from all his life. He saw people with serious illnesses. He saw decrepit people. He saw dead bodies. It was unsettling and disturbing. The story can seem a bit far-fetched: Could anyone *really* avoid facing such facts until their late twenties? But similar experiences can be found today, too. Showing any young person from a rich family how people actually live in areas of extreme poverty would be a shock to say the least. Reminders that your loved ones are getting older, when they forget names or can't make it up the stairs, are more than a little unpleasant. Trips to the hospital are difficult for many because it's hard to be face-to-face with really sick people. The first time you watch a person die in front of you is a deeply traumatic experience.

When young Siddhartha saw these things, they hit him like a ton of bricks. But he also saw something else. At this time on the Indian subcontinent there was a movement of people questioning traditions and giving up ordinary life to try to find solutions to these problems. He saw a man who had done just that and he seemed calm and collected, unfazed by the shitshow going on around him. Seeing this opened for Siddhartha the possibility of a solution that did not involve hiding from harsh realities, but one that was possible while facing them directly.

After that, he couldn't go back to his life as it was. He had to find a way to solve the problem for himself. It wasn't easy though—he had a beautiful wife and a new son. Social, political, and familial forces pulled him to stay, but he had to find a solution, a way to deal with the way the world now looked to him. Late one night he slipped out of the palace, got rid of his expensive clothes, and set off in search of a teacher.

For several years he studied with different teachers, many with extreme methods. They wanted to fight fire with fire, to beat pain with more pain. If you deliberately went through a lot of pain and suffering, they thought, you could eventually rise above it and find peace of mind. Others thought if you disengaged from the world in radical ways, by eating and drinking almost nothing, you could go beyond the problem; you'd be so disentangled from the world that its awfulness no longer touched you. Paintings and statues depicting Siddhartha during this period show a serious-looking skeletal figure, starved half to death (about as far from a laughing fat guy as you can get).

But he still felt that he hadn't solved the problem. Fed up, he sat down under a tree and resolved not to get up until he solved it once and for all. As you may have guessed, it was a long night. Traditional accounts describe fantastical events: A malicious demon tempts him away from his task with beautiful women; he recalls all of his many previous lives one by one; and finally, he sees the entire cosmos all at once. Some Buddhists take this as literally true, a description of events as they really happened. Others understand it metaphorically, with each of the beautiful women, for example, representing psychological obstacles to solving the problem. Of course, these two ways of understanding the story don't rule each other out, but it is a split we will see again in how different people understand Buddhism.

At the end of all this, he figured out the solution, and so is called a buddha. He spent the next forty-five years or so traveling around northern India explaining his solution. As you might expect, the solution is complex and difficult to put simply. But he cleverly packaged the broad strokes of his solution by adapting the steps of medical diagnosis into a foundational model for Buddhism. These are commonly known as The Four Noble Truths, but if we're in a philosophical frame of mind we might call them The Four Reasonable Assumptions or The Four Astute Observations. They are usually taken to be truths, but you might also see them as reasonable starting points for forming a worldview.

Think about what happens when you're sick and go to see a doctor. First you get a diagnosis: "You're having headaches and rashes because you have Lyme disease." Then the doctor tells you what the cause is: "You contracted it by being bitten by an infected tick." Then you get a prognosis: "But the good news is it's totally treatable!" And finally, if the prognosis is good, the doctor prescribes a remedy: "Take these antibiotics every day for the next month and you'll be fine."

The Buddha takes this structure and broadens its scope. Rather than treating a particular physical ailment, he applies it to the fundamental problems of life. We have seen the diagnosis. We want security, health, peace, and happiness (and we want them to *last*) but the world doesn't cooperate and, sooner or later, we lose these things. But, like a disease, this too has a cause. The cause is that our visceral ways of experiencing things misrepresent how the world is; we have mental habits that obscure how things are. Some of these are obvious, like frustration, misery, and loneliness, while others are more subtle types of insecurity or anxiety.

Buddhist writing often spends a lot of ink describing and analyzing the nature and causes of the problem. This can make Buddhism seem pretty depressing and pessimistic. But this is only half the picture. It is, after all, important for doctors to spend a lot of time thinking about the various types of illness and their sources. It's true that flipping through medical textbooks can be pretty depressing. But doctors do this so they're better able to treat people and get them healthy. Similarly, it's important to keep in mind that when Buddhists focus on the problem and its causes, it is in the service of better *solving* the problem by eliminating its causes.

Buddhism is optimistic about the prognosis. The terrible things Siddhartha saw on his trip out of the palace, the fundamental problem—all of it *is* solvable. This step is not discussed as much as the others. Some even think it is trivial: If you know that the problem has a cause then it must have a solution. But that's not true. A disease with a genetic cause might be totally untreatable. The world could have been made so that the causes of the problem are fixed and immovable; we could be both caused and fated to suffer. Buddhists, however, take a more optimistic view. A Buddhist is likely to point to the existence of buddhas; the evidence that the problem is solvable is that somebody actually solved it. But you can also take a more pragmatic view. If I have a disease, I want a doctor who is at least open to the idea that it's curable, because without that there's no chance of being cured.

Finally, the Buddha offers the details of the treatment. As with many treatments, it has several aspects. After all, doctors often don't just give medication but also recommend changes in diet, exercise, and sleep. Of course, it's not just *any* change in diet or exercise that will work. Sitting on the couch and eating nothing but hot dogs would also be a change, but it's not the right change. So the Buddha outlines the right way to make changes in various aspects of life (actually eight aspects, which is why this is sometimes called the Eightfold Path). The treatment includes outward changes, such as the right way to speak, work, and act. It also includes inner changes, involving the right way to change your motives, attention, and point of view.

After the Buddha passed away, his followers formed a community. Over the next 2,500 years Buddhism spread all over the world. In this time, people have developed new ideas (often under the guise of discovering old ones); they emphasize some ideas and quietly drop others; they develop and refine techniques relevant to their time and place. So, for example, some Buddhists think that the Buddha had *always* been a Buddha and only *pretended* to be a miserable prince as an instructive lesson. Others think of his life story as a mix of historical fact and instructive allegory. Still others think a particular version of the story is true to the letter. As we will see, Buddhism is a big tent with lots of room for disagreement. But Buddhists largely agree on the general framework: Our minds misrepresent how things are and we've got to wake up and make some changes. The story presents us with not only a diagnosis but also an example of what a successful treatment looks like.

4 | BUDDHISM AND REASON

The central aim of Buddhism is changing how you relate to yourself and the world. It's hard to overstate the depth, difficulty, and diversity of these changes. Rational reflection, thinking carefully about these issues, is an important tool in this process. The world is complex, and figuring out how it works is a task that sometimes requires careful thought and technical concepts.

Nevertheless, it's important not to see them as simply changes in what you *think*. Thinking differently is only one part of the required transformation; it also involves changes in how you feel, what you notice, and what you do. Focusing too much on what Buddhists *think* runs the risk of neglecting the other critical aspects of the solution that Buddhism provides.

Suppose you decided that you want to become a more relaxed person. Maybe you have a friend who is laid back and you want your outlook to be more like theirs. Simply adopting their beliefs is not going to be enough. It might help to *believe* that the traffic jam is no big deal, but your friend's relaxed outlook is much more than believing certain things—your friend doesn't just believe that the traffic jam isn't a big deal, they might hardly notice it. And if they do, they'll have a very different emotional response to it. The Buddhist solution is a bit like this: The problem doesn't get solved by simply having certain beliefs but also involves recalibrating a wide range of your responses.

Solving the problem also involves seeing through certain illusions that our minds present. Sometimes an intellectual thought *can* help dispel an illusion. When a good magician performs a trick, it can really seem like a rabbit came from nowhere or that a person was made invisible. We might intellectually resist it, but it really does seem that way. But once someone explains how the trick is done, it no longer even seems that way. Coming to know how the trick works can dispel the illusion.

But other illusions are harder to shake in this way. Consider superstitions. A passionate sports fan might *know*, in an intellectual sense, that viewing an important game has no effect on the outcome. And yet they can still feel as if they don't watch the game, their team will lose. Even if someone *knows* that calling in to work and saying that their kids are sick won't affect their kids' health, they might be unable to shake the feeling that they'd be "tempting fate" if they used their kids' health as an excuse. Even though they don't believe in fate, the feeling that it's a bad idea still pulls on them.

Sometimes changing your beliefs through intellectual thought just isn't enough to alter your overall outlook. But that doesn't mean that abstract thinking or reasoning is completely useless or bad; it means that it's only *part* of solving the problem. One way to understand the role of abstract, philosophical thought is as a kind of technology. Ideas, concepts, and arguments are tools to help with the project of understanding the world better and so help to solve the problem. In the same way that you can use a hammer to build a chair or weights to get stronger, you can use abstract thinking to help to see the world clearly. Of course, it's important not to confuse the tools with the goal. Hammers aren't chairs, weights aren't strength, and ideas aren't the solution. But they still help you do what you're trying to do. And like other tools, they can be used well or poorly. You can use a hammer to build a bad chair or even destroy one. In the same way, you can use ideas and concepts to obscure reality.

These tools are particularly useful for solving difficult and complex problems. You can take a short walk in your hometown without much thought; your feet just take you where you need to go. But taking a long trip to a new country requires some explicit planning ("Do I need a visa? Vaccinations? Which flight should I buy?"). A new program of diet and exercise is more likely to succeed if you spend some time beforehand thinking about what you'll do and why. The project of understanding reality and changing our mental orientation is even more complex, and it can benefit from careful examination of the facts about reality and what to do in light of them.

Many people think Buddhism is at odds with reflective, rational, or abstract thinking. Buddhism, for them, is something intuitive, emotional, and maybe even mystical. We have to be very careful here. As you might expect from a tradition whose history spans over 2,500 years and covers much of the globe, the Buddhist world is vast and includes many, many approaches. Like the Christian, Jewish, or Islamic traditions, Buddhism has both mystics and scholastics. More importantly, it's crucial to distinguish what Buddhism *is* from what we'd like it to be. We might find certain aspects more interesting and relevant, but that doesn't mean that's all there is. Highlighting those aspects often says more about *us* than it does about Buddhism.

Buddhism in the West is often placed on the emotion side of the divide between reason and emotion, but there are lots of reasons to question this. For one thing, there is good reason to question the divide itself. When we engage in reasoning we often rely on subtle emotional cues. When a scientist, for example, reasons about which experiment to run, she will not consider certain options because they *feel* ridiculous and might pursue others because they *feel* promising. If you are planning how to approach your work for the day, after a while you'll settle on a plan of attack because it *feels* like you're spending too much time planning and need to get down to work. Thinking and feeling are not separable domains and are often intertwined in complicated ways.

Even if we accept a division between reasoning and feeling, it is far from clear that Buddhism falls squarely on one side or the other. Sure, there are strands in Buddhism that advocate going beyond rational thought and aim at direct, non-conceptual awareness of reality. But Buddhists in India spent a long time developing and refining complex forms of logic. Schools of Tibetan Buddhism continue to engage in debate, defending and refuting rival philosophical positions. There are thousands of years' worth of texts containing highly detailed and technical debates between Buddhist philosophers. More to the point: Insofar as you can give reasons for the irrelevance of philosophical thinking in Buddhism, you've engaged in it and so demonstrate that it is at least useful for avoiding a common mistake.

Given that Buddhism aims at realigning our responses with how reality really is, this often means spending time thinking hard about philosophical questions dealing with the nature of reality.

We're going to discuss some intellectual arguments involving pretty abstract ideas, but the reason Buddhists do this is to get a clear picture of the world so they can better navigate it. Medical journals often contain discussions of complex and technical issues about physiology and biology, but it's all in the service of empowering doctors to better heal their patients. What seemed like a simple task, heal the patient, often requires thinking hard about the complex reality of the human body. Buddhist philosophy can also be technical and obtuse, but it is done in a similar spirit.

These issues bear on another dispute that Western Buddhists in particular are fond of having: Is Buddhism a religion? This often involves people who like Buddhism but do not like religion insisting that Buddhism is not a religion. "It's a philosophy," they'll say, "or just a way of life." The answer, of course, depends on what counts as a religion. This is far from clear. Can football be a religion? It does, after all, inspire a lot of zeal and organize people's lives around shared rituals. What about patriotism? That involves strong beliefs that bond a group of people together. But maybe those aren't supernatural enough to count. What about astrology? Perhaps, some will insist, religion requires a belief in an all-powerful capital-G-style God. But that oddly makes polytheistic religion an oxymoron; why should belief in *one* God count as religious, while belief in *many* doesn't?

Certainly many people in many places around the world relate to Buddhism in ways that are religion-like. Many people perform formalized actions within Buddhist institutions to convince supernatural beings to intervene in their lives in various ways. This is one aspect of what is sometimes called "traditional" Buddhism.

Others de-emphasize these aspects and attempt to fit Buddhist ideas into a scientific worldview, sometimes called "modern" or "secularized" Buddhism.

As we'll see, although these two ways of relating to Buddhism have much in common, they also differ in many important ways. I'll often suggest ways of making sense of Buddhism from a modern perspective, but it's worth noting that the vast majority of Buddhists, both historically and today, relate to Buddhism in a traditional way. I'm not here to say which of these is the "real" Buddhism (as if there is such a thing anyway) but merely to point out that there are many Buddhisms in this world, and being aware of these strands makes navigating the Buddhist world much easier.

Another important feature of the landscape of various forms of Buddhism is the presence of both popular and more esoteric levels. This happens in other contexts too. One Christian might think of God as an old, bearded man in the sky while a theologian might have a very different idea of God, something much more technical and abstract, like the "ground of all Being." Though both are Christian, one is part of a popular strand and the other a more esoteric or elite one. Buddhism is no different. Some might relate to the Buddha as a supernatural entity who can help them find a good marriage or business success, while other Buddhists will have a conception that, as we will see, is much more abstract and complex.

This is not to say that popular strands are bad. We often leave it to specialists to work out a detailed understanding of things. How I think of "easy to digest" food is very different from how a gastroenterologist thinks of it. And even that is different from how a biologist or a chemist thinks of it. Life is short, and for some people's lives it makes more sense to leave the details to the experts. I will discuss ideas found in popular forms of Buddhism, but my description of Buddhist philosophy will focus on ideas from the more esoteric strands.

Finally, keep in mind that Buddhism is a living and changing thing—particular people, myself included, present their own spin on things. But there's a difference between presenting what you think is the best version and insisting that *your* version is the only valid one. Here I'll be doing the former but not the latter. Still, it is important to keep in mind that what follows is *one* view of Buddhism. It is one that takes philosophical thought to be important, respects a wide variety of practices, and interprets those in ways that will be relevant to the lives of modern people.

Solving the problem means changing our responses to match reality. This in turn means figuring out what reality is actually like, which is one of the main tasks of philosophy. Before a doctor can properly diagnose an illness, they first need years of study. Much of this study involves concepts and ideas that don't obviously bear on any particular diseases, things like how cells function or how mitosis works or the Latin names of different parts of the body.

Buddhist philosophy is a bit like this. It involves thinking hard, often in detailed terms, about what reality is really like. This can seem far removed from the task of solving the problem, but as with medical study, it is critical to examine things carefully before you start a course of treatment. It means thinking hard about the most fundamental questions of reality, not as an intellectual exercise but as an important foundational step in solving the problem.

What exists? This is the most basic question you can ask when trying to figure out what reality is really like. It's also one of the trickiest. Part of what makes it tricky is the huge range of different kinds of things that seem to exist. Here are some things that at least *seem* to be real: a maple tree, friendship, the number 4, fire, a thought, a corporation, sunlight, a hole, a shout, a banana, plasma. Some of these might seem more or less real than some of the others. I can point to a fire, but I can't point to a thought. I can touch four maple trees, but I can't touch the number 4 itself. When I try to describe a hole, most of what I end up describing is *the stuff around* it.

Another part of what makes the question tricky is that we can talk about things that don't exist. We can meaningfully say things like "Vampires hate Italian food" or "Unicorn tears cure cancer" even though there are no vampires or unicorns. We can even talk about impossible things. "A triangle with four sides is unimaginable" is a perfectly reasonable sentence even though the thing it's about is impossible.

So our language is not always a good guide to what's really there; it can sometimes trick us. Even though we can talk about both "light" and "dark," there are not two different things out there in the world. We use the word "dark" just to refer to the *lack* of light. Sometimes these linguistic distortions are forced by grammar. In English we say, "It's raining today," but what's the *it* that's doing the raining? The rain? The atmosphere? Nothing? Buddhists are keen to highlight that many of the things it's natural and useful for us to talk about don't really exist. Things are not as straightforward as they first appear.

Another important task is figuring out which things are fundamental. That is, which things depend on other things? If I have a clay statue on my desk, maybe the statue depends on the clay, but the clay does not depend on the statue. After all, if someone comes along and smooshes it, I no longer have the statue but I still have the clay. Or think of people and crowds. There can be people without there being a crowd—say, if they are far away from each other. But there cannot be a crowd without people. So even if we think that statues and crowds exist, they are in a certain way less fundamental than clay and people. Buddhist thinkers will run with this idea, taking it as far as they can.

Even once you know which things exist, you still won't know which ones stay the same over time and which don't. If you stir it up enough, you can make butter out of milk. It's natural to think of this as one thing changing into another. The milk is now gone and has been turned into butter. Applying heat to the butter also brings about changes, turning it from a solid block into a liquid. But we don't say that the solid butter has been changed into *something else*; we say that it's still the *same* butter, but in a different form. Sometimes common sense says that a thing, like the butter, remains through changes. Other times it says that one thing ends and is replaced by a new and different thing.

These issues are difficult enough, but they become very thorny when it comes to collective things. The narrator of a nature documentary might say, "The sturgeon has existed for over 200 million years." But this does not mean that there is one *very* old fish out there in the ocean. So what is it that's 200 million years old? It's not one thing, but a series of linked things—generations of different individual fish parents and children that we call "the sturgeon" for short. What is 200 million years old is a lineage of fish descendants, a chain of individual fish with a special relationship. Buddhists defend the counterintuitive idea that most of what we encounter in life is like the 200-million-year-old sturgeon—not a singular thing but a continuum of many things.

Examining fundamental philosophical questions can be interesting, but it's also important for solving the problem. Not all philosophical questions are equally important to this task, and there is a danger of setting sail on the ocean of philosophical questioning never to return. The Buddhist tradition is sensitive to these dangers and offers lessons about when philosophical questioning is useful and when it's not.

There are, for example, a few episodes when the Buddha explicitly refused to answer certain philosophical questions. The details vary, but they typically involve questions like, Is the universe eternal? Is it infinite? What happens after death? Sometimes he even refused to answer questions about the relationship between the self and the body. And yet, some later Buddhist thinkers *do* discuss some of these questions, so it's important to understand different ways that the Buddha's refusal to answer them has been understood.

For some, the Buddha refused to answer because answering would not be beneficial *to the particular person who asked the questions*. This makes it less about the questions than about the person asking them. Sometimes people get carried away by their curiosity in ways that are unhelpful for what they need to do. Many students in an art class are able to ask which paintbrush to buy and then get on with their lesson. But some students will get distracted by such questions, spending hours online reading detailed reviews comparing different brands and types of brushes. For these students, it's better not to answer any questions about brushes, at least at first, because any answer will only prompt more questions and distract from the actual business of learning to paint.

For others, answering these questions might be unwise because *any* answer will push them to an extreme view. It's reasonable to ask a nutritionist which foods are healthy, but some people might think of health in an all-or-nothing way. For example, if they ask whether eating rice is healthy, a "yes" will lead them to load up on it, and a "no" will lead them to give it up entirely. And an even more nuanced answer, like "sort of" or "it's complicated," will lead them to press on for an answer that they can hear as a yes or a no. For people thinking in such stark terms, answering the question at all could be misleading and harmful.

Sometimes the question *itself* is flawed. Imagine being asked, "Have you quit being a jerk yet?" Here the very question presupposes that you were, at least at one time, a jerk. Answering either way implicitly accepts this assumption. Negative statements are particularly tricky in this way. You might say, "Vampires do not like lasagna" because there *are no vampires*, but someone might hear your answer and conclude that vampires *exist* and prefer other types of food. As we will see, Buddhist philosophers often make negative statements, arguing that many of the things presumed by our ordinary language and thought are not real. So it will be particularly important to keep this kind of ambiguity in mind.

The whole point of examining philosophical questions is to help solve the problem of how to live. People relate to these questions in different ways, and many of these are, from a Buddhist point of view, not very good. For some it's a fun way to pass the time, the way people in comic book shops can enjoy arguing about whether Superman is stronger than the Incredible Hulk. For others, making clever arguments becomes a kind of game they play. But none of these are very good reasons to tackle these questions since they don't help to solve the problem.

People can contribute to solving the problem in different ways, and in many cases solving it is a collective effort. In monasteries or universities, some people focus on thinking hard about these questions. Others contribute by cleaning the kitchen or balancing the budget rather than thinking about philosophy itself. In taking care of these necessary tasks, they enable philosophers to specialize and spend most of their time answering these difficult questions. They contribute to figuring out these issues too, but in a more indirect way.

Even though knowledge plays an important role in Buddhism, not all knowledge is equally useful. This is not peculiar to Buddhism. There are *lots* of things you might know that won't make a difference to your life. What is the serial number for the bumper bracket on a 1998 Honda Accord? That is something you could know. If you have internet access you could find the answer. But unless you have that particular car and do a lot of repairs yourself, knowing it is pointless. Sometimes philosophical questions are like this. Is the universe infinite or not? Knowing the answer to that probably wouldn't make a big difference in your day-to-day life, and looking for the answer might take you away from more important matters.

But some questions about the nature of reality *are* relevant to how we face life. If it turns out that there is an all-powerful invisible man in the sky who wants me to do certain things and will punish me forever if I don't, I may well change my life to make sure I do those things. The existence of such a being would change how I see myself and how I direct my life.

Questions about less religiously loaded issues can also change how we experience life. When you thought there was a monster under the bed, you felt afraid. After investigating and finding none, you were able to sleep easy. To use a more traditional example, you see a snake and jump back. You look closer and see it was only a rope and you're not scared anymore.

Or consider what philosophers call a category mistake. Suppose someone really wants to see New York City. They've heard people talk about how great it is and they want to experience it for themselves. But in overhearing people they make a mistake—they think that "New York City" is the name of a particular building, not the entire city.

One day they book an expensive tour because it promises to show them New York City, the building they've always wanted to see for themselves. The tour takes them to all the major sights: the Empire State Building, the Brooklyn Bridge, the Statue of Liberty, and so on. As the return home draws near, they start to get upset. They complain to a friend back home, "I paid so much money for this tour because I wanted to see New York City. But they spent all day taking me to all these *other* buildings and bridges. Those are fine, but when will they finally take me to see *New York City*?!"

This person makes a mistake about *the kind of thing* New York City is. They didn't realize that when they saw the Empire State Building or the Statue of Liberty, they *were* seeing New York City. New York City is not, as this person assumed, just another landmark on the list of landmarks. It's a name for the whole list. They didn't just make a mistake about where New York City is located or how big it is but about *its very nature*, about the kind of thing it is.

This angry tourist probably strikes you as foolish beyond belief. The mistake they make is so stupid that it hardly seems possible. But as we will see, Buddhists think that nearly all of us are making very similar mistakes all the time. For now, it's enough to understand that if this person saw more clearly what the world was like, if they understood the kind of thing that New York City really is, they wouldn't have been upset in the first place and in fact they'd have been happy with all the sights the tour took them to see.

Knowledge about yourself and your nature is particularly important for knowing how to get through life. If you know that eating peanuts will kill you or that spicy food gives you migraines, you can make decisions about what to consume that will make your life go better. If you know that you're apt to gamble too much or eat too much fast food, you can decide to stay away from casinos or burger places. On a less superficial level, knowing the *kind* of thing you are will make a difference in the plans, attitudes, and choices you'll cultivate.

The central Buddhist idea is that solving the problem in a sustainable way involves forming and executing a plan in light of how the world really is. This is more complex than the obvious truth that if you want to take a trip somewhere, you'd better know where it is and how to get there. Think of trying to be healthy. This means knowing about yourself, your allergies, and your body type, and it means knowing about foods, what's in them, and how they were prepared. It also means relying on technical knowledge about things like cells, bacteria, and carcinogens. Forming a plan means figuring out whether think there really are humors, *qi*, or vitamins. It can also mean facing harsh truths. It would be devastating to hear that you have cancer or that your lifestyle is killing you at an alarming rate, but it's still much better than ignoring those facts and remaining in the dark. Knowing how things are allows you to form a plan that is sensitive to the actual situation.

For Buddhists, a large part of this project involves finding and removing distorting ways of relating to the world. This often involves techniques specially targeted to the ways that certain mental states misrepresent things. It can also involve reflective thought about how the world is, which is why philosophical examination and argumentation can help us figure out reality. It is one lamp to cast light on the world.

Sometimes these illusions are subtle and don't seem to matter much. Often the mistaken way of seeing things is okay for getting through the world in a good-enough way most of the time. Only in the long run, with more specific aims, do the limitations become apparent. On the surface, a really big spheroid feels a lot like a flat plane. People got through life for thousands of years thinking the Earth was flat, and it made little difference. The fact that over the course of your life your head travels farther than your feet seems trivial and unimportant. Someone examining the Earth's shape, say, by putting two sticks in the ground, measuring their shadows, and doing a bunch of geometry, can seem to be wasting their time with abstract and impractical matters. But once you want to do something a bit more difficult and complex, like going to the moon, traveling across an ocean, or launching a satellite, it becomes *very* important.

In the same way, some philosophical questions can at first seem abstract and removed from the business of making it through the day. But once you see that solving the problem requires reorienting your experience in ways that are subtle, complex, and often radical, the significance of these questions becomes clear.

6 | HEAPS AND HURRICANES

The news is full of heaps. Not just piles of dirty laundry, but collections of all kinds. Anytime you check it, there are tons of stories about sports teams, companies, and governments. One article is about how the Norwegian government wants to maintain oil production. Another says Microsoft plans to launch a new product. In the sports section you see that Manchester United lost a match. We're so used to this kind of thing we never stop to wonder what these stories are really about.

Governments, companies, and teams are all kinds of collections. What collections are can be puzzling: Does Microsoft plan things in the same way that you plan a vacation? Can the Norwegian government want things in the same way that you want a cup of coffee? A natural response to these questions is no. To say that Microsoft plans something is just a short way to say that some subset of its employees plans it. To say that the Norwegian government wants something is shorthand for saying that certain citizens or officials want it.

Things aren't always so simple, though. Sometimes collections can want something even though *none* of the members that make it up want it. Suppose that half of Norway's government officials want to abandon oil production and half want to increase it. So they compromise and decide to maintain oil production. In this case the Norwegian government, the collection, wants something even though *none* of the officials that make it up want it. Nevertheless, it can still seem that the collection wanting or planning something still depends, in a complex way, on the wants or plans of the members that make it up.

The idea that there is nothing to a collection beyond its parts is a prominent Buddhist view of collections. To say that Manchester United lost a match is just a convenient way to say that the players and coaches that are members of the team lost. To talk about the wants, plans, and traits of a company or a government is really to talk about the members that make it up and their relationships. Although these collections can seem to be separately existing things in the world, they're just handy names for the things that make them up.

A classic example of a collection is a heap of sand. What is a heap of sand? It's just individual grains of sand organized in a certain way. A bunch of grains of sand scattered all over the floor isn't a heap, but if they're clustered in the right way they make a heap. All that's there is the grains and their arrangement. Even though we can talk about the heap, there's no extra thing in the world. There is nothing more to a heap than the grains that make it up.

Imagine that I have a pile of twelve eggs on a table in front of me. Suppose you ask me from the other room how many things are on the table. It doesn't seem right for me to reply, "There are thirteen things. We've got twelve eggs and one heap." That feels like double counting. Though I might be able to say true and useful things about the pile ("Now that's a neatly stacked pile of eggs!" or "Hey, watch out for the pile on the table!"), the pile isn't a thing in the world in the same way as the individual eggs are. The pile just *is* the eggs. When I'm talking about the pile, I'm really talking about the eggs and how they're organized.

Why might someone think that composite things like heaps don't really exist? One thing people have noticed about complex things is that they have a kind of nebulous existence. The classic Buddhist example of this is a chariot, but let's think about a car. A car is made up of a bunch of parts and so it's possible to remove some of them. If you take the bumper or hubcaps off of a car, it's still a car; it's just a more dilapidated one. But if we keep removing parts slowly, a bracket here and a spark plug there, eventually we won't have a car anymore. It would just be a bare frame or a pile of car parts. It can be hard, if not impossible, to figure out the exact moment when it stops being a car.

Philosophers call this "vagueness," and it's easiest to see when thinking about the heap of sand. If you have three grains of sand you don't have a heap. If you have four grains of sand it's still not a heap. You can keep adding grains and eventually you'll have a heap, but it's hard to say when exactly. There doesn't seem to be a sharp boundary for having a heap; there will be a time when the sand in front of you is sort of, but not exactly a heap. It is controversial, but some think that this fuzziness is evidence that heaps don't really exist, at least not in the way that the grains of sand do. The indeterminate nature of heaps and cars, at least for some, suggests that these are just made-up concepts that we project onto the world.

The history of Buddhism is long, and many different Buddhists have offered many different arguments about the nature of composite things. One famous argument is found in a text called *The Questions of King Milinda*, a dialogue between a Greek king and a

Buddhist monk named Nagasena (pronounced *Na-guh-say-nuh*). In it, Nagasena points out that if you think that both a collection and its parts are equally real, you run into trouble. This trouble is an important aspect of how we misrepresent the world—we think that both a collection and its parts are real. The best way to see why this can't be right is to think through the relationship between the two.

They must have some close relationship. After all, my car and the parts that make it up are both in my garage. When my car stops working, there must have been a change in at least *some* of the parts that make it up. Given this close relationship, Nagasena says that one of the following must be true: The car is the same as *one* of the parts, *all* of the parts, or *none* of the parts. None of these, he says, are very appealing.

Consider the first option, that the whole is just *one* of its parts. If that was true, then the whole would just *be* that part. But a car is not a carburetor or a steering wheel. A heap isn't any particular grain of sand. No particular player, however talented, *is* the team. Collections are complex, composite things, and the parts are not. So this can't be right.

So what about saying that the whole is *all* of its parts? Nagasena makes a point here that you will find either very clever or very nitpicky: A collection can't be identical with all of its parts because the collection is a single thing while the parts are many things. Two things with such different properties couldn't possibly be identical. Fair enough, but we also might reject this option because it makes collections too rigid and fragile. A heap of sand is still a heap if you remove one grain. The team isn't destroyed by losing one player. My car is still my car even after I lose a hubcap.

Maybe, then, the whole isn't *any* of its parts. Maybe it's just a separate thing entirely. But then it would be possible for the team to be on the field even though *all* of its members are at home in bed. I might then say to a friend, "Don't worry, your Maserati is still in your driveway. Just all of its parts are in my garage." This option destroys the close relationship collections have with their parts (and probably your friendship too).

You might think that Nagasena left out an option here—maybe the whole is identical with *some* of its parts. This does seem like the most reasonable option, but the thorny issues of vagueness pop up again. Which parts? Maybe a car is just the subset of parts that allow it to drive? But a broken-down car is still a car. There is also the problem of how to think of the other parts; the bumper is not a piece that's necessary for my car to run, but it still seems to be part of my car. If something happens to the bumper something has happened to my car. This option is also more difficult to explain in collections without a distinct purpose, like a heap of sand. It doesn't seem like any particular subset of grains is more important to the heap than any other subset.

So, Nagasena concludes, since none of the options for the relationship between collections and their parts seem to be any good, we have to deny the existence of one of them. We could avoid this by denying that the *parts* exist. This would be a bit odd. It's hard to imagine a composite without any parts; it would be like saying there is a team but there are no players. Aside from that, it does seem that we know the parts more directly. I can touch grains of sand in a way that I can't touch the heap itself. It's hard to make sense of knowing the *team* itself outside of knowing the particular players and their relationships.

This is just the tip of the iceberg when it comes to Buddhist philosophical discussions of collections and their parts. This might seem abstract, but it applies to nearly everything we interact with. We occupy a world populated with collections. Take a look around you right now. Most of the things you can see and name are collections, composite things like a heap of sand. Tables, buildings, cars, clouds—these aren't separate things in the world, but just labels for the sake of convenience. The world, Buddhists point out, is radically different than it ordinarily seems. Even though we use these labels, they're not extra things that exist in the world.

This isn't to deny that these labels can be *useful*, at least for some purposes. Sometimes talking about things that don't really exist can be helpful and even teach us things. Reading a novel, a story about things that didn't really happen involving completely made-up people, can help us to see truths about the real people and events in our own lives. Talking about the "average American" can illuminate truths about America and help direct public policy in beneficial ways. But it's important to keep in mind that there is no such person as the "average American"—you can't go to their house or invite them over for dinner. And despite the lessons you've learned, the characters in that novel that changed your life don't really exist.

These labels are just the names we give to a bunch of parts that interact in ways that are relevant to us. As we will discuss, this is a very strong tendency that's often useful but can also be deeply harmful and misleading. Using handy names for certain collections isn't necessarily bad, but when we start to think of those names as picking out something real in the world we start running into trouble. So it's fine to talk about what Manchester

United really *wants* or what Microsoft is *planning* to do or what China *believes* about tariffs, but it's important to realize, not just intellectually but viscerally, that these things don't exist and aren't doing the wanting, planning, or believing.

Things get extra tricky here because there is an interaction between how the world is and what our words mean. The concept of an atom was originally a particle that cannot be subdivided any further (the word literally means "indivisible"). So when scientists found certain very small particles they couldn't divide, they called them "atoms" and for a while everything was fine. But later they found out that the things they had been calling atoms could actually be divided into smaller particles (what we call protons, neutrons, and electrons). There are two ways to put this discovery depending on how you use the word "atom": One way to put it is that they discovered that *what they thought were atoms weren't really atoms*. Another way to put it is that they discovered that *you can split atoms after all*. These sound different, but the discovery is the same. You can either accept that much of what you thought was wrong, or you can change how you understand the meaning of certain words.

Something similar can happen with the Buddhist discovery about collections and parts. A more radical-sounding way to put this discovery is to say that much of what we thought was mistaken: Piles don't exist. Despite how meteorologists talk, there is no such thing as a hurricane. This is fine, but you have to be careful. Recall the pile of eggs—there is nothing to the pile beyond the eggs, but there's still a bunch of eggs on the table. You still need to be careful not to knock them over. So if you thought a hurricane was something extra beyond the bits of air and water that make it up, you were wrong. But there still are those bits of air and water and they really are a danger to you.

Another way to put the discovery is to revise how we understand the words we use: Heaps and hurricanes do exist, but the words "heap" and "hurricane" have a different meaning than you probably thought. When you're talking about the pile, you're talking about the eggs and their arrangement, nothing more. There *are* hurricanes and it's okay for meteorologists to talk about them. But all the word "hurricane" means is bits of air and water moving in a certain way. A hurricane *just is* a loose complex of air and water in constant flux and nothing more. All the things we said about piles and hurricanes are still true, but we have to be careful to remember that those words don't refer to anything extra in the world, just a bunch of parts.

Just like with the atoms, the discovery is the same, but how you put it depends on your willingness to revise what words mean. The important discovery, for many Buddhists, is that things that seemed to us to be singular, individual things are really collections. Experiencing reality as it really is means, in part, realizing that most things we interact with on a day-to-day basis are not the way they seem—they're composite heaps, nothing more and nothing less. As we'll see, this kind of mistake is a fundamental source of our misalignment with reality.

7 | EMPTINESS

Even if a *heap* itself isn't real, at least the individual grains of sand themselves are. Unlike the heap, which depends on the grains, the grains of sand don't depend on anything; they just *are*. Many Buddhists accept something like this, not for grains of sand, of course, but for *some* tiny instantaneous bits that make up all the things we see and interact with. We can split collections into parts and split those parts into parts, but eventually we hit bottom.

Since we can divide things not only spatially, but also temporally, these bits are less like atoms and more like tiny slivers of atom existence—the smallest possible instantaneous events. These slivers of happenings are called *dharmas* (with a little "d"), and there is a vast scholastic literature that meticulously catalogs and categorizes them. The point of doing this is to show very precisely and in great detail how all the things we interact with are like heaps. By rigorously analyzing the parts, you come to see that there's nothing more than these tiny bits interacting in certain ways. In the same way that taking apart a clock and examining each component helps you understand in a deep way what it really is and how it works, breaking reality down to its most fundamental bits helps you see what is really there and what makes it tick.

Other Buddhists, however, aren't so sure even about these tiny bits. The bits, they say, are *empty*. In fact, they say that *everything* is empty. But what does that really mean? First, here's what it *doesn't* mean. It doesn't mean that the bits don't exist at all. To say that things are empty is not to say they don't exist. Rather, it is saying that they don't exist in the way that they seem to, as free-standing and independent entities.

When we say that something is empty, we mean that it is empty *of* something. My mug is empty of coffee, but not of air. So when some Buddhists claim that all things are empty, it's critical to ask what they're empty *of.* The answer is a kind of essential self-nature. This is tricky to put into words, but it is an independent nature, a quality that makes something what it is without relying on anything else.

You might think, for example, that being hot is part of fire's self-nature. After all, fire that's not hot isn't fire at all. And, more importantly, fire doesn't need anything else to make it hot. It just *is* hot on its own, by its own nature. But a Buddhist would be quick to point out that even though it might seem like fire has heat as part of its essence, that it is hot independently of anything else, this doesn't hold up to close examination. A fire's heat isn't an independent quality at all; it actually depends on a lot of other things. Not only does it rely on something to burn and oxygen in the environment, but being hot doesn't mean anything unless there are things that are colder. Fire's heat isn't some inherent quality of the fire itself but relies on interactions with lots of other things.

Saying that things are empty of this self-nature means that things only exist in a relational way. What does that really mean?

Consider a playing card, a three of hearts. The card itself has no independent value outside of the deck and the game being played. Is it useless? Part of a straight flush? A trump card? What it means, what it *is*, depends on what game you're playing and what the other cards are. And this is true of *all* of the cards in the deck; they all depend on the other cards and the game in order to be what they are.

Or think again of the bits of air and water that make up a hurricane. You can't take a single drop of the water, put it in a bottle, and say, "Look! I've got a bit of hurricane!" Hurricane parts don't work that way. What it means for a drop of water to be part of the hurricane is for it to play a certain role with other bits of air and water, to be part of a complex web of relations. Being a hurricane part depends on all the other bits of air and water. And that's true for all the other bits of air and water in the hurricane too—they all depend on all the other bits in the same way.

Dependence means relying on something else. Without that thing being what it is, this thing can't be what it is. Some simple pairs have this feature: There is no left without there being a right and no right without there being a left. They both depend on each other to be what they are. This also happens in more complex ways. Think of the spoke on a bicycle wheel. In order to be a spoke, it must play a role in a wheel and a bicycle. And for a bicycle to be what it is depends on a certain relationship with human beings; we have to be things with two legs that need to travel certain distances quickly. There is no such thing as a spoke prior to bicycles and people. Being a spoke depends on all of these other things being in place. Sure, there might have been a long piece of metal, but its existence *as a spoke* depends on innumerable other things.

This web of dependencies stretches far and wide. To see just how far, imagine someone wanted to give a complete description of you. They don't just want a rough sketch; they want a *total* description, to understand every single detail of you in full. Doing this would mean not only giving a description of your mental and physical traits—right down to the cells that make you up and the bacteria that live in your digestive system, but also describing everyone you've ever met and everything you've ever touched, seen, tasted, and smelled. And, to be complete, they'd also need to describe everyone *those people* ever met and how all those things you experienced came to be. The more you try to be complete, the more you end up describing not only your entire culture, but the entire Earth and beyond. *Fully* describing what you are means describing a huge and complex set of relations that balloons to include everything.

A famous image to illustrate this is Indra's Net. Indra is a god from India, and, as you might have guessed, he has a huge net. So huge, in fact, that it stretches out infinitely in all directions. At each node of the net there is a jewel. Look closely at any jewel and you see, reflected in its surface, all of the other jewels. The look of each jewel, what it's like, depends on all of the other jewels. And this is true of *all* of the jewels. A similarly striking image is given by a Chinese monk named Fazang: Picture a candle completely encircled by mirrors. Each mirror reflects not only the flame itself but the other reflections of the flame, and their reflections, which in turn reflect all of the other reflections. And on and on and on.

To say that *everything* is empty is to make a claim about *a hell of a lot of things*. The snow on Mount Everest, the dogshit on the sidewalk, the number five, dust particles on the far side of the moon, this book—they're all empty. We have to be careful here. When we say "Everyone has a mother" we don't mean that all people share the same mother; we mean each person has a unique and different mother. So saying that all things are empty doesn't mean that there is one cosmic emptiness that all things partake in. The mirrors really are different mirrors, and the jewels in Indra's Net are distinct jewels. They have features that let you tell them apart (for one, they're in different places). But they all exist only relationally; they depend on everything else to be what they are.

And yet saying that all things are empty *does* point out something they have in common. What is it that all things share? It's not just sharing a similar quality—the way that a cherry and a fire hydrant are both red. That's not very interesting. Lots of things share similarities: All existing things are similar in that they exist. All things are identical with themselves. Saying all things are empty is not like saying that. The closest would be to say that all things share the relational quality of having only relational qualities.

But even this isn't *quite* right. It's important not to treat emptiness as just another quality things have. In this way, it's a bit like existence itself. A cherry has certain qualities: It's round, red, and sweet. But existing isn't like those qualities. It would be very odd to tell you about the cherries I bought, their color and taste, and then add, "Oh! They also have another important quality—they exist." It would be even stranger to describe the qualities of a wonderful car you have but add, "Sadly, it does lack one important feature: existence."

Existence isn't a feature of something in the same way that color or shape is. This is particularly important because emptiness is about *lacking* a certain independent nature. When I say that there is no milk in the fridge, I do not mean that there is milk in the fridge that lacks the property of existence. I mean that there is *no milk in there*. Similarly, when we say that something is empty, we're not saying that it has the positive quality of being empty; we're saying that a certain kind of essence or self-nature just isn't there.

In this way, saying that everything is empty is not like saying that everything is red or round. It's saying that everything lacks an independent self-nature. Such a nature just isn't there. It can be tempting, but wrong, to think of *this* as the self-nature of everything, that everything has some positive quality of what you might awkwardly call "naturelessness." This is a tempting mistake, one that's sometimes called "reifying emptiness." In the same way that my empty fridge doesn't have a thing in it called "emptiness," things don't have as their nature a thing called "lacking a nature."

When you take seriously the idea that *everything* is empty, you'll start to wonder if this also applies to emptiness itself. For some Buddhists, the answer is no; emptiness itself is the one and only thing that is what it is all the time, without relying on anything else. But for other Buddhists who accept emptiness, emptiness *itself* also lacks any independent self-essence. The truth that everything exists only relationally is itself only relational. Emptiness is itself empty.

You might be wondering what this has to do with you or your life. Working out this idea, though a challenging theoretical task, isn't just a fascinating intellectual puzzle. Getting glimpses of the emptiness of all things can change how you relate to everyday experiences. If the problem is a subtle buzz of anxiety that underlies everything, emptiness highlights some of the very faint overtones that can be easy to miss. That sip of coffee may seem to be inherently pleasant, but it's intimately connected with the dead bugs that lived in the soil in Ecuador, the painful sores of those who picked the beans, the shipping industry (and so too the oil markets and all involved with those), and so on and so on.

This is true of unpleasant things too: A mosquito bites you. Bad, right? But then again, your blood not only feeds the mosquito but also the birds and bats that eat it, and the larger animals that eat them. A single drop of your blood actually helps sustain countless other animals. Internalizing the relational nature of everything is no easy task, but doing so illuminates complex interrelations that are otherwise very difficult to see.

8 | WHO DO YOU THINK YOU ARE?

Put as abstract questions about independent self-essence or existence, these philosophical questions can seem impersonal and academic. They certainly can be, but one way to see their importance beyond philosophical theory is to remember that these issues also apply to *you*. You, the person currently reading this sentence. In the same way that there isn't really a pile, there isn't really a you. If *all* things are essentially relational, one of those things is *you*. These aren't merely questions about how the world out there works, they're also about *you* and what kind of thing you are.

Self-knowledge is critical for solving the practical problems involved in getting through life. If you want to be healthy, you have to know not just about the human body in general, but also about your own particular allergies, habits, and ailments. Choosing a job or a partner means knowing something about what you find meaningful and what you just can't stand. An awareness of your own quirks, character, and preferences is important for figuring out what works for *you*.

Self-knowledge is also tricky—tricky because it is especially elusive. We commonly learn about ourselves only indirectly. Often it is only by reading the reactions of *others* that we can see how harsh, kind, or annoying we are. It is also because when trying to know ourselves, the thing we are trying to see is the very thing that does the looking. Buddhism offers many evocative images to illustrate this special challenge: Just as a knife can't cut itself, the mind can't be directed toward itself. This makes knowing yourself, especially in a deep way, a particularly difficult task. An eye needs a special kind of object, a mirror, in order to see itself. Knowing yourself requires special kinds of tools and methods.

Someone might talk about discovering their *true self*. It can be hard to explain what the "true" adds. What's the difference between a friend and a true friend? A hero and a true hero? What these phrases mean is that we want a friend and not just someone who only *appears* to be a friend. We want a hero, not something approximating one. So discovering your *true* self means learning what you're actually like, as opposed to what you appear to be. For Buddhists, this means seeing that you are like most other things: composite and empty.

Just as there's nothing more to a pile of eggs than the eggs and their relations with each other, there's nothing more to *you* than the bits that make you up and how those bits are organized. Talking about "me" or "myself" or what "I" did today is just a convenient name for those bits and their relationships. You are a convenient fiction, like the pile or Microsoft.

The pile is made up of eggs and Microsoft is made up of employees. What are the bits that make you up? Again, different Buddhists give different answers. Ancient India did have materialists, people who thought there was nothing more to you than your physical body, but the Buddhists of the time rejected that view. For most Buddhists, the bits that make you up are both mental and physical; instants of thought, perception, feeling, and consciousness along with the physical stuff are all parts of the pile. Other Buddhists, however, defend an even more radical idea. For them, physical stuff is just a projection of our consciousness. Though Buddhists disagree about what *exactly* the parts are, they agree that what we are is very different than what we appear to be.

Not only are we a collection of parts, but those parts are in constant flux. Most of the cells that make up your body are constantly changing, with older ones being replaced with new ones. The thoughts and feelings you have bubble up and then fade away. Think back to yourself as a six-year-old. What is the connection between that kid and the person currently reading this sentence? That kid had a body made up of very different physical stuff and had a mind composed of very different thoughts and perceptions. Of course, you have *some* special connection to that six-year-old kid, but that connection is much weaker than it first seemed.

It can feel like the changes that occurred between then and now happened to *you*, the same person. It can seem like butter melting; the same butter was solid and became liquid. But, if Buddhists are right, then it is more like milk turning into butter. There's nothing that persists through the change—first there was milk, then there was butter. First there was the six-year-old, now there's you. The six-year-old is more like someone you grew *from* rather than the very same person. Talking about *you* is like talking about Microsoft or Manchester United—it's an easy way to pick out a certain chain of causes and effects, but there's nothing extra there.

And, if later Buddhists are right, you are also empty. That means "your" existence is also essentially relational. The best way to start seeing this is to think of everyday ways in which we think of our identity as relational. Think of the many roles a person can take on: They might be a mother, a daughter, a boss, a citizen, a neighbor, and on and on. These make up who the person is, and they're all relational—being a daughter depends on a mother, being a boss depends on a company and its employees, being a citizen depends on a government.

It can be easy to forget this relational nature. Consider the task of choosing a romantic partner. Many people think of this as mainly about choosing another person, picking a person that will fit well with who they are. But that's not the whole story. When you pick a romantic partner, you're not just committing to another person, but also to the version of yourself that emerges when you're with that person. A relationship is not a static person picking another static person; you both influence and change each other.

In the same way, the world isn't just the place you live, the setting for the events of your life. You *grew out of the world* and exist in a way that depends on it and everything in it. You aren't plopped into the world with fully formed wishes, hopes, beliefs, and traits. You emerge and develop along with everything else in the world, formed by everyone you've ever met and everything you've ever seen and heard.

Think too about your parents. Being who you are depends on your parents, which in turn depends on their parents, and on and on.

Your existence, your various roles, all depend on everything else to be what they are. Again, this doesn't mean that you *are* everything or anything mystical like that. It means that your being what you are relies on everything else being what it is. You don't exist *prior* to relationships and then enter into them. You *emerge out of them*, in a web of mutual dependence.

This can all sound bleak. What seemed like a self was just a composite series in constant flux, dependent on everything else. This might sound like bad news. The person who mistakenly thought there was a particular building called "New York City" might be sad to learn that there isn't, and never was, such a building. But they're better off knowing how things are than endlessly running around, looking in vain for a landmark that can't be found.

Many forms of Buddhism talk about how you really are in more optimistic sounding ways. One important approach says that you, and every living creature for that matter, have what is called Buddha Nature. Buddha Nature is a slippery concept and is talked about in different ways by different Buddhists. The heart of the idea is that the problem Buddhism aims to solve comes from experiencing the world in misleading or distorting ways. There's nothing essentially wrong with us; we just need to stop making the mistake. It's like being unhealthy because you think that eating only hamburgers is good for you. There isn't anything wrong with your body, you just need to clear up the misconception about what's healthy and what's not.

Not all Buddhists emphasize Buddha Nature, but for those who do, it refers to something in you, actually in *all* beings, that's uncorrupted by the mistakes and distortions that lead to the problem. There is some kernel in there that *does* respond to reality as it is; it's just that all these layers of distortions are caked over it.

This isn't a self, and it's not really *yours*, but it is in you. Often it is talked about as a potential or capacity. A classic image is one of a seed containing oil. The seed has a *potential* for oil in it. Somewhere in the seed there is oil, or at least the possibility of oil—it just has to be brought out. This is contrasted with a stone; no matter what you do with a stone you can't get oil from it. In the same way, the potential to experience reality directly and accurately is there in you. Of course, that doesn't mean you actually *do* experience reality that way. You can have a seed without having oil. Nevertheless, there is something in a seed that's not in a stone when it comes to producing oil, and there is something similar in you when it comes to seeing reality as it is.

The *Lotus Sutra*, a famous Buddhist text, gives some famous analogies to illustrate this potential. In one, a really poor guy goes to visit his rich friend. Naturally, they have a great night and end up getting wasted. They're so drunk that the poor guy decides to just crash at his friend's house. The rich friend has to leave on a business trip so he wakes up early and, seeing his poor friend still sleeping, decides to sew a jewel in the lining of his friend's jacket. The poor friend wakes up later, surely hungover, puts on his jacket, and leaves. In the following months and years he has a rough time and lots of problems making ends meet, but he struggles and makes do with whatever little money he can scrape together. One day he runs into his rich friend who is shocked that he didn't find the jewel—he shows him that it was right there in his jacket the whole time.

The jewel, of course, is supposed to be Buddha Nature—the idea being that it's always there even if we don't realize it. In fact, we have constant access to it; it's just that we don't know about it. The poor friend's problem was that he was looking outwardly for what he was trying to find, oblivious to the fact that what he needed was with him all along.

This applies to the problem itself too. If you thought that the way to solve the problem, to end the essential dissatisfaction of life, was to get something from out in the world, you were wrong. You had the solution to the problem the whole time. Just as in other cases when you correct an error, nothing about the world changes. Instead, your relation to it changes; you realize how things really were all along. You see a spoon in a glass of water and it looks bent. When you look again and see that it was just an illusion, nothing about *the spoon* or *the water* changes at all. You simply realize your mistake and now see that the spoon was never bent to begin with.

This is why some Buddhists will say that Buddha Nature just *is* emptiness. Once you really get that you don't have any static, non-relational essence, that there's nothing to you but a dependent series of related mental and physical events, the problem evaporates. This is because the only problem to be solved was that you mistakenly experienced the world in a way that implied the problem. But the spoon was never bent, New York City was always a collection of buildings, and you only thought there was a problem because you made a mistake about what kind of thing you really are.

9 | NOTHING IS FOREVER

The composite nature of things entails some harsh truths: Things that are put together eventually come apart. When something is made up of pieces, it's only a matter of time before those pieces go their own way. Part of understanding the composite nature of things means seeing their fragility, their temporary nature. Buddhists often talk about impermanence, but this idea covers a range of meanings, some fairly obvious and others more subtle. They all, however, highlight aspects of reality that we must face in order to solve the problem at hand.

Some of these harsh truths are pretty easy to see: People die. Nations fall. Cookies crumble. When something is just smaller bits organized a certain way, it can't last. Sooner or later those bits move someplace else, or at least are no longer organized in the same way. When alliances and loyalties change, nations cease to be. When the cells in a human body stop working together in a certain way, that person's life is over. It's no accident that when philosophers and theologians talk about the immortality of the soul, they also often talk about its indivisibility. The only way something could last forever, it has seemed to many, is if it wasn't made up of parts at all.

It's not just that things will end *eventually, someday*. Even when they seem to remain, they're in a constant state of flux. The parts that make up a car are constantly, imperceptibly wearing out. Tiny bits of metal chip and flake off; rust slowly forms, one speck at a time. That's why things that seem to exist through time—cars, bodies, companies—all require constant maintenance to endure for any substantial amount of time. You need to keep eating food and drinking water to keep living. To keep a company, team, or government going requires a lot of effort because they are impermanent; they are in a state of perpetual transformation.

One way to understand this type of impermanence is to think about what it means for something to persist through time, to continue, to endure. It's a complex subject to be sure, but for many, time and change are intimately related. After all, how do you know that time passes other than by observing some change? Watching the hand of a clock tick, the leaves fall, or the series of waves emitted by a cesium atom—those are all changes. Imagine a universe where *nothing at all* changes. Does time pass there? What would that mean? These are difficult issues, but the point is simple: Many ideas about time *presuppose* this kind of impermanence, that things are continuously changing.

If this seems dizzying, it gets worse. The discussion so far has implied that there is *something that changes*, but as we've seen, many Buddhists deny this. A hive is just a succession of different groups of bees; when a hive changes, there's no *hive* that is changing. There are only different bees coming and going, living and dying, interacting in different ways. So if we say that Manchester United changed— for example, that it got worse or better—it might seem like there is something there, a team, that changed. But teams are made up of a constantly changing roster of players. They might even change their logo or move to a different city. There's no *team* getting worse or better, just different players and coaches doing different things.

At the level of collections, it's not quite right to say that things are constantly changing because there aren't really any things to change. It's better to say that *changing happens*. Think of a river. A river is just a bunch of water; there's nothing to a river beyond the water that makes it up. But that water isn't sitting there; a river isn't just a very long pond. The water is constantly moving and any particular stretch of it is made up of different bits of water from instant to instant. Most everything in life, Buddhists will say, is a lot like that—a convenient name for constantly changing parts.

For Buddhists, impermanence means that everything comes to an end, and in fact, things are constantly ending. But what does any of this mean for you and your life? Thinking about collections, the concept of time, and impermanence can get very theoretical. But these aren't supposed to be just intellectual puzzles to kick around late at night or to split hairs about in academic articles. They're aspects of reality that we have to confront and adapt to if we're going to find a way to live that takes full account of how things really are.

A particularly stark reminder of impermanence is death. Contact with death often prompts re-evaluation. The loss of a friend, a close call on the street, a medical diagnosis, these can prompt us to rethink what we value. Being reminded that your time is limited can make you reconsider how you're spending it. It's one thing to waste time when you have a lot of it; it's another when you see how limited it is.

This can be a mixed blessing depending on your temperament: Knowing that you have limited time on a vacation can be motivating for some, getting them out of bed and out seeing the sights. For others it can be paralyzingly stressful, causing them to fret over each moment wasted in traffic or waiting in line. As with limited time on a vacation, it's good to know that time in life is limited so you don't waste it, but focusing too much on it can be counterproductive. Ideally, it will motivate you to actually focus on the things you want to do and experience doing them rather than putting them off until it's too late.

Impermanence means that death, for you and for everyone you know, is inevitable. It's easy to forget this. Schools sometimes talk about your "permanent" record; it's not really permanent, it just lasts longer than most other records. All tattoos are temporary; they last only as long as the body they're drawn on. Many Buddhist texts warn against thinking of this life, this body, and this world as a home. You are less like a resident at home and more like a visitor at a hotel. You get ninety or a hundred years tops, then you have to move on.

We often think of doctors, medicines, and hospitals as *curing* diseases and *saving* lives. This is true, but what these things really do is provide a small and finite amount of extra time. You might not be killed by *this* illness, but you *will* be killed by something. Doctors play a game where winning simply means extending the game a bit longer. There's nothing wrong with extending the game, but we have to accept that we can't extend it forever. Even if we could, it's worth reflecting on what that would mean on a Buddhist view.

Would it be a good thing? Suppose you wanted to live forever. Try to really imagine that. Forever is a *long* time. Does the world keep changing without you? Thinking this through means thinking about *what* you are outside of your cultural, political,

and social context. After all, if you live forever all of that will radically change. Does it mean outliving all your relationships? All the
cultures, nations, and people that you've ever known? The collapse
of our sun? You would be constantly separated from what matters
to you, for eternity.

More importantly, do *you* keep changing? You're a constantly
changing collection, so all of the physical and mental bits that
make you up will have changed many, many times over. Would
you even recognize yourself after a thousand or a million years?
In what sense would that person still be *you*? Saying that you're
200 million years old starts to seem a lot like the nature documentary narrator saying, "The sturgeon is over 200 million years old."
At that point both you and the sturgeon are just a loose collection
of connected states.

That's a lofty series of questions, but impermanence also touches
more day-to-day matters. We often do not deal with changes well.
Think of visiting a place, maybe the place you grew up or maybe a
place that was very special to you, after a long time away. Likely it's
different. There are new people there; old places are either completely gone or different in various ways. This can make you feel
a range of emotions: happy, sad, bewildered, surprised, wistful.
You might say the place has really changed, but really it was always
changing, even when you were there. The place in your mind is just
a snapshot, a still photo of something that was in motion. Facing
up to that can make it easier to accept and adapt to the reality of
the places you occupy.

The same is true of stuff. Having things presupposes not only
that the thing continues to exist but that the owner does too: If

I own a bicycle, there is a thing, the bicycle, and an owner, me, and I *own* the bicycle. But think of modern ideas about ownership. Often people understand ownership as involving certain rights and permissions. These can even be divided up, so for a single plot of land, the mineral rights, airspace, and building can all be owned by different people. We can even own a fictional character, a process for refining magnesium, or a slogan. And the owners can be a company, with ever-changing stockholders distributed throughout the world. Ownership starts to look not only abstract and ethereal, but also very impermanent. But, Buddhists can say, the same is true of my owning the bicycle.

Since both the owner and possession are collections, made up of parts and constantly changing, the question is not *whether* you will lose what you have, but *when*. Having something just means having the opportunity to use it for a certain window of time. We think of wealth and money as things we *have*, but they're really things we can *use*. They're things that allow us to do stuff, to alter the course of life, and nothing more.

This applies not just to material possessions but also to less tangible things like success and reputation. These too can't last— they're composite and constantly changing. Not only are you constantly changing but so are other people's ideas about you and about what success is. You might have it or you might not, but either way it's not a permanent state and it's not an essential property of you. Like material wealth, it might be useful for certain things, but it's not something *you have*; it's a temporary relation. Part of what this means is that basing your worth and sense of identity on things like success or a good reputation is not only a bad idea because it's an unstable foundation, but it's a mistake. Success isn't something you get. It's a transient and provisional position you occupy.

Perhaps most painfully, our relationships are impermanent. For the bad ones, this can be a source of comfort, but for the good and meaningful ones, it can be a painful fact to face up to. In fact, these relationships (along with the people in them) are constantly changing. This can be good: Someone trying to have the same relationship with you now that you shared when you were six is not going to work very well. Part of what makes relationships, the good ones at least, relevant and meaningful is that they change and adapt as their members do.

Every relationship with every important person in your life will end. You will be separated from each and every person you care about. As with other kinds of impermanence, this means you have limited time and have to use it well. This can turn the volume down on certain things: Is that perceived slight really worth having a big argument over? Does it really matter where you go to get lunch? When time is limited, what's important comes into sharper focus. It can help you to cut out the bullshit and make the most of the limited time you have together. This doesn't mean you have to give up trivial things. Sometimes the most meaningful connections are formed when you're doing seemingly unimportant stuff—shopping for groceries, playing a game, waiting for a bus. Internalizing the fact that your time is limited can help you see these moments for the important opportunities they are.

10 | BUDDHIST PSYCHOLOGY

We've seen some important aspects of how the world is from a Buddhist point of view: Things are composite, relational, temporary, and in constant flux. But that's only half of the story. It's also important to examine the nature of our mental habits, our normal ways of perceiving, thinking, and feeling. The source of the problem is a mismatch between our usual way of relating to the world and how it really is, so it's important to closely examine our mental habits and understand how exactly they obscure reality.

Some Buddhists take this even further. It's not that our mental projections don't match reality, they'll say, it's that there *is no reality aside from our projections*. For them, the problem isn't a mismatch. Rather, the projections themselves are defective, obscuring not an external reality but the nature of the mind itself. Of course, this raises difficult issues: Is saying that there is no reality outside of our projections itself saying something about how *reality really is*, or is it too just part of the projection? Philosophical tangles aside, even these Buddhists will agree that our mental habits are messed up in a deep way and need to be corrected.

The mental habits that distort reality are often called hindrances or poisons. These are things our minds do that prevent us from seeing reality clearly. These habits are often pleasant, at least in the short term. The poison analogy here is a useful one. A poison is something that is toxic for you, but that doesn't preclude it from having a sweet taste. Buddhists offer a striking image to convey this: These habits are like honey on the blade of a knife, sweet but ultimately painful to eat.

We've already run into some of these habits. Our habit of giving names to composite things, for example, can lead us to think of them as real. We use "Microsoft," "Manchester United," "New York City," "car," "table," and most infamously, "me" as convenient names for collections. But after a while, we start to feel like it's more than just useful shorthand. We talk about lots of things—chairs, traffic, books, careers—and forget that these are categories we invent and project onto the world. Though these names are useful for day-to-day living, they start to cause trouble when we begin to mistake such names for reality.

Our minds also construct fictions in more subtle ways. We take a variety of different experiences and merge them into a singular idea, which we project back out into the world. Think of a coffee bean. It's small, brown, fragrant, hard, round, and bitter. Some Buddhists point out that what we really have are different experiences—of bitterness, of brown, of roundness, and so on. Our mind then links them, connecting them to form a single thing. We assume, usually subconsciously, that there is a single object out in the world, a coffee bean, that has all of these different qualities. But this is merely a mental shorthand our minds use, not part of reality. There are, they'll say, only these various experiences. But we project our idea of a coffee bean out into the world and experience it as an independent and singular object.

A similar thing happens when we think of objects over time. It often seems to our minds as though there is *one thing* that goes through various changes over time. But like the coffee bean, this is also a mental construction. Our minds make it seem as though there is *one thing* that starts as milk, which changes into cream, and then finally becomes butter. It also seems like there is *one person* who started as a baby, then became a toddler, then finally an adult. But Buddhists will point out that this too is a mental projection, not reality.

To use a classic analogy: There's no *thing* that first is summer, next turns into fall, and then becomes winter. There is summer, then there is fall, and after that winter. In the same way, there is a baby, then there is a toddler, and after that an adult. There is no one thing that goes through this process, only *different things in sequence*. We might *say* that the season changes from summer to fall, but that's just an easy way to talk about the weather. It's not what is really happening. There is no *season* out there in the world going through these changes. In the same way, we might *say* that you were a baby and became an adult, but that is the same convenient talk.

Another important source of trouble is our psychological tendency to experience the world in a self-regarding way. This takes many different forms and is described in many different ways. One way Buddhists describe it is through the categories of good, bad, and indifferent. The basic idea is that our experiences are implicitly filtered through a mechanism that sorts them based on how they relate to us and our goals. You're about to start a trip—but wait, there's a huge traffic jam. "Ugh," you think, "that sucks!" But you learn the road you'll be taking is clear: "Ah, that's great!" Through all of this, your experience is filtered through what is good or bad for *you* and *your aims*.

Even things you experience as *neither* good nor bad have this feature. A traffic jam (or maybe a housing crisis or natural disaster) happens somewhere far away, where you don't know anybody. You're pretty indifferent; you aren't particularly moved one way or the other. This is because deep down you know that it won't make a difference for *you* or your immediate goals. Implicit in your very experience of indifference is a sense of self.

Judgments often depend on our aims in very subtle ways and can be implicit in seemingly harmless thoughts. We often, for example, distinguish between a drug's effects and its side effects. But the difference depends on what *we* want: When it's something we want to happen it's an effect, and when it's not we call it a side effect. Effects as opposed to side effects aren't *inherent features of the drug itself* but depend on us and our aims. We move from a relational quality that's based on our aims and slip into thinking it's a free-standing feature of the world.

Buddhists also talk about our mental lives in terms of craving and aversion. We want the good things in life for ourselves, or at least for our friends. A bigger salary, fancy title, glossy photo, prestigious awards—we want them for ourselves. We want everyone to clap for *us* and to know and appreciate what *we've* done. This is a common tendency; flattery works for a reason. Of course, it's the opposite for bad stuff. We want to avoid looking foolish or losing a contest. Let it happen to someone else. Let *them* get booed or humiliated, let *them* lose their money.

Most of the time this happens without your ever realizing it. You just find yourself drawn to the smell of warm cookies and away from that stinky dumpster. You find your eyes lingering on a person you find attractive and looking away from someone you find repulsive. Without a second thought, you skip a song you find annoying and bob your head to one that you like. These habits might not seem particularly bad. After all, there's nothing wrong with skipping a song. But these habits shape our experiences around a false idea of self, obscuring how things really are.

It's not just that we *want* these things, but there is an attitude of attachment that often accompanies and underpins this. This is sometimes called grasping or clinging. It involves not just wanting something, but being hung up on it. It connotes a kind of stickiness, like sharp nettles that get stuck in your clothes or a price tag that you just can't seem to peel off. This stickiness is a pull to possess things, to *have* them and to *keep* them.

There are many, many objects of attachment, things we can get stuck on. Group membership, things like national identity, political affiliation, schools you attended, hobbies you have. Opinions or interests, being a musician or a gardener or a foodie. Careers, romantic status, familial roles. Life provides an embarrassment of riches when it comes to what you can get hung up on. This attitude of attachment reorganizes your experiences around a sense of self, which makes it very easy to act in ways that are insensitive to how things really are.

It's important to keep in mind that attachment isn't the same as mere enjoyment or pleasure, though they often go together. It's possible, though often psychologically difficult, to enjoy something without being hung up on it. One can enjoy a delicious meal or an amazing concert without being sad that the meal is over or wishing that the concert went on forever. But that is partially because, as we get full and as the concert goes on, our enjoyment starts to wane. Psychologically speaking, as long as we enjoy something it's easy to get hung up on it and want it to continue.

Attachment is particularly important when it comes to our identities. It's not simply that I want to get the promotion or award; it's that these things become part of who I think I am. I'm no longer some mere sales associate; I am a *regional manager*. I don't just want to own the car, but to be a *Porsche owner*. An *award winner*. This involves not just wanting some thing or event, but latching on to it and making it part of your sense of who you are.

Part of the reason this is a hindrance is that it leads to accumulating not just experiences, but a sense that you're an independent, separate self. Once you start to identify with being smart, cultured, a failure, a manager, or whatever else, it's easy to start getting stuck on this idea of yourself. This reinforces a distorted picture of the world in a few ways. It makes relational and temporary features, being a manager or popular or rich, feel like essential qualities of you. This in turn makes you feel like there is a *you* that isn't merely an impermanent collection of mental and physical states.

This false sense of self can often be pleasant. It's a bit like being drunk. It can feel good even when, and often *because*, it's deeply distorting. And like being drunk, though it can be pleasant for a while, it creates another level of anguish later on. You get fired. Your Porsche gets stolen. When things like this happen, not only did you lose something you enjoyed and liked, but now you have to question your identity. You lost the car *and* your status as Porsche owner. But it all started because you treated something temporary as permanent, and something relational as an essential part of who you are.

It's not just ordinary identities that are hindrances, either. You can also get attached to an identity like being morally good, being a Buddhist, or even one of *not being attached to things*. Without noticing, you can slip into an identity of not identifying with things. You can get hung up on not getting hung up on stuff. This can be especially painful when exposed because not only do you feel bad, but you feel bad for feeling bad. This kind of hang-up poses special challenges and, as we'll see, Buddhists have developed special techniques for dealing with them.

All of these different mental habits we have prevent us from seeing reality clearly. That's why Buddhists often talk about ignorance as the most fundamental source of the problem. Calling it ignorance, however, can be a bit misleading. Talk of "ignorance" sounds like you simply don't *know* something, cognitively or reflectively. We often use the word to mean not knowing something in an intellectual way: I don't know the capital of Estonia and then someone tells me it's Tallinn. Now I know, so I'm no longer ignorant of what the capital of Estonia is.

The Buddhist sense of ignorance, however, involves more than just intellectual knowledge. Ignorance in a Buddhist sense is more like a lack of awareness. It's also about not getting something about the world, viscerally, in your bones. Consider someone who says something like, "I know there's beauty in this world, but I just don't feel it." Is that person *ignorant* of the beauty in the world? What they're missing is closer to what Buddhists are interested in. Someone can know, intellectually, that traveling by plane is safer than traveling by car and yet still *feel* more afraid on the plane than in the car. I can know that a certain spider is harmless or that there's no point in being angry about a small inconvenience, and still feel afraid or furious. It's just not as simple as learning a few facts.

Ignorance is typically illustrated with visual metaphors like fog or darkness. In trying to walk a trail in dense fog or make your way through a pitch-black room, you can't see how the world is and so have difficulty navigating through it. This is what Buddhists mean when they're talking about ignorance. You just can't see the way things are. You don't get the collective, empty, and impermanent nature of things. Even though you might understand it intellectually and be able to explain the ideas, if you don't fully experience things that way, the problem will linger. The mental habits discussed here act as blocks to this richer kind of understanding.

If all of this sounds radical, that's because it *is*. Since Buddhists are in the business of diagnosing the subtle and fundamental mistakes our minds make, often the errors they find will not seem like errors at all. They are so natural that questioning them can seem absurd. But the whole point is that what initially seemed obvious sometimes doesn't hold up under closer examination. When you're watching a film, it can seem obvious that there is a seamless, moving image. Only upon closer investigation can the counter-intuitive truth be revealed; it's actually a series of distinct images shown in rapid succession that exploits certain features of your visual perception. What seemed to be an intuitive and obvious truth about the world turned out to be a mental glitch.

So far, this doesn't paint a pretty picture of the human mind. But this is because it's a list of things to fix. You need to understand what you want to correct before you start trying to correct it. And it is by using our mind's abilities and capacities well that we can correct these mistakes. After all, the prognosis is good. The problem is solvable, even if it is difficult and takes a long time.

11 | REBIRTH AND REDEATH

Maybe nothing is forever, but some processes do go on for a long, long, *long* time. For many forms of Buddhism, especially more traditional ones, one such process is a cycle of birth and death that stretches back zillions of years. One of the biggest splits in popular teachings on Buddhism is over how to understand rebirth. For some, it's part of Buddhism's cultural baggage. For others, it's absolutely essential to the Buddhist outlook.

Like it or not, a worldview that assumes this cycle of birth and death forms the context for the vast majority of Buddhist thought. It is inescapable when reading virtually any Buddhist text written before the modern era. Many Buddhists, especially in the West, have de-emphasized and reinterpreted rebirth. But even if you think it's just a metaphor or that it's merely part of the historical context, it *is* there and is an important part of Buddhist thought.

It's hard not to roll your eyes as hard as you can when you hear someone blabbing about how they were Cleopatra or Napoleon in their previous life. This is partly because such talk is often boring. Like talking about your dreams or your workout routine, it's just not interesting for people to listen to. But it can also be self-indulgent. After all, why Cleopatra or Napoleon and not some moderately successful cobbler, a housefly, or a parasite living on the shell of a snail? Those aren't nearly as sexy or interesting, but, if previous lives are real, they're far more likely.

It's important to distinguish rebirth from reincarnation. As we've seen, Buddhists will deny that there is any independent and persisting essence, so they will deny that beings have immaterial souls. Reincarnation is the transfer of a soul from body to body. To say that you're the reincarnation of Cleopatra or a snail is to say that you share the same soul. Rebirth, on the other hand, is a cycle of many births and deaths, without any soul linking them. It's commonly called rebirth but it could equally well be called *redeath* since each lifetime involves both a birth and a death.

How, you might wonder, could a being be reborn without some kind of underlying essence? What is it that gets reborn if not some kind of soul? This is a thorny question for many Buddhists. Here's one way to think about it: If Cleopatra was a snail in a previous life, what makes Cleopatra and the snail the same is just what makes Microsoft in 1981 and Microsoft in 2030 the same even though it might change all of its employees, its logo, and the products it makes. Think about the nature documentary that talks about how "the sturgeon" is 200 million years old even though there's no single thing that has been around for all that time. What is 200 million years old is a chain of many, many generations of different fish. Just as "the sturgeon" is a convenient name for generations of different fish, the "you" that gets reborn is just a name for mental and physical parts that have a special connection.

Another way to think about the difference between rebirth and reincarnation is like this: Reincarnation is like a boat sailing over the water. There's a special thing, separate from the water, that is moving through it. That's the soul moving through different bodies and different lifetimes. Rebirth is more like a wave. We might say that a wave moves through the water, but the wave just *is* water doing a certain thing. When a wave moves through the water there's not a thing that's separate from the water moving through it; it's just an easy way to talk about what the water is doing.

In many traditional forms of Buddhism this cycle of rebirth and redeath includes supernatural beings and places. The cycle involves not only humans and animals but also various types of supernatural beings. There are gods with very cushy but finite lives, lives that are pleasant, fun, and all-around wonderful. That is, until they start to die. Knowing they'll certainly be reborn into a more painful life, death is an incredibly traumatic experience for them. There are also lesser gods, who live in constant jealousy of the easy lives of the more fortunate gods. There are even beings called hungry ghosts, with huge stomachs and tiny mouths that leave them perpetually starving and in search of food.

The cycle of rebirth also includes hells. Yes, Buddhism does have hells. Traditionally, there are *many* different hells: There are hot hells, freezing hells, hells where you are cut up over and over again, and more. These are agonizing and are understood as the results of previous actions. Though Buddhists use terms like "heaven" and "hell" to describe some of these realms, we have to be careful not to import various connotations of these words. So, for example, time in the heavens and hells is not eternal. Instead, like other lives, they last for a finite amount of time and then they're over. And, as we'll see, it can be misleading to think of these as a reward or punishment rather than simply the natural result of previous mistakes.

Many traditional Buddhists think of these places and beings as real, just as real as the world that we occupy. In fact, this is central to many traditional statements of the fundamental problem Buddhism aims to solve: These different kinds of lives all make up what is called samsara. Beings are constantly being born and dying in these different realms, over and over and over again. At least for the more pleasant ones, this might seem like a good thing. You get to stay on the ride for a long time. But, like all rides, it gets old. It might be fun playing Monopoly with your family for the first hour. At hour five, however, it's no longer so fun. Samsara is like playing Monopoly *for millions of years*. It might have its moments, but overall it sucks.

On this traditional understanding, Buddhism solves the problem by ending this cycle of birth and death. The solution, sometimes called nirvana, is about getting out of the cycle. Though it might not be obvious, *all* of the realms, heavens included, are characterized by the awful buzz of anxiety and dissatisfaction. This is obvious for hungry ghosts and those in hells, but it is true of the gods too. After all, they're having too much fun at the party to think about anything important in life and, when the end comes, they have to deal with the fact that they're leaving the best party in the universe. Even though they ignored it, their good times were fragile and temporary all along.

This context is important because it makes a difference to how you understand Buddhism's practical advice. It can change how you understand the timescale for solving the problem. If you think there are many, many, many lives to experience before you get out of the cycle, you start playing the long game. Rather than trying to solve the problem directly, you start doing things like being just a little nicer and supporting Buddhist institutions so that maybe next time around you'll be in a better position to start seeing things as they are. Rather than solving the problem *right here and right now*, you focus more on more incremental progress that spans over many lifetimes. In fact, many people around the world relate to Buddhism in just this way.

Some people are only able to make incremental progress, but others have the opportunity to do more. Traditional Buddhists emphasize that having a human life is very rare and puts you in a great position to make larger steps toward solving the problem. There are various striking images to illustrate this. Picture a huge, blind turtle swimming in the ocean. The turtle is so huge it only needs to surface once every hundred years. Floating somewhere out in the ocean is a doughnut-shaped ring, just big enough for the turtle's head to fit through. Each time the turtle puts its head through the ring, that's *one* human birth. Given the number of humans, this gives you a sense of just how many *other* types of beings there must be.

It's not just that a human birth is rare, but it includes the ideal mix of factors for escaping the cycle. Hungry ghosts and jealous gods are too distracted to try to solve the problem. Animals aren't smart enough to think hard about reality. In the hells, everyone is in too much pain. And the gods, well, they're having too good a time to bother. But as a human you're smart enough to think hard about life and have enough pain to motivate you to do so, but not so much that it takes over your entire life. The traditional understanding of rebirth changes the scope of the problem. It isn't just about escaping the dissatisfaction of *this* life but of a whole cycle of lives. This is the standard framework most teachers in Asia use when explaining Buddhism, and it's assumed by a majority of Buddhists, at least in popular (rather than esoteric) forms of Buddhism.

If you're a modern reader, however, this probably doesn't sound very plausible to you. It can seem supernatural, too fantastical, and a bit too *religious*. For many Buddhists in the modern world, the background of rebirth isn't central to what they find interesting or inspiring about Buddhism. They often see it as the cultural equivalent of the wrapping that Buddhism arrived in; you open it up to get what you really want and then discard it. This isn't unusual for modern people making sense of historical ideas. Isaac Newton, for example, was both Christian and very interested in alchemy, but those things are often discarded when thinking about his contributions to science and mathematics.

But the fact remains that many important texts and teachings of the historical Buddha make explicit reference to supernatural aspects of rebirth. There are a number of strategies modern Buddhists make use of when confronted with such texts and teachings. An unfortunately common one is to simply ignore these parts. This isn't great—not only because it can set an uncomfortable precedent (you can just ignore any Buddhist texts that say something you don't like?), but also because references to rebirth are so pervasive you run the risk of ignoring huge numbers of foundational Buddhist texts.

Another strategy is to understand these aspects metaphorically. On this approach, hungry ghosts and hell beings aren't understood as *real creatures* but as representations of psychological states that we all experience. Anyone who has been desperate for food or acknowledgment has been a hungry ghost. Anyone who has passed a kidney stone or lost a close friend has been in hell. Anytime you've experienced a day where everything just falls into place perfectly, where you couldn't want to be anywhere else, has been in heaven. This way to understand rebirth isn't an exclusively modern one, but it is a common way to make sense of these ideas within a contemporary scientific worldview.

Stepping back, there is an important way in which thinking about the literal truth or falsity of these stories misses the point. That is, focusing on whether or not such beings *really exist*, and if so how and where, is like hearing the story of Robin Hood and focusing on whether or not there ever was such a guy, and if so where exactly he lived. You might think about such questions, but a more rewarding way to relate to the story is to reflect on the lessons about wealth, inequality, justice, and vigilantism that the story raises. You can accept and learn from these lessons *whether or not* you think Robin Hood was a real person.

Of course, for many people the literal truth of the story is an important source of its power. Americans sometimes tell the story of a young George Washington who, after getting a new hatchet, tested it out on his father's cherry tree. When his father saw the damaged tree he asked George about it and, because of his honesty, young George owned up to his vandalism. The story isn't true. Of course, it could still be true that George Washington was very honest and that honesty is a very good trait to have. But for some Americans, it's particularly important that this episode *really did* happen, that young George *really did* cut down a tree and own up to it. Some Buddhists relate to rebirth in this way, seeing it not merely as a story that illuminates other truths, but as an important truth in its own right.

But reflecting on rebirth can be beneficial even if you don't think it's literally true. Even thinking about whether or not it's true forces us to think hard about what *exactly* it would mean to have been another kind of creature. If you were once a cockroach or a god or an elephant, in what sense is that *you*? Answering this means, in part, reflecting on the interests, experiences, and well-being of such creatures. What is it that you might share? That you want to avoid pain and suffering and you try to make your way through a world you only understand a tiny fraction of? Such reflections can change your attitudes toward these other creatures, producing if not empathy, then at least a kind of solidarity with them.

Even if rebirth isn't true, the change in perspective these reflections bring about can make a real difference to how you go through life. We can learn something about human life by reading a story, even if that story isn't true. We do this all the time when trying to get others to be more empathetic. We say things like, "Imagine that was your daughter!" or "Think about how hard it would be for you to be a single parent!" Someone who responds to these prompts with "Well, she's *not* my daughter" or "But I'm *not* a single parent" misses the point. The point is that imaginatively entertaining something, even something that you know isn't true, can get you to see features of the world you previously missed. It can help you connect with others in a way you couldn't before. The thought that you've had every possible relationship with someone can change the tone of your current relationship. Imagining that every person you meet has been your friend, enemy, sibling, and rival in a previous life can change how they seem to you, even if it's not literally true.

Rebirth is most generally about how you see your life and its place in larger cycles in the world. Different Buddhists interpret this in very different ways, which not only sets the context for other ideas in Buddhist thought but also illuminates the different background worldviews Buddhists can have.

The history of Buddhism is one of different people in different times and places struggling with the task of figuring out what's the gift and what's the wrapping. Buddhism, for its part, has managed to remain relevant because it is a living, changing thing that adapts to the needs of different groups of people. Understanding Buddhism means understanding a wide variety of points of view on various issues. Rebirth highlights the differences between a modern, scientific take on Buddhism and a more traditional, supernatural one. You might prefer one over the other, or think one is more authentic or more plausible, but it's important to keep these different views in mind when trying to understand Buddhism as a whole.

12 | KARMA

What are you doing right now? This seemingly simple question can have surprisingly complex answers. You are, of course, reading a book. But you might also be relaxing, doing something on your to-do list, spending time at home, riding on a bus, or putting off an important task. What you're doing can also be spread out over a long period. Someone might be studying for their law degree, even though *right now* they're having lunch with a friend. What exactly you are doing depends on features of your situation, plans, aims, and desires.

Karma literally means action. Initially, a *very* long time ago, it meant specific ritual actions performed to bring about certain results, a good harvest or rain or whatever. Later, the meaning of the term expanded and started to refer to *all* actions. Not only that, it's also used to refer to the *effects* of your actions and the *connection* between your actions and those effects. So when someone says that something is your *karma*, they're saying that *you did it*, you acted in ways that made this happen.

The most basic idea behind karma is that your actions have effects. Drinking booze makes you feel drunk, screaming aggressively makes another person feel bad, exercising regularly makes your body stronger. There are regularities in these connections.

Planting tomato seeds will, if the weather cooperates, produce tomato plants. It will never produce wheat or corn.

As we saw, these effects are incredibly complex and difficult, if not impossible, to know. Buying a pound of coffee beans has the effect of supporting countless growers, traders, shipping and fuel companies, marketing firms, investors, and on and on. In fact, if you take emptiness seriously, each action is connected to *everything else* in the universe. Nobody said karma was easy.

Given this basic idea of karma, it's important to highlight what it is *not*. People will sometimes talk about the "law of karma"—this phrase is a modern one. Karma is not traditionally talked about in this way. This doesn't mean that it's necessarily wrong or misleading, but it can be. We sometimes think of laws as having a lawmaker and an enforcer: The traffic laws are written by a legislature and enforced by police. But karma is not like that—there's nobody writing the law and making sure it's enforced. In this sense, it's more like the law of gravity—it's a regularity in the way the world is, which nobody has to write or enforce.

Similarly, traffic laws often result in punishments, but when you fall, gravity isn't punishing you. Karma isn't some form of cosmic justice; it need not be about *deserving* the effects. If I eat hamburgers every day, I will gain weight. Gaining weight is the *result* of my eating choices, but do I *deserve* to gain weight? Drinking whiskey will get me drunk, but do I then *deserve* to be drunk? More to the point, Buddhists will highlight that beings in fact act in ways that lead them to suffer. It is perfectly compatible with pointing this out to also think that none of them *deserves* to suffer. Karma is about the regularities between actions and their effects, not about enforcing punishment for certain forbidden actions. To be sure, some effects are bad; falling down is bad. But not all bad effects are punishments.

Finally, karma isn't fate. The Buddha is clear that not all events are determined by karma. Think of your health. Sometimes being healthy or not is the result of what you do, your diet and lifestyle. But sometimes, it isn't; it's just the weather or genetics. In fact, talking about action presupposes actions are importantly different from other kinds of events.

Again, things get complicated here. There is an important difference between what we *do* and what *happens to us*. There's a difference between eating and digesting, between a sharp gesture and a muscle spasm. Some things, of course, muddy the waters. Sometimes breathing just happens and sometimes we decide to breathe in a certain way. Sometimes we decide to recall a certain event and sometimes a memory just appears.

Infamously, sometimes *not* doing something counts as an action. If someone is drowning right next to me and I just sit there, it seems like in *not* helping I *did* something: I *let* that person die. Other times, of course, not doing something isn't an action at all. After all, there are infinite things you're not doing right now, and if they were all actions you'd be a *very* busy person. Part of what helps to separate these is what's going on inside a person's head.

Buddhists distinguish different aspects of an action. Suppose a bully picks on someone by saying cruel things to them. There are many phases of this action. First, the bully sees the person he wants to pick on and recognizes who it is. Then he decides to say something to hurt them, maybe considering what would sting the most. Next, he actually says the words out loud, directed at them. Finally, the person hears what he said and feels bad. These are all different aspects of that single action, and for Buddhists, they're *all* harmful. Even if the person couldn't hear it or if the bully got interrupted before he could actually say what he planned, he still did something bad.

To see why, it will be important to consider both the range of effects and the critical place of intention. Buddhists are unique in placing particular emphasis on the role of intention in karma. All the steps are relevant, but the one where the bully *decides* to say something hurtful is the most critical one. One reason for this is that the intention, the fixing of a goal or a plan, is essential for determining what the action is. Think of someone going to get their stuff from an ex after a breakup. What their goal is determines what exactly they're doing: Are they trying to get their stuff back? Are they trying to reconcile? Are they trying to inconvenience the ex in a final act of retribution? The only way to tell the difference is to think about what their aims and intentions are.

Or think about apologizing. Two people might say the exact same words in the exact same tone of voice, but one might be apologizing while the other is just manipulating. What's the difference? The difference is whether the person actually feels sorry about what they did and whether they really plan to do anything differently in the future. What a person's intentions are makes the difference between whether saying some words counts as apologizing or not.

There are other reasons it makes sense to emphasize intentions. Killing someone and hiring a hitman to kill them seem importantly similar, but Buddhists can rightly emphasize that such actions are similarly bad because they involve the same intentions. Shooting at someone and missing is, of course, not as bad as hitting them, but you don't get to avoid bad karma just because you have bad aim.

Some non-Buddhists in India have emphasized the *effects* of actions as being the most important. They were quick to make fun of Buddhists for their emphasis on intention. If intentions are so important, then it looks like stabbing a gourd while mistakenly thinking it's a baby would be worse than unintentionally stabbing a real baby. After all, they said, the former involves a bad intention and the latter does not. Or think of dreams. If you had a dream where you intended to murder your boss, is that just as bad as actually murdering them? After all, the intentions are the same. This is, of course, an uncharitable understanding of the Buddhist position. Emphasizing one aspect doesn't mean that you must ignore all of the others. The effects of our actions are also very important to Buddhist thought, but it's important to understand the wide range of things that this includes.

We can think about the outward effects of our actions. Saying cruel things makes someone feel bad, and feeding someone will make them less hungry. Some actions are karmically good in the sense that they lead to more happiness and less pain and suffering in the world; others are karmically bad in the sense that they do the opposite. As we've seen, these ripple outward in complex ways and are difficult to know with much certainty.

But there are also inner effects on your own mind. When we act, we develop and reinforce mental and physical habits. This is obvious when learning a skill—at first you can't play the piano or drive a car, but after doing certain actions over and over, your hands just know what to do. The same is true of our minds. Acting in certain ways shapes how we experience the world. After a while, a surgeon can start seeing patients as bags of organs and tumors instead of as people, or a lawyer can start to see a rowdy party as a collection of potential lawsuits. This is also true, Buddhists will point out, of mistaken and harmful ways of seeing the world. After a while, a bully can start to see social interactions as a series of opportunities for biting and cruel comments.

More importantly for Buddhists, actions can reinforce mental habits that make it hard to fully realize the true nature of the world. The bully, for example, acts to develop habits that reinforce many of the mistakes we've seen. He thinks of himself as persisting through time and as having an independent essence that is disconnected from others. In this sense, even actions that produce good outward effects, as when the surgeon performs a successful surgery, can still be bad by reinforcing distorted ways of seeing the world.

Many Buddhists, especially ordinary people, talk a lot about merit. Actions that produce good effects, both inner and outward, are thought to bring merit to the person who does them. There's something almost fiscal about it; after investing time and energy into good actions, merit starts to accrue for you. Merit is typically thought to result in insights into reality or, more supernaturally, memories of past lives and the prospect of better future ones.

It is also commonly thought that doing certain practices in certain places or on special dates produces even more merit. This can certainly seem like superstition, since the dates are sometimes astrologically determined. You might gain more merit when visiting a certain temple when the planets are in a certain position or during a certain phase of the moon. But one way to relate to this is to reflect on similar attitudes in your own culture. For many people it seems natural that making a promise while wearing a white dress in a special building in front of your family is weightier and more transformative than making it privately in sweatpants at a gas station. Many people who aren't even Christian feel that it's especially meaningful to see their family on Christmas. Some people think there's something special about a kiss at midnight on New Year's Eve. These are all ways that make the time and place of an action more weighty or significant. We need to be careful of discounting other people's social meaning simply because we're not used to it.

Many Buddhists also think that merit can be dedicated and transferred. That is, when you do something that gains you merit, you can give that merit to others. Somewhat paradoxically, this act is itself meritorious. This can work to change your outlook in important ways. For example, it can undermine a kind of selfish greed for merit. Rather than doing things to gain merit for yourself, you start to see that the best way to get merit is to do good things *without trying to get more merit*. Merit is something good, but also something you, at least eventually, don't want to be too hung up on.

Traditionally, karma is situated within the context of rebirth. That is, it's the fuel that keeps the engine running. The cycle of rebirth and redeath keeps going because we act and so produce future effects. The way you solve the problem in this kind of context is to escape the cycle by no longer acting, no longer producing any more karmic effects.

This can sound odd. So the solution to the problem is to stop acting at all; does that mean you turn into something like a robot or a complicated thermostat? That does not seem very appealing as a solution. What Buddhists are getting at here is that people who understand how reality is in a deep way don't act in the same way as the rest of us. What they do is spontaneous and selfless. Imagine you're taking care of a child. If the child falls or hurts themselves badly, you instantly rush to help. You rush over spontaneously, without any extra thoughts, certainly without thoughts about how you're such a good person for helping or the problems you'll face if the child dies. It's not quite right to call this response automatic; that feels too mechanical and stiff. Better to call it natural. You're self-lessly in tune with the world and so act in a special way. The idea is that a buddha, someone who is no longer acting from ignorance, acts in this way *all of the time*.

Many modern Buddhists, however, understand karma in a more scientific register. For them, the cause and effect involved in karma is the very same cause and effect that you find in the sci-ences. When a physicist says a certain element causes a chemical reaction or a psychologist says that certain beliefs cause distress, that is the sense of cause involved in karma.

Of course, these two views on karma each raise issues that need to be explained. For example, traditionally, the effects of our actions occur over many lifetimes. If this is the case, one needs to explain how causation can work over such huge gaps in time and space, what your current habits and tendencies would look like in a snail or hungry ghost, and how this kind of causation relates to the kind discussed by scientists.

But modern Buddhists who see rebirth as metaphorical rather than literal also have some things to explain. If rebirth isn't literally true, then the effects must occur in this very lifetime. What then do we say about terrible people who die peacefully in their beds surrounded by loved ones? A traditional Buddhist who accepts the reality of future lives has an easy answer: That person has some very bad lifetimes ahead of them. But if rebirth is just a metaphor, what can be said? Perhaps they weren't *really* happy, deep down. Perhaps their actions weren't *really* terrible. Neither of these is particularly plausible, but whatever the modern Buddhist says, it cannot appeal to the idea of future lives.

These are of course complicated issues, but it's important to keep in mind that different ways of understanding karma give rise to different problems. What both approaches can agree on is that our actions have effects, both in the world and in our ways of experiencing things. They can also highlight how our thoughts, plans, and feelings change the nature of what we're doing. These are important insights when taking on the difficult project of reorienting our outlook on life.

13 | THE TWO TRUTHS

We've seen that Buddhists see the world as full of composite, relational things in constant flux. We've also seen that there are important Buddhist ideas about rebirth, merit, action, and intention. But if *everything*, including the self, is empty and impermanent, how can we make sense of these ideas? We've seen that Buddhists grant that talking about collections can be a useful fiction or a practical simplification, but what does that really mean? If Buddhism is about seeing reality as it is, how could it be useful to talk about something that isn't real?

A common image in Buddhism is to liken Buddhist teachings to a raft. A raft is useful for crossing a river, but once you've crossed it, carrying the raft with you can become a burden. Like the raft, the Buddhist teachings are a vessel to get you someplace where you won't need them anymore. The Buddha often adjusted what he taught to the particular people he was teaching at the time. Most people aren't ready or able to grasp the full truth, so he tells them things that are helpful for their progress toward the truth *given where they are*.

When the truth is complex, teaching often means saying things that aren't *exactly* right, especially at the start. Nearly everything a professor says in an introductory history or physics class is not true in light of cutting-edge work in contemporary history or physics. Even though these lessons aren't *exactly* true, certain falsehoods are taught in an introductory class because saying the full truth would be incomprehensible to students starting from scratch. What's taught in these classes allows the students to progress and eventually see that what they learned at the start wasn't really true.

Perhaps the most famous example of this is from a classic text called the *Lotus Sutra*. In one scene, a rich guy's house catches on fire. His kids are playing inside and so absorbed in their games that they don't respond to his shouts for them to leave the house; they don't fully grasp the danger and find their games too engrossing. So, he gets their attention by telling them that he has brand new carts with each of their favorite animals waiting for them outside. This gets them to run out of the house and eventually see the danger they were in. The story ends with the dad presenting them all with a single cart, different from any he promised.

Here the dad represents the Buddha who, because of people's limited understanding, sometimes teaches things that aren't really true. The three promised carts, representing different Buddhist approaches, end up all being the same, though different from the ones he promised. Just as the dad promises different carts to each kid based on what they like, the Buddha adjusts his teachings to different students. It's not that anything goes, though. He always does this with the aim of benefiting the student and eventually increasing their understanding. As with the introductory course, sometimes long-term understanding requires short-term falsehoods. This is part of what makes teaching anything so challenging.

Buddhists care deeply about getting at the truth and as a result have thought a lot about what truth is. One of the most important philosophical ideas to emerge from Buddhism is that of the two truths. The best way to understand this idea is with an example: Suppose your friend is watching a Mickey Mouse cartoon. You missed the start so you ask, "What's happening?" Your friend is likely to reply with something like, "Mickey just met Minnie and he fell in love." This is true insofar as this is what happened *in the show*. Within a set of assumptions, it is the correct answer, while an answer like, "Mickey just robbed a bank" is an incorrect answer—that didn't really happen in the show. This type of correct answer is conventionally true because it is true within a certain set of conventions you both accept.

And yet, the conventionally true answer isn't *fully* true. What is *really* happening, a philosophically minded friend might insist, is that a flow of electrons has caused pixels in the screen to glow in different ways. These glowing pixels cluster in ways that resemble lines and produce light that hits the rods and cones within your eyes. When these lines change in rapid succession, your brain interprets this information, organizing it to form a representation of two mice. Onto these representations, you project human mental states like love and desire. If your friend is more long-winded, of course, the story will be more detailed. This, they'll insist, is what is *actually* happening. What is really true, not just within a set of conventions, Buddhists call ultimate truth.

We can relate to the Mickey Mouse cartoon on two levels, one embedded within the norms of our everyday lives and the other not. The question was asked from within a set of assumptions, that there are characters who act and experience emotions, and the conventional answer is true within that context. It does not, however, capture the full reality of what is going on in the world.

This doesn't entail that conventional truth is always bad or to be abandoned. Talking about a show with your friend can be an important source of value and even knowledge. Conventional truth can be useful as long as it doesn't blind you to what is really happening. A physicist or vision scientist could give the conventional answer to their friend while knowing full well the complexity of what is really happening.

This idea plays two different roles in Buddhism, both as a philosophical idea about the nature of reality and as an interpretive strategy to make sense of a variety of Buddhist texts. Think of a subject you know a lot about. Now imagine that you've discovered a trunk full of papers containing things that an expert in this subject said at various times and places, and unfortunately they're all mixed up. Sorting through them you'd likely find that some things they said contradict other things they said. What do you do? This is similar to the task Buddhists face when confronted with the vast range of texts that claim to record the Buddha's teachings.

There are, of course, a variety of strategies available. You could say that some stuff was written down wrong or that the expert didn't really mean it or that they used certain words in a special way. These, of course, exist in the Buddhist world, too. But you could also see the two conflicting claims like the two claims about the Mickey cartoon. One day your friend said the complicated story about electrons, pixels, and eyes, and said that there is no Mickey. But on another day, at home with their kids, they said that Mickey fell in love with Minnie. One way to interpret these so that they fit together and are true is to see that one was made within a particular system of assumptions and conventions. The same is done with things that the Buddha said, allowing them to be true (at least in a system of conventions) and fit together well.

Truth here has two senses. One applies to sentences, like when we talk about whether what someone said was *true*. Here we're asking if what a person said matches reality. The other applies to the world. When walking in the desert we might ask if we're *truly* seeing palm trees and water in the distance. Here we ask if what we see is *real*, if the world really is the way that it seems. Though it's more commonly known as the two truths, it could also be called the two realities.

Let's consider conventional truth first. There are many different systems of assumptions and conventions. Some countries drive on the right side of the road and others on the left; this is a convention, one that is very important for safety. People in those places came together and decided that one or the other side was the correct side to drive on. Sometimes these are deliberately decided, as when governments write traffic laws, but other times they just emerge. So even though nobody had a meeting to decide that people should not stand very close to the only other person in an elevator or that they should say "please" when asking for something, these are conventions, too.

It's important to keep in mind that there are still truths within these conventions. The game of chess is a convention—its rules are something we invented and all agree on. But there are still facts about good and bad strategies, facts about what is an illegal move, facts about who can win with what pieces remaining. Just because the game of chess is merely a convention doesn't mean that anything goes. But it does mean that truths about chess are of a special kind; they're inextricably intertwined with the conventions that make it up.

One really important kind of convention is language itself. Is the little ball of dough with a filling called "dumpling," "*jiaozi*," or "*momo*"? What the right name is depends on what language you're speaking, on what set of conventions you're operating in. We can see language itself as a set of rules and sounds that we agree on, as a convention. This, as we'll see, has important consequences for how we relate to speech and writing. After all, if language is just a convention, then anything we say or write (including *this*) can only be conventionally true.

As you might have guessed by now, it's difficult, bordering on impossible, to say much about ultimate truth. Different Buddhists have understood ultimate truth in different ways. Most generally, you can think about it as how things *really* are, in the important italicized sense of really. It's often identified with emptiness itself, as the changing, relational nature of the world. Another way to get at ultimate truth is to think about what the difference between the conventional and the ultimate is supposed to be.

One way to think about this distinction is as different levels of reality. The world has two levels or aspects, one conditioned by our norms and conventions, the other not. Traffic laws, cartoon mice, and language really do exist, on one level of reality, while the ultimate, how things *really* are, exists on another. When thinking of a human body, a physician will think in terms of different organs, while a biologist will think in terms of cells, and a chemist will think in terms of different elements. We might think that none of these specialists are *wrong*, just looking at different levels of reality. This way of understanding the difference between conventional and ultimate makes them function in the same way.

Another way to think of the distinction is experientially. We can think of reality as experienced by clear-eyed people who really get how things are, as opposed to how it is experienced by the rest of us. Think of a magician who is watching another magician's act. If the two magicians have the same bag of tricks, the magician in the audience will see through the illusions and experience the show in a very different way from non-magicians. By analogy, conventional truth is how things seem to people who don't really get the full picture. A classic image is that of someone with cataracts who sees floating hairs. They really do see them, but they're not really there in the world.

Of course, this way of understanding the difference between the conventional and ultimate puts the conventional in an uncomfortable position. Thought of this way, what is conventional *can't* be true, because it's defined as a mistaken experience of the world. By making the conventional erroneous, the idea of conventional *truth* can be hard to preserve.

Yet another way to understand the difference between the two is based on analysis. The conventional evaporates when analyzed closely, while the ultimate does not. We saw something similar when thinking about heaps and piles. When analyzed closely, when broken down into its component parts and their relationships, the *pile* of sand disappears. The analysis shows that it doesn't really exist, so it's merely conventional. Whatever can withstand this kind of close analysis is ultimately real. Again, there is disagreement here about what might withstand such analysis. The individual grains? Emptiness itself? Nothing that is expressible in language? Buddhism offers a large menu of options.

What about the relationship between the two truths? Does conventional truth exist ultimately? Is ultimate truth just a convention? As you might have guessed, Buddhism again offers a wide range of viewpoints. One view is that all truth is conventional. If you think that all of our concepts are rooted in conventions, then ultimate truth, since it is itself a *concept*, is also conventional. The distinction between the conventional and ultimate *itself* is like the rules of chess or traffic laws, merely a product of our joint agreement to pretend that there is such a thing. Just as traffic laws aren't out in the world waiting to be discovered, there is no such thing as ultimate truth out there either.

Another view is that there is only ultimate truth. This fits naturally with an understanding of the ultimate as the reality experienced by clear-eyed people. On that way of thinking, the conventional is just what ignorant people *think* the world is like, so it's no surprise that it's not real. Just as when you see how a magic trick is done and realize what was really happening on stage all along, on this view when you see the ultimate, you realize that's all there ever was. This makes conventional truth something to overcome, to get past.

Finally, you might see the two truths as identical. This is the dominant, but by no means only, view in Tibetan Buddhism. For these Buddhists, the two truths are just two aspects of the same thing. A lemon is both yellow and sour. You can know about its sour taste without knowing that it is yellow (say, if you taste it when blindfolded) and you can know that it's yellow without knowing that it's sour (say, if you only saw a photo of a lemon, but never tasted one). These are two different things you can know about the lemon, two aspects of it. In the same way, the two truths are about a single reality, but they get at different aspects of it. Both answers about the Mickey Mouse cartoon are true and are truths about a single thing. They're just truths about different aspects of that thing.

You might wonder how the two truths could be identical given that they seem so different. Conventional truth is often misleading and relies on social agreement, while ultimate truth doesn't. One way to get in the mood of seeing the two truths as identical is to think about times when the same thing presents itself very differently. You might wonder, for example, how Superman could be Clark Kent when they seem so different. After all, Lois Lane loves Superman and not Clark, Superman inspires people and Clark doesn't, Clark pays taxes and Superman doesn't. The reason they seem different is they appear in different ways, under different guises. But they're still the same person: Superman *is* Clark Kent. So you might also think of the two truths as presenting in different ways but still being fundamentally identical.

Why should any of this matter for the practical business of getting through the world each day? For one thing, if you're interested in reading what the Buddha said about how to live (or records of what *any* wise person said for that matter), you'll have to think about *who* they're addressing. What system of conventions and assumptions is their advice embedded in? Keeping in mind the context in that way can help you make sense of seemingly contradictory advice and see what assumptions to further examine and test. (Is there really a Mickey? Is there really a line on the screen?)

It's not just texts and cartoons that call for this approach. If you want to see reality clearly, it might help to know a bit about what you're looking for. Is there a reality apart from our language and conventions? If so, can you *say* anything about it? When you're trying to get at truth, what exactly are you getting at? And how can you relate to others who haven't ever thought about collections or emptiness? These are thorny questions, but the framework of the two truths can be a useful tool for finding answers to them.

There is also a more practical lesson. Keeping in mind the context in which we're relating to what someone says can help us to appreciate what's true in it without dismissing the whole thing. It allows for real engagement and discussion with people in different conventional systems while keeping in view the provisional and contingent nature of the interaction. Figuring out what's true in a system of conventions, fictions, religions, and cultures can help to illuminate the nature of those conventions and, hopefully, help us see more clearly what the world is like outside of them.

14 | LIVING SELFLESSLY

Seen in a certain light, the two truths and emptiness can seem depressing and discouraging. Our lives are mostly made up of conventions, stories we tell about things that don't exist. Ultimately, we're just composite, relational fictions. How is seeing *that* supposed to help you live a better life? Understanding how means seeing these facts in a very different light, one that illuminates how they hold the key to living a more compassionate and engaged life.

First, it's worth reflecting on the importance of conventions. Conventional truths are still *truths* and are relevantly different from conventionally falsehoods. Even though chess is a constructed and empty game, there are still good and bad moves within the game. One can still be better or worse at playing chess and, perhaps more importantly, one can still play and enjoy it even while knowing these facts.

Realizing emptiness doesn't preclude genuine interaction with others on a conventional level. Think of someone who sees the complex reality of many situations, who knows about what really happens on an atomic level. They can still discuss what happens in a cartoon with their kids even though they understand what is really happening more fundamentally.

More importantly, internalizing the emptiness of all things brings with it an important ethical shift. It helps you to break out of the confines that the idea of a self imposes, allowing you to live a life that is less isolated and more compassionate. To see this, think back to where we began: We started with a problem, but it was *your* problem. It was how to fix the subtle buzz of dissatisfaction that rings in *your* ears. But seeing that the self is empty and relational expands the boundaries. It changes from a problem essentially about you and your life, to a problem for *everyone*, for every creature with experiences.

When you see clearly how things are composite and relational, solving the problem is no longer just about getting some peace and quiet for yourself but ending the sound of the buzz entirely. It's no longer enough to focus only on *my* life going better because that involves a fundamental mistake— "my" life going better is deeply intertwined with life going better for everyone else. There was a subtle error buried in the problem. The scope was too narrow and too segregated. Understanding emptiness blows this apart.

This ethical shift is central to a very important concept in many forms of Buddhism: the bodhisattva. The term is present in early Buddhist stories of the previous lives of the Buddha. Since he didn't fully understand the nature of reality, he wasn't a buddha yet. So in those stories he is called a bodhisattva, meaning someone working toward being a buddha. Later Buddhists expand the meaning of this term and use it to characterize a particular selfless ideal. The bodhisattva becomes someone who works toward helping *others* better see reality and live in accordance with it. They aim to solve the problem not just for themselves, but for *all beings*.

In a traditional context, this is cast in terms of rebirth. If the problem is that you're stuck in the cycle of rebirth, solving it means escaping that cycle. Some figure this out and manage to escape. But others, the bodhisattvas, see things clearly and yet knowingly and deliberately *decide to remain in the cycle.* They do this in order to help others get out. In fact, they make a vow not to leave until they help all other beings out first. It's the difference between running out of a burning building and staying in until you're sure that everyone else is out.

In the context of rebirth, this is a *huge* task. Caring about "all beings" doesn't just mean all people, but also all animals (even things like snails, worms, and cockroaches) and all of the other-worldly beings too. Even though bodhisattvas are still in the cycle of rebirth, they're not like the rest of us in an important way. They're completely clear-eyed, fully understanding how reality is. They're not someone oblivious to how bad the fire is; they're staying in the burning building to help, knowing full well what's going on.

A more general, and modern, understanding of the bodhisattva is simply as someone who sees the nature of the world clearly, particularly emptiness. And so they've left behind all self-centered motives, working to benefit all of the beings in the world. Since they fully realize the collective and empty nature of things, they see how self-regarding aims build in faulty assumptions about how things really are. They no longer get in their own way, and so they can help everyone.

This isn't about making sacrifices so you can help others; it's about changing your outlook so that you don't even experience helping others as a sacrifice. It means helping others in a way that flows from a more fundamental change in your experience of the world. This shift is, of course, an extraordinary one, but something similar can also happen on a smaller scale. Think of ways that a strong moral identity can turn bad. For some well-meaning people, it's not enough for good things to be done; *they* have to be the ones who do them. This is pretty admirable, but it can become harmful when this identity turns helping others into a kind of competitive game. Suddenly they're invested in a contest where someone gets to be the morally superior winner and others are shamed into accepting their moral inferiority. Even though they're helping others, they do so in a way that doesn't seem so good anymore, partly because the whole thing centers on feeding their own self-conception.

One way to understand the Buddhist practice of dedicating merit to others is as a counter to just this kind of temptation. You do a good thing that produces some credit, reinforcing your sense of yourself as a really good person. How do you respond? A natural impulse is to accept the credit, or even flaunt it. But when seen in light of emptiness, it becomes clear why you shouldn't do that. It's not just because the credit is another gift you can give, but because *the credit itself* can be a dangerous thing. It can reinforce a misleading identity, one of yourself as a champion in a competitive ethical game. You don't need to quit doing good things to avoid this, just quit doing them in ways that reinforce an identity. Do them with the full understanding that *any* identity is a dangerous illusion when taken too seriously.

Much of the transformative power of finally getting emptiness comes from helping us to see through our various identities. Identities are complex and we have many of them. Not only do we often think of ourselves as the main character in the story of our lives, but we identify with different roles within that story. We identify with being a sibling, a boss, a citizen, the funny one, and on and on. Seeing emptiness doesn't mean completely throwing these off; it means recognizing them for what they really are. They're useful fictions, convenient ways to organize our lives. But they're not essential or intrinsic properties of us. They're changing, fluid, relational, and most importantly, conventional.

Realizing these facts about identities can help to open up your experience of life. You no longer need to experience life as the protagonist in a world full of antagonists and supporting characters. Maintaining an image for others is hard enough, but maintaining one to yourself can be stressful, especially when your entire self-worth is wrapped up in it. Realizing that you and the world are constantly changing means possibilities open up, and you're less trapped by a specific image of yourself.

Part of maintaining an identity means that it's never enough to just *do* something; you have to *be* a certain type of person. It's not enough to sing; you have to *be a singer*. The aim of being a certain kind of person can at times be useful and motivating, but it also creates serious problems. It brings attachments and threats to this identity. What if something happens and people don't think I'm really a singer? Other singers become rivals, competing for the same role. Non-singers, like drummers or violinists, feel like very different kinds of people now.

Seeing the empty nature of these identities allows for a certain kind of freedom. You can just sing without taking seriously all of the baggage that goes along with maintaining and defending an identity as a singer. Moving beyond this kind of interest in identity lets you directly experience singing the songs, without the extra layer of experiencing yourself as a singer. This opens things up—you can be glad to hear other singers without feeling threatened. You can meet violinists and drummers and not feel like they're fundamentally different from you. Whether people think you're a singer or not isn't threatening to an identity you're holding onto.

Consider the role identity plays in our experience of failure. Sooner or later everyone fails. It's incredibly frustrating and discouraging for things not to go as we'd hoped. But it also stings on another level too. Not only did I *fail*, but now *I am a failure*. It can seem like part of who I am—the stink of failure emanates from me. Seeing emptiness clearly means seeing that this is not part of my essence; it is a temporary and relational feature of a collection. The same, of course, is true of success. The timbre of success and failure changes. It's no longer revealing anything about the ultimate worth of who you are.

Being less invested in certain identities can also help you make changes in your life by making it easier to face up to the badness in yourself and others. Lots of irrational behavior relies on a strong sense of identity. When everyone around us can see we made a mistake, we can be in denial because of what it suggests about our self-image. After falling for a scam, we say to ourselves, "I'm a smart person and a smart person wouldn't have fallen for a scam, so this *can't* be a scam." Not being as attached to an identity can help us see mistakes more clearly and fix them without having to deal with an existential crisis on the way.

The same goes for judging the identities of other people. This can often happen when meeting someone in the same role as you or who likes the same things. What should be an occasion for bonding over what you have in common can turn adversarial. You can end up like two wild animals, skeptically circling each other. But if you understand emptiness, rather than sizing other people up, trying to determine if they're a *true* fan or a *real* singer, you can appreciate what they do and share in what you have in common. This is because you realize that you're both changing and interrelated collections. When you shake the habit of categorizing people into different identities, you're free to relate to them in more direct and flexible ways.

Most fundamentally, internalizing emptiness allows us to stop getting in our own way. It's not that we have to reject any of our many identities, but rather we see them for the changing conventions that they really are. Letting go of a fundamental, static identity can be scary, but it also opens up the world. The bodhisattva lives with a clear sense of being part of a complex, changing, and interrelated world. This opens them up to participating in it, rather than just guarding what they think of as their own little corner of it. The noise of insecurity, competition, success, failure—their volume gets turned way down. When you realize that you don't actually have anything to lose, you're not afraid of losing it. When you see yourself and your identities for what they really are, you can participate in the world more fully.

15 | ENLIGHTENMENT

Once you've reoriented your experiences so they better match how reality is, *what does it feel like?* Some Buddhists call this enlightenment, others awakening. Whatever you call it, does it mean you're happy all the time? Is it even possible to say anything about what it's like? Many modern writers describe Buddhism as a path to happiness, but there are a few important ways in which enlightenment and happiness can be quite different.

Happiness, for example, is often thought of as an entirely subjective state. If you *feel* happy, then you are happy. If you want to know if someone else is happy, you ask them. Assuming they're being sincere in their reply, if they say they're happy, then that settles it.

The problem that Buddhists are trying to solve, however, isn't merely a subjective state. Sometimes the experiences that reinforce the problem can be really pleasant. Success, compliments, and applause all feel great, but they also reinforce a deep sense of self. Recall the image of eating honey on the edge of a knife; it might taste sweet in the moment, but it's doing damage to you in the long run. The problem for Buddhists isn't just that we feel bad but that we have a precarious and destructive way of being in the world, one that we often fail to recognize at all.

In this sense, the Buddhist goal is more like being healthy than being happy. Just because you *feel* healthy, doesn't mean you actually *are*. It's possible to have many health problems like high cholesterol, heart disease, or even early cancer all while feeling fine. This isn't to say that how you feel has nothing at all to do with how healthy you are, but just that there's more to health than how you feel. In the same way, it's possible to feel like you have solved the problem when you haven't. Even if you *feel* enlightened, you might not be. This is the same as other ways of getting it right about the world. You might be mistaken about the answer to a question even though you feel like you know it. Someone who needs glasses might *feel* like their vision is perfectly clear.

Another difference between enlightenment and happiness is that happiness can often refer to things going the way we want *within our mistaken worldview*. Think of a person who is caught up in all of the illusions about the world that Buddhists aim to break out of. They experience the world through the lens of a persisting self, and they relate to success and material benefits as permanent and deeply identify with them. If this person gets what they want, say they get the special title or salary they want, it's natural to call them happy. They wanted something and they got it so they're smiling and happy.

This, of course, isn't the kind of solution Buddhists are aiming at. Some ways of being happy don't *solve* the underlying problem at all but actually rely on it. The goal isn't just to have a pleasant delusion but to break out of the delusion altogether, to get enlightened. Some call enlightenment a deeper type of happiness, while others don't like to call it happiness at all. Whatever kind of labeling you prefer, the solution isn't like the good feelings that come with winning the game. Rather, it's the deeper and more stable state of no longer playing it. Winning can feel nice, but once you're not invested in the game anymore, you're no longer tossed around by winning or losing.

Even within more traditional forms of Buddhism that don't often talk in terms of happiness, enlightenment is thought of in very different ways. For some, the cycle of rebirth is real, and solving the problem means escaping it. We're in a bad place, and by realizing certain mistakes we can break free. Put in this way, it can make you wonder where the enlightened person goes when they escape. The traditional answer is that this question misses the point. Escaping the cycle is likened to a flame being snuffed out. Nirvana, the word used to describe freedom from the cycle of rebirth, literally means to extinguish or blow out, as when you blow out a candle. Asking where the flame goes after it's snuffed out is a mistaken question. Even though it's not here anymore, it doesn't *go* anywhere. It's like asking where Santa went when you realized he wasn't real.

Other Buddhists, especially those who emphasize emptiness, have a more philosophical take. They point out that both the problem and the solution lack any independent existence. After all, they rely on each other: Problems and solutions need each other to be what they are. For these Buddhists, the solution isn't some separate place or state that you arrive at; it's simply fully internalizing the way things really are. There's no other place, only here. On this view, being enlightened isn't a *change in you* because there never was a you. Just like your idea of self, your idea of enlightenment was just another conventional fiction that you projected onto the world.

Think back to the spoon that looked bent because it was in a glass of water. It really seemed to be bent, but upon closer inspection you realized that it only *looked* that way. When you realized this, the spoon didn't get straightened out—it was never bent at all. In fact, nothing about the world changed; you just cleared up a mistake your mind was making. On this understanding, when we say a person "gets enlightened," all that happens is they recognize and correct a certain illusion, though a *very* subtle and difficult one.

What is it actually like to be enlightened, to see through these illusions? For many, this state is indescribable. Language is good for many things. It can be useful to be able to say what you want or explain an idea or connect with another person. This book is, after all, full of words. But part of how language works is by sorting the world, carving it up into categories: self and other, problem and solution, enlightenment and misery. Since this categorization is part of what obscures our view of reality, it won't do a very good job of explaining experiences that transcend these categories.

Impermanence, the lack of self, and emptiness aren't just interesting intellectual ideas, they're aspects of reality that you're supposed to internalize and experience directly. As we've seen, ordinary, unenlightened experience is full of shorthand. Our lives are full of fictions, stories about events that didn't happen to characters that don't exist. These stories can be useful enough to get by in life, and even beneficial. But once we start *believing* the stories we tell, mistaking our projections for reality, we get into trouble. The trouble is so deep that it's hard to even realize how it happened or how bad it is.

Getting out of this trouble means giving up many of the ordinary ways of relating to the world. A critical part of this is breaking the habit of seeing life through the lens of a self. This means realizing there was never a you; it was only ever a projection, a story applied to the world. It's not a matter of trading one self-image for another. It means giving up the habit of relating to the world through a self-image at all. Doing this doesn't mean you never use the word "I" or that you don't respond to your name. But it does mean that when you say the word "I" or hear your name, you feel very differently about it—you aren't taken in by the story anymore.

Part of realizing this is seeing that, even if there is no persisting self, actions have effects. Even if there's no pile, eggs can get broken. Even if there's no you, more hamburger means more cholesterol. These effects can be big or small, and they can be beneficial or harmful. But more importantly, doing *anything* means developing and reinforcing habits. The first day of a commute is hard, but after a few years you don't need to think about it anymore. Each and every time we act to avoid something we don't like or to get some success, we deepen our sense of self. Without thinking about it at all, we fall into the habit of believing a fiction where we are the main character.

Enlightenment involves a radical reorientation of our outlook on the world. It's one that takes into account the ways in which our habits of seeing, feeling, thinking, and responding to things fool us into having a visceral sense that the world is one way when it is really very different. The process of breaking out of these habits can be difficult and even painful. Extinguishing a raging flame can be hard and unpleasant—smoke gets in your eyes. Despite the pain, once you get it, the mistake might seem almost silly. To a child, tic-tac-toe seems like a difficult game, but to an adult the right move is glaringly obvious. It may be that once you see how things work, you'll be amazed that you could ever have missed it.

Intellectually believing that the world is composite, relational, and impermanent isn't the end of the line. Neither is having a direct experience of reality as it is. It's important to integrate these insights into your everyday life. Imagine you have a flash of insight, a glimpse of how things really are. Sitting alone, you see through all of the illusions and delusions that your mental habits conjure up. But a moment later someone knocks on your door, saying, "Hey, what's up? You wanna grab lunch?" This insight isn't very beneficial if it evaporates at the sound of that knock on the door. You need be able to take it with you into the mess of real life.

One way to understand how this can work is to think of how we relate to games. When you play a game you know that it's not real—it's an invention and the pieces on the board don't have inherent value or meaning. We can lose sight of this and feel all kinds of things like frustration when things don't go our way and satisfaction when they do. Understanding that it's just a game doesn't mean you stop playing altogether; instead the significance of the game changes. Winning is still nice, but when you keep your sense of what the game really is, it doesn't affect you in the same way. You get a kind of peace of mind, one that's different from the simple joy of winning, because you relate to the game for what it really is.

16 | PHILOSOPHY AS PRACTICE

Solving the problem requires more than just an intellectual understanding of how the world is and what needs to be done. Knowing about diet and exercise isn't enough to make you a healthy person; it's important but not enough on its own. A philosopher might reason themselves into Buddhist philosophical views, accepting and defending the idea that everything is impermanent or empty but still not have any motivation to live their lives any differently. So far we've been thinking of philosophy as a set of views about the world and considerations for and against them. But there is another way to understand the philosophical aspects of Buddhism.

Instead of seeing philosophy as about abstract things to know, you can think of it as a kind of mental exercise, an intellectual training regimen. Rather than something to know, it's something to work through, something to *do*. Science, for example, also has this dual aspect. On one hand, science is a body of knowledge, a set of theories and data about the natural world. But science is also a pursuit, an activity that people engage in. Both senses are important and both have value.

Or consider the difference between description and instruction. Someone can *describe* the perfect chocolate cake, its various aspects and what it is like. But they can do that without telling you how to make one. A recipe for chocolate cake, on the other hand, tells you *how to go about making one*. Of course, a recipe doesn't primarily aim at describing reality, but it depends on reality being a certain way. It depends on truths about physics and human taste and digestion. And by executing a recipe you can learn things about the world—maybe general things, like "heat drives out moisture," or maybe specific things, like "my oven runs about fifty degrees too hot."

Much of Buddhist philosophy can be read on both levels: as a description of how things are and as instructions for how to realize it. An argument establishing that a whole cannot be identical to its parts is meant to show something about the world, about wholes, parts, and their relationship. It is also meant to be a series of steps for you to consider in sequence which will, over time, help you to experience the world differently, as impermanent, relational, and inter-dependent. It's *one* step in a recipe for solving the broader problem. After all, the Buddha left home looking not for abstract answers to philosophical questions, but for a way to solve the problem.

Of course, if you take seriously the idea that language and concepts are themselves merely conventions, then philosophy might seem like a self-undermining practice. How can pushing around concepts help you see through the distorting influence of those very concepts? One answer is that philosophy involves turning conceptual thought on itself. In thinking hard about your concepts and ideas, you will start to see their limits more clearly. We can, after all, use language to talk about the limits of language. We can use words to gesture, albeit in an indirect way, to what is beyond them.

Of course, even if you think that all language distorts reality, saying *that* is also distorting. But maybe it's a *more* helpful thing to say than saying other things. So one way to understand all of the Buddhist philosophy we've seen so far is as a low-resolution picture of the world. It's like a fuzzy map to get you in the right neighborhood, but once you're there you'll look around for yourself and won't need it anymore.

When understood in this way, Buddhist philosophy is like an exercise you go through to help you get started in the right direction—it's a process you go through to get your mind out of its old habits. This means that, like any practice, it's not for everyone and, eventually, you may not need it anymore. Luckily, and perhaps dauntingly, the world of Buddhist philosophy is rich enough to provide several lifetimes of material to explore.

So despite the format of this book, Buddhist philosophy and practice are not so easily separated. Philosophy itself can be a practice. And, like engaging in philosophy, engaging in any of the wide range of Buddhist practices can teach you about the world. These other practices can also illuminate unexamined assumptions and reveal things about the world and yourself that were previously hidden. Of course, it's possible to do them separately. Many people think about Buddhist philosophy in an intellectual way and without doing any other Buddhist practices. Even more do Buddhist practices without ever thinking about Buddhist philosophy. But taken together, they can aid and support each other in the difficult task of solving the problem.

Part II

Practice

17 | VARIETIES OF BUDDHIST PRACTICE

Tenzin lives on the Tibetan plateau. As a child he was brought to live at the local monastery and has been a Buddhist monk ever since. As a monk he has a shaved head and wears traditional monk's robes. He is required by the rules of the monastery to be celibate. He loves eating yak meat, though he gives it up for holy days. He's memorized many Buddhist texts, though he is unsure of the exact meaning of many of them. He recites prayers every morning in the assembly hall of the monastery and occasionally recites texts at funerals for extra money. He doesn't think he will get enlightened in this lifetime but hopes that his devotion to Buddhism in this life will help him to secure a good future life.

Tomoko lives in rural Japan. Her first exposure to Buddhism was hearing her grandmother recite a special Buddhist phrase over and over. She also saw Buddhist statues at local shrines, often mixed in with objects sacred in Shinto, an indigenous Japanese religion. Most of her friends interact with Buddhism very little outside of funerals, which are typically Buddhist. Tomoko, however, is a practicing Buddhist. On special holidays she visits temples and lights incense as an offering to the statues. Like her grandmother, Tomoko recites a special phrase which she believes will cause her to be reborn in a special place where getting enlightened is easy. She has chanted and sometimes even recopied the *Heart Sutra*, a very short and famous Buddhist text. She has some vague idea of its meaning, though much of it is unclear to her. This is unimportant to her as she believes that chanting and recopying the text give her good merit even if she doesn't understand the meaning.

Somchai lives in Thailand and for him, Buddhism is the family religion. Following Thai custom, he spent one month living as a monk before he got married. He thinks of this period as tough but character building and as giving his family good merit. He doesn't really meditate or read Buddhist texts, but on special days he goes to his family's temple and makes offerings of flowers and incense. He also gives food to monks who come by his house each morning. He doesn't think about this very much; it's just what his family has always done. If pressed, he'd say it gives him and his family longer lives and success in business.

Jennifer lives in America and recently moved to Seattle for work. She became a Buddhist after taking a world religions course in college and joining a meditation group on campus. Her family is not Buddhist, but they support her interest in it as they think of religion as a personal choice. Jennifer, for her part, dislikes what she sees as rituals and would describe herself as "spiritual, but not religious." She practices Buddhist mindfulness meditation at a local center that also offers yoga and tai chi classes. She reads popular books on Buddhism and occasionally will also read translations of classic Buddhist texts. She is vegetarian and politically liberal, both of which she sees as an extension of Buddhist principles. She sees Buddhism as essentially compatible with a scientific worldview and sees Buddhist practices as helping her to manage the stress of having a career and a family, a way to be less stressed and more calm in her day-to-day life.

These are, of course, stereotypes, but they give a window into the wide variety of Buddhist practices. Though these people would all self-identify as Buddhist, what Buddhism means to them and the role it plays in their lives is *very* different. This is not to say that Tenzin's Buddhism is more authentic than Tomoko's or that Jennifer's practice is better than Somchai's—it is just a slice of how different people in different places relate to Buddhism. To get a fuller picture of the range of Buddhist practice it's worth highlighting a few of the differences.

Think about the social context for each. For Somchai and Tenzin, Buddhism is deeply intertwined with both family life and powerful social institutions. Neither of them ever considered other religions as live options, and their Buddhism is assumed by everyone in their social world. For Jennifer, however, Buddhism is largely a private matter. Her family and most of the institutions she interacts with are not Buddhist. For her, Buddhism is a matter of personal choice, one that goes against the traditions of her family. She is skeptical of organized, institutional religion. Though she attends a meditation group, she doesn't see the meditation teacher as a spiritual authority in the way that Tenzin sees his lama as one.

This social context affects how practice looks for each. For Somchai and Tenzin, what they do and how they do it are largely determined by the Buddhist authorities and institutions in their lives. Tenzin doesn't have to choose which texts he recites for prayers and Somchai doesn't have to decide how to offer flowers or incense. Jennifer, however, can pick between various Buddhist practices and often mixes them together with non-Buddhist practices like yoga or tai chi.

The role of ritual is also different for each. Ritual is a tricky term. We often use it to describe things other people do that we don't really understand. Someone from America might describe bowing as a ritual but not shaking hands because they're used to one and not the other. We also use ritual to refer to actions in special situations that have to be done in a particular way. For Tenzin, it is critical that he recite a funeral text in the proper way, by ringing a special bell at the right time and clapping at the right time. For Somchai, it is important to make offerings at the temple in the right way and at the right time or else they won't bring merit. Jennifer's Buddhism has rituals too, but they're fewer and less rigid. She often practices when and how she likes.

There are also different background assumptions about the supernatural in play. For Somchai, the world contains many spirits who can be managed, helped, or angered. Part of gaining the favor of these supernatural beings is performing the proper rituals at the proper time. He sees a consecrated statue of a buddha as being the literal embodiment of that buddha. Jennifer's Buddhism does not assume any such spirits. For her, Buddhism is compatible with modern science and often taken to be explicable in those terms. Supernatural references are understood symbolically, so when she bows to a buddha statue it's because she sees it as a *symbol* of the Buddhist teachings rather than the literal body of a buddha.

Another difference is the place of meditation in the lives of each of these Buddhists. For Jennifer, meditation is central to Buddhism—that's what it's all about. Tomoko's practice of reciting a special mantra might be understood as a form of meditation, but it looks very different from the kind of mindfulness that Jennifer practices. For Tenzin and Somchai, meditation plays little to no role in their Buddhist practice. Tenzin's monastery might have some monks who specialize in meditation, but he leaves it to them. Somchai may have meditated during his month-long period living as a monk, but now he rarely if ever does.

Their motivations for engaging in these different Buddhist practices are also different. Jennifer does it to bring about positive emotional and ethical changes in her day-to-day life. Somchai does it to bring merit to himself and his family, to bring good fortune and wealth. Tenzin's Buddhism is, at least in part, motivated by social and familial pressure. Being a monk is just part of his role as an upstanding member of his community and family. If this seems sad, reflect on how many American college students you think decided to attend college out of a genuine love of knowledge. Some do, but many attend because their family expects it of them and, in their social world, that's just what an upstanding young person does.

None of this is to say that any of these people are practicing "real" or "authentic" Buddhism. It is merely to highlight the ways in which Buddhist practice varies around the world. Jennifer's Buddhism is sometimes called modern, while practices of those like Somchai and Tenzin are often called traditional. Of course, many people in Asia practice Buddhism in ways that resemble how Jennifer does things, and many people in America and Europe practice it in ways that look more like how Tomoko and Somchai do things. When learning about Buddhist practices, it's worth keeping in mind that people like Jennifer are a minority, both globally and historically. That doesn't mean that this relationship to Buddhism is bad or wrong, but it does mean that it's not the only one around.

There is wide variation not just in what people do but in why they do it and when they expect to see the results. Like all practices, they're not isolated activities, but fit into an entire life. Jennifer and Somchai face different struggles with their families when it comes to Buddhism. Tomoko has a job and bills to pay while Tenzin does not. Some things that work in one context might not work as well in another.

As Buddhist thought highlights, traditions are not inanimate fossils; they're living and constantly changing. Part of what has allowed Buddhism to survive for so long is that it adapts and changes to fit the needs of different social and cultural situations. Buddhism stays relevant to people's lives by adapting, by emphasizing and developing what works and dropping what doesn't.

Our cultural, familial, and financial situation shapes our habits and experiences, so it's no surprise that different techniques are called for in order to change these habits. What works for a monk in Tibet might not work for a middle manager in the American suburbs. What worked for an Indian monk in the eighth century might not work for a Canadian lawyer in 2022.

Buddhism contains a wealth of practices and techniques, things you can actually *do* to improve your life. Of course, lots of practices can help you improve your life that aren't *Buddhist* practices. Buddhists don't have a monopoly on beneficial activities. Eating well, seeing good friends regularly, and taking a long walk in the woods all might make your life better and happier, but they're not exclusive to Buddhism or to any religion or philosophical school.

So what makes a practice *Buddhist*? This is a more difficult question than it might seem at first. Imagine you're an anthropologist trying to understand a Christian family. You notice that they go to church every Sunday and afterward they always go out to have brunch together. Is going to brunch together part of their *Christian* practice? On one way of seeing it, the answer is no; the Christian part happens at church and what follows is just a regular family gathering. After all, many atheists also go to brunch. But on the other hand, the family might feel that spending time with each other isn't separate from their Christianity; if they skipped brunch their religious practice might feel incomplete. So is brunch part of their Christian practice or not? It can be hard to say.

Many Buddhist practices are like this. Burning incense, lighting candles, sitting alone in a calm place: None of these are exclusive to Buddhism. Anybody can light a candle or burn incense, but these things will only be Buddhist practices when done for certain reasons in certain situations. Ideally, Buddhist practices aim at realizing, on a fundamental and experiential level, how the world is, to see that things are composite, impermanent, and, for many Buddhists, also empty. They aim at changing our fundamental orientation to ourselves, others, and the world as a whole.

They might aim at this in very slow or indirect ways. After all, for many Buddhists, getting used to how things really are is a process that takes up many, many lifetimes. Offering incense to a statue might not seem like it changes your sense of self and the world, but it can be part of a long process. Doing a single push-up or buying an apple doesn't immediately make you healthy, but they do help, even if in just a small way. This is especially true for things early in a process. Asking a friend about their gym really doesn't seem like it makes you healthy, but it can be an important initial step.

18 | A FEW GRAINS OF SALT

I once saw a group of young monks chanting the *Heart Sutra*. That's a text that means a lot to me and had a big impact on how I see the world. But for these kids, it was just another boring chore in their day. It makes sense—when you're a kid, grown-ups make you sit still and repeat all kinds of things. For them, in their lives, the *Heart Sutra* really *is* a boring chore. Some of them might come to feel differently about it; some probably won't. People come into contact with Buddhism in different ways and in different situations. For some it's the house religion; others have a convert's zeal.

It's important to keep in mind that there's more to Buddhism than one's own idealized version of it because there's a real danger of projecting what you want onto Buddhism and ignoring the rest. Though the descriptions of Buddhist practices here are idealized, not all Buddhists relate to them in this way. Some people, especially those who have found Buddhism to be beneficial, start to project everything they want onto it. This is unrealistic and leads to ignoring or denying anything that doesn't fit within this idealized image.

To avoid this, it's worth reflecting on some common cultural associations that many Western people have with Buddhism and where these associations came from. In early nineteenth-century Europe and America, two groups, the Romantics and the Transcendentalists, started to take an interest in ideas from Asia in general and from Buddhism in particular. If you think Buddhism is mainly about "getting in touch with your feelings" or "using your intuition" and "going beyond rational thought," this is because that's what the people who first imported Buddhism were interested in, and so that's what they emphasized.

Of course, you can find these themes and ideas in Buddhism, but you can also find much that doesn't fit with this at all. Buddhists in India, for example, developed a robust system of formal logic and engaged in rigorous philosophical debates. Life in a Buddhist monastery was, and often still is, rigidly regimented with rules about what you wear, who you see, when you eat, and much more. It's about as far from "do what you feel" as you can imagine.

Another early source of Western interest in Buddhism is a religious movement called Theosophy. Started in New York City in the late 1800s by a Russian immigrant, the Theosophical Society was a religious group with a wide range of interests. They claimed to communicate psychically with beings called the Masters, originally from Atlantis, but who they thought resided in Tibet. The Masters were said to be the keepers of an esoteric religion that was implicit in the teachings of Daoism, Christianity, Confucianism, and of course Buddhism. In addition to uncovering the secret meaning shared by all of the world's religions, the Theosophists were also interested in various occult subjects like speaking with the dead, auras, and mysticism more generally.

It's through these channels that many in the West first came into contact with Buddhism. It arrived filtered through people with very particular agendas and interests. These people had little, if any, command of Buddhist texts or the languages they were written in. Though they popularized ideas and texts from Asia, they did so with a very specific spin, one that still can be felt today.

The heirs to these movements, the Beat Generation and later the Hippies, were also interested in Buddhism and found in it validation of what they liked: drug use, rejecting materialism, and sexual liberation. These morph into an even more eclectic movement called New Age, one that includes a wide range of subjects like astrology, crystals, homeopathy, and mysticism. So Buddhism, because of the history of its reception, came to be associated with these other things too.

Recently, many in the West have reacted strongly against these trends. They see Buddhism as compatible with a scientific and rational way of seeing the world. They're interested in doing brain scans of meditating monks and hosting dialogues between Buddhist teachers and physicists or neuroscientists. Here it's not emotion or personal experience that's emphasized but empirically measurable data and scientific rigor. These Buddhists emphasize the rational and scientifically respectable aspects of Buddhism and downplay anything supernatural or mystical.

This is a deep cultural conflict: astrology versus astronomy, homeopathy versus randomized controlled trials, the mystics versus the scientists. It's also a conflict that is not really about *Buddhism* at all. Buddhism existed before any of these conflicts and exists in places where these conflicts aren't particularly relevant. Both sides find in Buddhism what they like and ignore the rest. Both want to claim Buddhism for their side. So when considering not just what Buddhism *is* but also what it *can be*, it's worth reflecting on how you got your current view of it and how that view might be limited.

There are other dangers when adopting practices from a different culture. One is making it too exotic, hanging on to the feeling that this is a strange, ancient, and mysterious thing from a land far away. This overlooks the reality that these practices are done by real people, people with relationships, frustrations, hopes, and feelings. Seeing them as alien practices done by otherworldly beings keeps them at a distance. They're always strange things that *those people* do. One problem with this is that it flattens out a lot of differences; people in feudal Japan, ancient India, and contemporary China are very different. Seeing them all as "exotic" misses these important differences.

Other versions of this problem take different forms. Sometimes it's condescending: "Let's go see what those silly, strange people are doing." This resembles a kind of gawking, wanting to learn facts about the weird stuff that other people do. Other times it's patronizing, just unquestioningly accepting anything someone says: "Oh yes yes, that's right." If I'm conversing with someone and all they ever do is agree with what I say, we're not really having much of a conversation. This is how you humor an unreasonable child, not how you interact with someone you respect.

Another danger is forcing practices to fit into your existing categories. If what *they* are doing is reasonable or beneficial, it must be basically the same as something *we* do. There's nothing wrong with trying to understand something new in terms of what you already know, but taken too far it erases what is new and interesting. A well-intentioned Christian trying to learn about Buddhism might mistakenly assume that Buddhism and Christianity are basically the same, just using different words ("I see, they call God 'Buddha'"). There's a kind of faux tolerance here. In order for your thing to be okay it must secretly be *my* thing. But sometimes people are doing *different* things, and understanding that means accepting that it's *unlike* what you're familiar with already.

Navigating these issues is difficult and trying to take up Buddhist practices brings with it special challenges. This book contains a wide range of practices from different Buddhist traditions. It's very unlikely that any Buddhist would engage in *all* of the practices discussed in this book. It would even be inadvisable; doing all of them would mean you would not advance much in any particular one. Some might even interfere with others. This is because practices are chosen taking into account context and individual tendencies. Imagine reading a book that explains a wide range of therapy techniques or exercise routines. Even though they all might be based on the same research, doing *all* of them at once would be overwhelming and counterproductive. Which you choose involves taking into account what your situation is and what your specific body is like.

As someone with the luxury and burden of having a wide range of practices available, a special problem arises: Cafeteria Buddhism. In a cafeteria you get a tray and as you make your way down the line you pick whatever foods look good to you. If you feel like a burger, you get a burger. If you hate fish, you don't take any. You take what you want and leave the rest. The danger of Cafeteria Buddhism is that you might take from each Buddhist tradition whatever is easy and convenient and ignore what is difficult and challenging. Like taking only pudding and french fries at the cafeteria, taking just what looks good can be nice in the moment but not very sustaining in the long run.

This is particularly difficult for those practicing in the absence of institutional authority. If two Catholics disagree about how or when to pray, for example, they can go to their priest who has the authority to settle the matter. For members of an institution there can be, for better or for worse, an official verdict on the matter. But if two people practicing Buddhism on their own have a similar disagreement without any official authority around, there is nobody to settle the matter. So there's nothing for them to do but simply forge their own way. Sometimes this is good, but sometimes it means people are just doing whatever they want and calling it "Buddhism."

This is a tricky problem. On one hand, there is something bad about shaping an existing tradition into whatever you'd like it to be. There's something unsavory about just picking out the things you like and ignoring the rest, since it assumes a certain kind of superiority. The underlying assumption is that you know best, better than people who have been devoting entire lives to this for thousands of years. And you can just swoop in after reading a few books and decide what's important and what's not.

On the other hand, there is something bad about forcing yourself to accept something just because it's traditionally part of the package. Sometimes views and practices are linked by historical accident. One might have good reasons for accepting one and not the others. Sometimes traditions *need* to be changed. Many Buddhist institutions, for example, limit the role of women by ranking the most senior nun below the most junior monk. A Buddhist shouldn't have to accept this situation simply because that's how it's always been.

People in the modern world have an embarrassment of riches when it comes to ideas and practices they can learn about. This makes it tempting to take bits and pieces from many different ones. This can be both good and bad. Burdened with information and choice, it's important to do this thoughtfully and carefully. It's important to confront the aspects of a tradition that you don't like or agree with. Even if you ultimately reject them, it's important to wrestle with them and examine them carefully. It's important to be reflective. Why do I want to skip over this? Why is it part of the tradition? What does the tradition say about it?

Another nearby danger is cultural appropriation, taking over practices that belong to another culture. This is especially thorny since Buddhism is not the exclusive property of any single culture. It originated in various cultures on the Indian subcontinent but soon spread to others in Tibet, China, Korea, Thailand, Japan, and beyond. In many ways, the history of the spread of Buddhism is a long chain of cultural appropriation. Each of these cultures, America and Europe included, alter Buddhist ideas and practices to suit their own needs. This is part of what has made Buddhism survive for so long and spread all over the globe. If you like the adaptations, you call them "developments," and if you don't, you call them "corruptions"; but the point remains that Buddhism has always changed to adapt to new situations.

Of course, much of what is bad about cultural appropriation is taking something important in a culture and using it in ways that strip away its meaning. This is why wearing moccasins is different from wearing a headdress; both are Native American clothing items, but one has a special significance in the culture and the other does not. Someone wearing a camouflage jacket for fashion does something different from someone wearing a medal of honor that they didn't earn. Making a good faith effort to engage with Buddhism is different from using a buddha statue to decorate your bathroom.

Part of making a good faith effort is actually listening to Buddhists and trying to understand what they think and what they do. It means accepting that others know things that you don't. It also means being honest about what you're taking, what you're leaving out, and what you change. Rather than saying, "I like doing it this way so this must be the *true* Buddhist teaching," you can simply say, "Traditionally, it's done like that, but I found that doing it this way works better for me."

When thinking about Buddhist practice it's important to reflect not only on the context the practice comes from but also on our own context. This means, in part, reflecting on what we think Buddhism is and how we came to think of it that way. It also means reflecting on what we want from Buddhism and why.

19 | GETTING READY

As when starting anything new, it's a good idea to spend some time getting ready, and Buddhist practice is no different. It's important to be careful of certain dangers. Developing bad habits early will make things more difficult later on. You need to be careful not to put too much pressure on yourself, become lazy, or expect results too soon. It's a long road, so you have to be consistent. Starting off well gives the best chances for making progress.

Especially in the early honeymoon phase, new practices can burn brightly and flame out quickly. The thrill of starting something new can make it easy at first to avoid certain foods or use a daily planner every morning, but that excitement only lasts so long. Meaningful change is often a long, hard road. Think of the last time you tried to give up a bad habit. It's hard to overstate how difficult this is. Even seemingly simple things like trying to stop biting your nails or swearing or checking your phone every few minutes can be very difficult and often involve periods of success and failure. If changing simple habits like that is hard, then changing your fundamental feeling about the world is bound to be even harder. It's not something that's going to happen in a week or two.

Some Buddhists think that seeing reality clearly can happen suddenly, in a flash of insight. Somewhat romantically, this sudden insight could strike anywhere, prompted by the most mundane experiences: the light reflecting off the hood of an old car, dropping your ice cream on the sidewalk, staring at the tile while taking a shower. These mundane experiences all have the power to hit you just right and shake you free from your illusions. Other Buddhists have denied this. For them, seeing reality as it really is comes only after long and hard training. Seeing reality accurately is more like how experts learn to see things that others can't, the way a skilled mechanic can immediately see what's wrong with a carburetor or a master baker simply sees when the dough is ready to bake. Experiencing things in this way happens only after years and years of hard work.

Still other Buddhists have taken a mixed view; practice is important, but only to make space for sudden insights to happen. You work hard to encourage sudden insights so that when they happen you can handle them properly. Even if insight comes in a flash, your habits and how you behave matter for how long it lasts and how well you can integrate it into your life. A sudden flash of insight into the nature of reality while in the shower might be nice, but it's not very helpful if it wears off by the time you're dry.

Whatever the speed of realization, it's important to practice regularly. To do that it's important to start well. So, how do you do that? Buddhism has a wide range of what are often called preliminary practices. Some of these are very simple—bowing or offering incense to a statue of a buddha, listening to a Buddhist teacher speak in person or via a recording, donating money to a monastery. It can be tempting, especially for people doing more advanced practices, to look down on these things. But this reaction misses the important role preliminary practices play. They demonstrate and develop an intention to understand the world and act accordingly. Even though this intention might be a whim or a tiny spark, it's critical. After all, every buddha and bodhisattva started sometime, somewhere, with just such a small spark. Practices that kindle these sparks are incredibly important.

Another common early step involves finding a teacher. Some people inherit one through their family or community, while others have to choose one. In many forms of Buddhism the relationship between teacher and student is very important. Many traditions trace a line of teachers and students from the current teacher, through important figures in the history of Buddhism, all the way back to the historical Buddha himself. Many of these lineages are historically dubious, including connections between people who could never have met. But these lineages are more about expressing values than documenting historical fact. Which figures you trace your lineage through says something about your outlook and what aspects of Buddhism are important to you. Nevertheless, in many Buddhist circles who your teacher is, and who *their* teachers were, is of critical importance. It places you in the Buddhist world and says much about the views and approaches you've been exposed to.

But do *you* need a teacher? Depends on who you ask. After all, the Buddha had several teachers before eventually striking out on his own. Then again, very few of us are as advanced as he was. Compare the question to learning a musical instrument or a foreign language. Do you need a teacher to learn to speak Japanese or play the piano? It depends. It depends on your ability, level of dedication, access to resources, learning style, and so on. Some people become great musicians or fluent speakers on their own, while others need the guidance of a teacher to give them direction or to force them to practice regularly.

Having a teacher has its advantages. Think of the benefits of having a teacher in other contexts. Part of what makes learning something from books difficult is that there is nobody around to demonstrate what you should be doing. Having a living teacher in front of you while learning the violin means there is someone who can not only demonstrate the right way to move your arm or place your fingers but who can also correct mistakes that you can't see for yourself. It can be hard to distinguish actual improvement from *the feeling of improvement*. Sometimes we don't feel like we're making progress when we actually are, and sometimes we feel like we're getting better when we're really stalled. A teacher is not only a competent judge of your progress but also someone who has taken partial responsibility for it. For some people, having a teacher who is invested in their progress can make a huge difference.

More importantly, experienced teachers know what habits will create problems later on and so can help you avoid having to go back and unlearn the bad habits you developed at the start. Not only do they know the common missteps and how to avoid them, but they get to know *you* and the kinds of mistakes that *you* tend to make. No book, however clear and well-written, will be able to respond to you like that.

If you decide that you do need a teacher, it's important to choose carefully. It is not something to be taken lightly. It's an important relationship, one that requires someone you can really trust. For many Buddhists, part of having a teacher means seeing that person as a buddha. After all, in teaching you one-on-one, they become a physical embodiment of the Buddha's instructions. There is an aspect of mutual responsibility here: The student is responsible for practicing and listening to the teacher, and the teacher is responsible for protecting the student and guiding their development.

Like any relationship, especially one involving trust and a power differential, it can turn ugly fast. Not all teachers are *good* teachers. Think about all the meals you've had at restaurants. Now think about the chefs who prepared that food. How many of those have been completely dedicated to their work and amazing at what they do? Some are, but many more are just so-so or even bad at what they do. The same is true of Buddhist teachers. Some chefs make food you won't like even though they have a great reputation. Some don't care that much. Some care, but are overworked and tired. Some just don't have the knack for it.

Sometimes the teacher is bad and sometimes they're just a bad fit. Being a bad teacher is a bit like being a bad spouse. Some people are bad spouses period. They're abusive, cruel, or oblivious and aren't suited for that kind of relationship with anyone. Other people might just be a bad spouse *for you*. Given your personality and character, they're not a good fit for you, even though they're a fine fit for some people. Buddhist teachers can be like this—some are bad for everyone, but some are just bad for you.

None of this is to say that you *must*, or even should, find a teacher. Having a teacher also has its drawbacks. These relationships are often formed in an institutional setting, with all the complications of power, money, and bureaucracy that go along with it. Your teachers can start pressuring you to do more and more to sustain and grow the institution. You can start hearing things like, "The director told me to make sure you book vegan caterers for the fundraising gala for the new meditation center." You started out aiming to solve a deep problem and now you're spending your time booking caterers, sending invitations, and soliciting donations. This isn't a danger for everybody, but some people can get sucked into logistics and management at the expense of their own practice.

Having a certain teacher can also end up becoming yet another identity: "Well, *I* am a student of His-Holiness-Venerable So-and-So!" This can make your Buddhist identity yet another source of competitiveness and jealousy. It can fuel endless thoughts and disputes about who is the favorite student or whose teacher is most amazing. A teacher is supposed to guide you through solving the problem but can also end up being another factor that reinforces a misleading social reality and only adds to your problems.

As with other positions, being famous or popular isn't the same as being good. In fact, there are ways in which *everyone you meet* is a teacher. This isn't to say they'll be able to deliver an informative lecture on Buddhist teachings or give you specific guidance about particular practices, but they can still offer an opportunity to learn. They not only show you by example how to deal with difficulties in life but can serve as a gauge for your own progress. As we'll see, they need not even mean to help you. Being insulted can illuminate the ways in which you are still hung up on an identity as a smart or sophisticated person. Falling victim to a theft can show you how you really haven't internalized that *all* things are impermanent. Your reluctance to give up your seat when on a crowded bus or train can help you to see the ways in which you still prefer the suffering of others over your own. Of course, it's no replacement for a qualified Buddhist teacher, but it is still a place to learn. In this sense, diligent students will find teachers everywhere.

Whether or not you have a formal relationship with a Buddhist teacher, there are limits to what this person can do for you. Just as a piano teacher cannot practice or perform for you, a teacher can help you along but it's *you* who needs to do the practice. Buddhist practices aim to change the way you experience the world and get through life. No teacher can experience things for you. Nobody else can live your life.

This is evident in another common aspect of Buddhist practice: taking vows. Vows are common in many strands of Buddhism. When someone becomes a monk or nun they often take many vows that restrict their behavior in various ways. Even people who are not in a monastery often take vows to refrain from things like stealing, lying, killing, sexual misconduct, and getting drunk. Bodhisattvas, in making the deliberate decision to help others before themselves, take a vow to eliminate all suffering, wherever it may be.

Vows are often made in front of an audience, often in the presence of someone very important. But they're not forced. Taking vows is something that the person decides to do because they understand that it will help them to better see how the world is and live accordingly. Like a marriage vow, it's a promise that you make in front of others, ideally because *you've decided* to take on a long-term course of action in your life. Like a resolution, it's not really a promise *to* anyone but a way of solidifying a decision to do something, a way of keeping you on track for a long-term goal when it's tempting to veer off course in the short term.

Of course, as with resolutions, vows need to be made at the right time and in the right context. Making ones that are too harsh or too ambitious virtually guarantees they'll fail. If I've never run before, making a resolution to run twenty miles a day is not going to go well. Failing at them can also be discouraging and counterproductive to your goal. In the same way, it's important to make vows suited to your level and situation; determining this is another area that teachers typically have experience with.

Changing your outlook in life is hard, and Buddhism includes a wide range of approaches to starting out. Figuring out what works for a particular person means reflecting on these issues: Do promises or resolutions help you to stick to your plans? Do you need the support of a community? Do you do better under the direct supervision of a teacher? Of course, for many Buddhists these matters have been decided for them by family, tradition, and society. For others with the luxury and burden of choice in the matter, being thoughtful at the start, can avoid a lot of wasted time and effort later on.

20 | RELICS AND VENERATION

For the vast majority of practicing Buddhists in the world, the veneration of relics and important places is absolutely central to what Buddhism means to them. Words like "relic" and "veneration" can often feel too religious and too supernatural. For many with a modern outlook, practices involving the veneration of relics can seem archaic and irrelevant. As a result, they're too often overshadowed by philosophy and meditation in many contemporary discussions of Buddhism in the West. Nevertheless, these practices can not only be deeply meaningful and transformative but are among the most widespread and popular in the Buddhist world today.

Most generally, these practices are ways of expressing respect and admiration, but they also bring about changes in your outlook. They typically involve an especially important object or place, and there are, as you might expect, many, *many* variations. Since they often involve magical or supernatural elements, they're sometimes ignored or downplayed in modern forms of Buddhism. They are, however, important in the Buddhist world and offer important lessons, even for those who don't accept the supernatural aspects.

The Practices

These practices, at their heart, are about relating to special objects and places. Think about a time when you've met with someone important to you, a mentor or a family elder. Or think about visiting an important place, like the grave of someone you were close with or a person who inspired you. Doing this often means behaving in special ways that acknowledge this importance: You get dressed up, you bring flowers or a small gift, and your body language and speech change.

These are ways that we acknowledge that a person or place is special. Something similar happens with physical objects too. A family member hands you a watch that belonged to your great-grandfather, and you not only handle it with more care than you handle other objects, but you feel a more direct and immediate connection with someone who was previously an abstraction.

Buddhist practices of veneration work in a similar way; they're special ways of relating to important places, objects, and people. If it's a physical place, it might be a Buddhist temple or monastery. Or it might be the place where events from the lives of important Buddhist figures happened, like the birth, enlightenment, or death of the Buddha or another influential teacher. It might also be a geographic feature like a mountain or lake. Often these were important places before the arrival of Buddhism and, after its arrival, took on new significance.

Many of these special sites are marked with special structures. This might be a pagoda (a tall tower) or a stupa (a big dome). These often contain special objects and are consecrated with special ceremonies that certify their status as important landmarks in the Buddhist world. Often these structures will contain a relic, an object connected with a special person or event. This might be part of a teacher's body, like a bone or tooth, or something they used during their lifetime, like robes or a bowl.

Other objects of veneration are images, paintings, or statues of buddhas or bodhisattvas. Sometimes these are created by people. The creation of these images involves not only trained artisans but those trained in consecration ceremonies, particular ways to make the image more than just a representation. After consecration, the image more fully *becomes* the buddha or bodhisattva. It's a bit like when an artist signs a mass-produced copy of one of their works and by doing so make it something more. It's no longer just a copy, but an important and meaningful artifact.

Sometimes writing is also an object of veneration. Such objects include texts containing important Buddhist teachings, texts explaining and elaborating the meaning and implications of those teachings, as well as biographies of important teachers, translators, and practitioners. It might also be a scroll containing special prayers or invocations printed many times over. These might be objects of veneration sitting on a bookshelf or altar in a home or they might be placed inside a temple or stupa. Often it's not just what a text says that's important, but the physical object itself.

There's a huge range of things to venerate, but what do you actually *do* to venerate them? One very popular practice goes by the awkward English name circumambulation. This is a long word for something simple: It means you walk in circles around something as a way of valuing it. It's typically done only clockwise. This is because that way your right side is always closest to the thing you're venerating, and the right side is traditionally thought to be cleaner. Of course, it's not *just* walking around something; you have to do it with the right state of mind. It is, after all, a way of respecting a special place and so the importance of that place should be on your mind while you do it.

People sometimes do many circumambulations, especially on special holidays. It's common to do them daily as part of your normal routine. Circumambulation is also often combined with other practices, so you might do it while doing an imaginative practice or even just reflecting on Buddhist ideas. As with other practices, you should dedicate the merit you generate to all beings.

Another very common practice is prostration. This can be done when you encounter a special place or teacher but is also commonly done at home facing an image of a buddha or bodhisattva, or even a shelf of Buddhist texts. While facing the object, you put your hands together, raise them up and touch them first to the top of your head, then to your mouth, then to your chest. This symbolizes your aim to retrain your body, speech, and mind to be in better accordance with reality.

Next you drop down so your body is face down and flat on the ground. You extend your hands out in front of you. Then you get back up and again put your hands together and touch them to the top of your head. If you're meeting a teacher or just making a quick visit to a temple, you'll do this three times (one each for the Buddha, his teachings, and the Buddhist community). If you're doing prostration as a stand-alone practice, you might do this several hundred or thousand times. Some Buddhists do hundreds or even thousands of these *every day*.

Prostration is also sometimes done together with circumambulation. Here after you've dropped flat on the ground, when you get up, you step to where the tips of your fingers were. As you do this you can slowly move toward or around an important place, one prostration at a time. In a less common and much more difficult variation, you face toward the place you're circumambulating and move only the width of your body with each prostration.

You can also use imaginative techniques at the same time. There are many variations on this. You might imagine that you have a huge body or many bodies all doing the prostrations with you. One variation involves picturing all of your previous bodies doing the practice along with you. This helps emphasize the strength and depth of your commitment and the worth of what you're venerating.

You might also travel to a special place, making a pilgrimage. This can be done alone or with other people. Not only can visiting a special image, teacher, or place be meaningful and transformative, but when done with others, the journey itself builds a supportive community, even if just a temporary one. While on the pilgrimage you can learn from others and, since the trip is often difficult, get the chance to help each other. Here it's not just the place itself that's important but also the trials and setbacks on the road and the others on the journey with you.

The Purpose

This stuff can seem spooky to some people. The idea that objects and places have a special power can seem too supernatural or magical. For many people who do them, these practices have just this kind of power, and that's a large part of their importance. Certain places and things are worthy of veneration precisely because they have an otherworldly power. As common as this view is, it isn't the only way to understand these practices.

It's not so easy to maintain a sharp division between what is spooky or magical on one hand and what's mundane and worldly on the other. Imagine you have to leave your home suddenly and can only take a few things with you. What would you take? You'd probably want to take at least some things that have sentimental value: a watch that belonged to your grandfather or the cork from the champagne bottle opened at a close friend's wedding. These objects have a special kind of value that is more than their material worth or their price on the open market. They have the power to connect you to past events, to trigger vivid memories and intense emotion. They're not exactly *magical*, but they do hold a special psychological power.

Often that particular object's history, where it's been and who's touched it, are critical parts of this kind of value. After all, why lug that souvenir for your friend all the way back from a distant vacation when you could buy the same thing online and have it shipped right to their house? Part of why you want to bring the object with you is because it's important that *you* bought *that particular thing* at *that particular place and time* and brought it all the way home, just for them. The history of the object and the effort you put in to bringing it back become part of its value, its special meaning.

Places themselves can also have this function. When an Elvis fan visits Graceland, the very place has a special meaning and triggers a flood of emotions. This is where Elvis, the real person, lived and made music. This can also happen on a more personal level. Think of someone visiting their hometown after having moved away long ago. When they visit one of their old hangouts they're confronted with the past because of that particular place and their personal history with it.

It's possible to have these kinds of experiences with objects and places even if you don't believe in supernatural or magical stuff. You can understand Buddhist relics and pilgrimage in a similar way: The Buddha's jawbone, an important teacher's robe and bowl, or a famous statue are all meaningful and important in the same way as the objects you'd save from your house. The places are important in the same way that Graceland is for the Elvis fan, and the objects are meaningful in the same way as the souvenir from an important trip. They serve as a bridge from the material world to the world of values and relationships.

These things can also connect you with people and places that are far away from you in space and time. Maybe you never met your grandfather, but here is the same watch he used every day right in your hands. Your friend and their spouse may be thousands of miles away, but nevertheless that cork from their wedding day can serve as an important connection to them.

Historical artifacts in particular often have this power. Imagine how you'd feel if you got to hold an ancient Greek coin or John Lennon's guitar. These objects have a special meaning and significance that other objects don't. Part of the feeling of holding one of these objects is of being connected to things from the distant past, things otherwise known only from books or documentaries. In the same way, you can't meet the historical Buddha or many of the thousands of famous Buddhist teachers throughout history. But you can sometimes interact with a relic that connects you with them in a direct and physical way.

Relics, both personal and Buddhist, have the power to make larger-than-life things feel approachable and real. Why does it feel different to see Van Gogh's original *Starry Night* than to see one of the hundreds of copies and prints you've likely seen over the course of your life? Part of it is that seeing the original means seeing the *actual* smears of paint that Van Gogh, *a real person*, made. He put this very paint on this very canvas and here you are seeing it right now.

Seeing the actual painting can make you realize that Van Gogh wasn't some fictional or mythical character, but a real person. He was someone with a physical existence who could feel itchy or catch a cold. Seeing Elvis's clothes and papers can remind you that Elvis isn't some fictional rock-god—he was an actual guy. Ancient Greek culture can feel like a purely academic idea, something that exists only in books, until you hold a real physical object in your hand. Then it hits you that these things really happened in the same world that you occupy. These were real people with real experiences just like you.

The same is true in a Buddhist context. Karma, emptiness, and enlightenment can start to seem like intellectual abstractions, historical and theoretical curiosities that exist only in old texts and faraway temples. But direct physical contact with relics can help you to recognize that these are living things that permeate every moment of your life.

This recognition serves to reinforce your values and motivate you to act in certain ways. An Elvis fan might get more excited about listening to Elvis's music after a pilgrimage to Graceland, and you might call your friend more often after visiting a place where you spent time together when you were young. In the same way, making a pilgrimage to a special place or handling a special relic can make you more motivated to actually make changes to how you live your life and to actually *do* other Buddhist practices.

Some Buddhists emphasize that you can get these benefits even if you just *think* that something is a relic. In one Tibetan story, a guy is traveling for business near holy places in India and his mother asks him to bring a relic back for her. As happens on business trips, he gets busy and forgets. Just before he gets home, he picks up a dog's tooth and gives it to his mom, telling her that it's one of the Buddha's teeth. She believes him and is deeply moved by the tooth, which motivates her to better align her outlook with how reality is. Even though the tooth was just an ordinary object, it still brought about a real and valuable change in her experience of the world.

This isn't to say that it doesn't matter if a tooth was really the Buddha's, just that sometimes relics that aren't genuine can have the same effect. This happens in other contexts too—in medicine, placebos can be very effective. Giving someone a sugar pill can actually relieve pain or help with an illness as long as the person *thinks* the pill is really medicine. This doesn't mean that there's no difference between medicine and a sugar pill, but it does mean that the effectiveness isn't just in the pill but involves our minds too. If what you thought was your friend's wedding cork turned out to really be just another cork, it might have still helped sustain your friendship for years. It might have still made you think of them, communicate with them, and prompt reflections about your shared time together.

This highlights that these practices aren't just behaviors you do with your body but must be done with the right frame of mind in order to work. For example, Bodhidharma (pronounced *Boe-dee-dhar-muh*), the Indian monk who is said to have brought Buddhism to China, dismissed people who circumambulate stupas thoughtlessly. Just walking around a stupa without the right frame of mind might get you exercise and fresh air, but it won't help you solve the problem.

The relationship between your body and your mind is complicated though. Sometimes we have to fake it till we make it, going through the motions first and waiting for the mental stuff to come later. This is particularly clear in prostration practice, which can change your mental outlook through doing certain things with your body.

Our bodies often affect our minds. Think about trying to make an important decision when you're sick or trying to make small talk with a headache. Reading and writing can be much harder in a cramped, hot, and noisy place. If you're sitting with friends around a table and one person has a very low chair, they can feel like they're a kid at a table full of adults. It can affect how the conversation goes—which jokes get a laugh, which suggestions get taken seriously, which questions get answered. The physical situation alters not just the conversation but people's entire experience of the evening.

You can think of prostration as working the same way. It can change your orientation to yourself and others. For some of us, it's natural to go through life with a feeling of confidence and, if not superiority, then at least self-assurance. It's the feeling that *I* know what's what and can immediately evaluate things clearly and accurately. It's responding to someone with a nod of the head and a smug, "Hmmm, fair enough." It's the feeling that other people might make *suggestions*, but *I* am the expert and final arbiter.

Not everyone is like this. But many of us are, at least *some* of the time. Prostration involves lowering your body before something else. Circumambulation involves literally altering your course to acknowledge the importance of a place. A lowered, humbled body can help cultivate a more humbled mind. It can develop a mind that is more willing to acknowledge that other people might know better than we do, one that listens to what others say and seriously considers it. This consideration isn't just comparing it to our own preexisting opinions and seeing if it fits in, but taking what others say seriously on its own terms. It means losing the impulse to dominate conversations and developing a willingness to listen, be open, and not simply wait for your turn to speak.

Prostration is hard. If you're not used to it, you feel sore and achy for days after. For some Buddhists this is a way to purify bad actions from the past. But you can also see it as changing the very habits that produce those deeds. By lowering yourself before something that represents certain ideas, you can start to bring about psychological changes that put those ideas ahead of your own self-image. As a painful activity, it prompts you to reflect on that experience more broadly and on what kinds of mental habits produced it.

Of course, like other practices, it can itself become part of a self-image: "*I* did ten thousand prostrations yesterday. What did *you* do?" This is a danger of any practice and is one reason you might do it in private or not want to discuss the details as it can easily turn into a competitive game with holier-than-thou winners and dilettante losers. Another danger is coming to see the relics or places as having some special essence and so to focus on them rather than their meaning. The cork is a symbol of your friend's wedding and you'd be foolish to value it above your friend and their marriage. Coming to fetishize objects and places in this way is a real danger of these practices.

Many Buddhists will point out that these objects and places are, like everything, impermanent and empty. The cork from a friend's wedding or the Buddha's tooth are composite and relational things. They can be tools that help bring about motivational, emotional, and spiritual changes, but they are still composite and relational. Just as a story you hear as a kid can help change your outlook even though you later understand that it wasn't really true, these objects can work the same way.

Because of the supernatural and physical aspects of these practices, it can be tempting for modern, academically minded people to be dismissive of them: "I'm a serious Buddhist practitioner so *I* study texts and meditate." This is rooted in a kind of spiritual or intellectual pride that reinforces a sense of self-superiority and perpetuates the underlying problem. It's important not to get too philosophical and underestimate the role of the body and physical objects in retraining your outlook.

It's hard to understate how popular these practices are in the Buddhist world. It's true that many people who engage in them do so in order to accumulate good merit or secure a better re-birth next lifetime, but they can play other roles too. They can serve to connect you with the past, make abstractions more tangible, build community, and bring about a less self-involved outlook.

21 | SOLITUDE AND MEDITATION

In the Western popular imagination Buddhism conjures up a particular image: the lone seeker, dressed in religious robes, meditating in bliss on a high mountaintop. Like much in popular perceptions of Buddhism, this image bears the fingerprints of those who shaped and promoted it. It's emphasis on self-sufficiency, personal experience, and spiritual reverence for nature promotes the agendas of *Western* cultural movements, agendas that previous Buddhists didn't have in mind. Of course, these aspects *are* present in the Buddhist world, but they're only part of the story.

Solitude does play an important role in many Buddhist practices. The problem you're out to solve is very difficult, and the intellectual, perceptual, and emotional habits that stand in the way are deep-seated. This means that attacking the problem requires focused time and energy. Life provides a nearly endless parade of distractions: bills, gossip, social obligations, groceries, politics, not to mention the uncountable tiny interruptions each day brings. This is partly why many Buddhist practices involve establishing some degree of separation from everyday life.

Establishing some distance from the diversions and pace of life allows for the space to confront the problem in a sustained way. Many practices involve not only sustained focus but also a greater degree of perceptual sensitivity to what is happening in your body and mind. This is already difficult to develop but can be even harder in a chaotic or intense environment. It's much easier to think something over during a quiet walk in the woods than it is during a walk through a crowded and noisy shopping mall.

It's not just being away from distractions that helps, but being away from the demands of the social world. Being with other people means not only interacting with others but also monitoring their responses and managing how you present yourself. This is important for people to get along, but it requires mental processing to accomplish, even for those who are very good at it.

The expectations of others can also push us in other, more subtle ways. When visiting your parents or an old friend you haven't seen for a long time, something strange sometimes happens: You find yourself behaving the way you did when you regularly spent time with them. You've changed, but they expect you to behave the way you used to, and sometimes even without realizing it, you end up playing into those expectations. You complain about things that you used to complain about; you use a tone of voice that you haven't used for years.

The expectations of a social role can have the same effect. Your kids expect you to respond the way they think a parent should and your employees expect you to respond the way they think a boss should, so you end up talking, acting, and even thinking like a parent or a boss. If you're trying to adopt one of these roles, this can be a good thing. But if you're trying to step outside of them, to see and break free from their associated mental habits, people's expectations can make it even harder. Since expectations often reinforce our habits, changing them can mean removing yourself from these situations, at least for a little while.

Buddhists, particularly those who specialize in meditative practices, can take retreats that last for years. For many of us, that's not practical. It requires preparation, social support, and of course money. For many, even taking a three-day weekend retreat is impractical—we may not have jobs that make this possible. We may have people to take care of. We may not live anywhere near a place that's suitable to retreat to, and may lack the money to get to a place that is.

Practical obstacles aside, a retreat into solitude isn't for everybody. For those just starting out, such long periods of solitude can be dangerous. There's a reason that solitary confinement can be traumatic: Being suddenly alone for long stretches without preparation is psychologically risky. Long retreats usually happen within a specific social context. Those who take them typically have a long-term association with a particular Buddhist institution and so have a lot of preparation and social support, even if they lack social contact during the retreat.

So even for a retreat into solitude, social support plays an important role. Being around others with the same goal, especially those you know and trust, can help you better achieve it. Again, different people are different in this respect. Some people learn a skill better by taking a class and some learn better from books and informal lessons. Some people need a workout buddy to keep making it to the gym, while others can exercise on their own perfectly fine.

Even if you're not going to retreat into the mountains for years and can't even get two or three days to yourself, there can be ways to adapt ideas about solitude to your life. Solitude often comes in small servings: taking a shower, driving to work, sitting on the toilet. It won't work for all of them, but some practices can be adapted to fit in these smaller slices. You can also try to organize your day in ways that create space for these small islands of solitude. Maybe you park farther away from work and so get ten minutes to walk alone. Maybe you wake up a little earlier or stay up later, finding time alone while others are sleeping. Maybe you spend an evening with your phone turned off.

All of these preliminary practices are about creating a space for you to change your outlook. Making that space can be difficult and depends a lot on your personality and situation. This can change—what works now might not have worked for you five years ago and might not work five years down the road. But successfully doing any of the practices we'll examine means finding a space in your life that is peaceful, regular, and reliable.

As for what fills that space, for many in the West it's one thing: meditation. If someone reveals they're Buddhist, the usual follow-up question is something like, "How often do you meditate?" Not "How often do you do prostrations?" or "Do you offer incense at the temple?" *Just meditation.* Buddhism is often talked about in Western circles as a "contemplative" tradition, which reinforces the misleading idea that Buddhism is all about meditation.

Buddhists do meditate, but it is only one practice among many. Buddhists also participate in rituals, festivals, and pilgrimages. There are many Buddhist practices that have nothing to do with meditation at all. Thinking that Buddhist practice is all about meditation is like thinking that Catholicism is all about confession or working out is all about doing bench presses. Sure, that's *part* of it, but it's not the whole thing.

As we've seen, there are many Buddhists who do not meditate at all. Monks and nuns often specialize in particular practices. Some might specialize in memorizing texts, others in doing funeral rites, others in debate. Some specialize in meditation, but many do not. Some do think that meditation is *the* central part of Buddhism and that all Buddhists, even those who are not monks or nuns, should meditate. This is, however, a modern idea and doesn't reflect the reality of Buddhist practice in all places and times.

What is meditation, anyway? The English word is often used to mean simply considering something in a careful or deep way. In this sense you can meditate on a painting or piece of music. Here it refers to mental activity that puts you in a special kind of state. It's also often associated with sustained focus, relaxation, and careful observation. Meditation in this sense includes *a lot* of different activities: Christian or Muslim prayer, stargazing, and reminiscing about the past.

Advocates sometimes pitch meditation as having a huge range of benefits like curing insomnia, depression, or sickness. But as we'll see, in a Buddhist context this isn't the point of meditation. It is a tool for a very specific task, though a fundamental one. It can have benefits for what therapists sometimes call the "worried well" but it is, at best, a complement to and not a replacement for professional mental health treatment.

Buddhists sometimes distinguish three tasks involved in coming to see reality clearly. One is learning about the ideas. This means hearing about how things are, listening to what smart people say about how the world works. Next you have to think it over. You need to reflect on these ideas for yourself and apply them to your own life. The final task is typically translated as "meditation," though most accurately it means internalizing the way things are, getting used to it.

These three tasks—listening, thinking, and meditating—happen in other cases of learning too. If you learn to play an instrument, for example, first someone will tell you how it works and all the different things you need to do to make certain kinds of sounds. Then you think about these things, what they mean, and how they relate. Finally, you practice so that you internalize how the instrument works and you get used to playing. After a while your hands make the sounds you want naturally, without your thinking about it. Meditation in a Buddhist context is like the latter phase except what you're getting used to is experiencing the world in a radically different way.

The kind of skill that Buddhist meditation develops is what makes it unique. What is the difference between a Buddhist monk meditating and a kid in the backseat of a car playing games on a tablet? After all, they're both in a special state, developing perceptual sensitivity, and focusing their attention on solving the problem at hand. They're both developing skills to advance, though the games they're playing are very different. The difference is that the kid develops skills to complete the tasks in the video game, while the monk is developing skills to retrain his fundamental experience of the world. The monk has particular motives and aims, to realize certain facts about the world. So the techniques he uses are particular tools to retrain his mind to internalize the relational, composite, and impermanent nature of all things.

Still, it's important to keep in mind that in most places and times, meditators make up a *minority* of Buddhists. Perhaps more importantly, meditation *isn't one single thing*. Just as working out isn't a single activity, meditation isn't a single practice but a wide range of different techniques. There are many different methods Buddhists have developed to bring about the relevant changes in your mental life. Some will count as meditation in a broad sense; others will not. Some will involve thinking or imagining; others won't. Some will require doing certain things with your body; others won't. All of them, however, aim to change your outlook to one that fully internalizes a radically different orientation to yourself, others, and the world as a whole.

22 | MINDFULNESS OF BREATHING

These days the word "mindful" gets asked to do *a lot* of work. People advocate eating, driving, working, and doing pretty much everything else *mindfully*. Being mindful gets used to mean everything from being "fully present" or "in the moment" to simply being careful when doing something. Though it has taken on a wide range of meanings, all of them center on how we direct our conscious mind.

As a Buddhist technique, mindfulness involves sustained attention to particular things in special ways in order to change how we experience the world. The Buddhist concept of mindfulness includes not just attention but also memory. This might seem to be at odds with "being in the moment." After all, being in the moment is about the *present*, and isn't memory about the *past*? Sometimes yes, but the division isn't so clear-cut. Being *mindful* of how long you leave your bread in the oven means, at least in part, keeping track of the time that has elapsed and *remembering* to take it out. Talk of "living in the moment" or being "fully present" can be confusing for just this reason. Can I be living in the moment if what I'm doing *at this moment* is planning next year's vacation? Can I be fully present in what I'm doing if what I'm doing is reminiscing about the old days with my mom? Even if you think it's important to be fully present and engrossed in the task at hand, some tasks involve the past or future.

To represent this connection with memory, some scholars use the term "retention" instead. This captures the idea of not only fixing your attention on something, but also *keeping* it there. But mindfulness or retention isn't just noticing something; we do that all the time without any effort. It means deliberately fixing your attention on certain things in a sustained way. This is much easier said than done—our minds love to wander away at a moment's notice. Breaking this habit is an important early step in Buddhist practice and one that mindfulness can help to correct.

There is a wide range of mindfulness techniques. Here we'll start with a very common beginning exercise centered on breathing. The technique is simple to describe but difficult to do well. On the bright side, it's something that you can get better at when you do it regularly. It is a technique that has become widely taught and practiced outside of Buddhist circles, so it'll be important to highlight how it works when done as a distinctly Buddhist practice.

The Practice

Though most commonly done while sitting, traditional sources are clear that it can also be done while lying down, standing, or walking. There are some advantages to being seated. Lying down can make it easy to doze off, and walking can be dangerous, requiring you think about where you're going. So it's best to start by finding a comfortable place to sit.

It's also important to find someplace that is relatively quiet and distraction free. You are, after all, trying to train your attention, so having more distractions around is going to make it more difficult. For similar reasons, it's a good idea to close your eyes. It's natural to notice things in your field of vision and start thinking about them, so closing your eyes removes a big source of potential distraction.

You start by simply fixing your attention on your breathing. You take in air and then let it out. As you do this you keep your attention fixed on this cycle of inhaling and exhaling. Some versions of this technique focus on the feeling of the breath in your chest or lower abdomen; others focus on the feeling of the air around your nostrils and upper lip. Whatever the location, it's important to keep your mind fixed on that particular place. As you continue, you'll start to notice more subtle aspects of how each breath feels.

You shouldn't try to breathe faster or slower than you normally do. Don't try to make your breathing conform to some idea of how you think it should be; don't try to slow it down or speed it up or take deeper or more shallow breaths. Just allow it to happen naturally and observe it. The aim is to *observe* your breathing closely for an extended period, not to force yourself to breathe in a particular way.

Some forms of this technique recommend counting your breaths, sometimes up to five or even ten and then starting over. This can be useful for maintaining your attention as it gives you a task to focus on. Other teachers, however, will explicitly discourage this as it can lead to focusing on *the counting* rather than the breathing itself. You want to attend to your breathing, not just close your eyes and count to ten over and over. Counting can also distract you to from noticing the details of each breath.

As you focus your attention on your breathing, sooner or later your mind will start wandering to other things: something a co-worker said earlier, what you're going to have for dinner, stuff you need to get done today, and on and on. When this happens, as it definitely will, don't get mad at yourself or feel like a failure. As soon as you notice what's happened, acknowledge it and calmly return to your breath. "Ah, there it goes again! Okay, back to the breath." Especially when first starting out, this will happen a lot. But with regular practice, your ability to keep your mind on your breathing will improve and you'll start to notice more and more subtleties of how it feels.

The Purpose

Since it involves being deeply focused, this technique might seem similar to being hypnotized or in a trance, but it's different in important ways. Though it can produce a kind of peaceful feeling very much like these other ways of being engrossed in something, being entranced or hypnotized is often something that happens to us. This type of mindfulness, on the other hand, is self-induced and self-directed. It's something *you* decide to do and that *you* carry out.

Another critical difference is why you do it. Though it involves being unresponsive to many things around you, mindfulness aims at being in a state of heightened awareness. Of course, it's an awareness directed exclusively at one particular thing, your breath. But it's less like *tuning out* and more like *tuning in* very, very carefully. It's not losing your mind, just directing it in a precise way.

Even though from the outside it can look like you're not doing anything, you are in fact honing and developing a mental skill. This isn't to knock doing nothing, which is often beneficial and undervalued. Sometimes people like to call anything they want to do a "practice" but in this technique you really are *practicing*. You're doing a very specific mental activity with the aim of getting better at it. In this case, the skill you're developing is one that gives you more control over your conscious mind: the ability to fix your attention on something for a long time.

Buddhists commonly liken the mind to a wild elephant or a crazed monkey—erratic and very difficult to wrangle. Being mindful and focusing on the breath is an early step in the process of calming and controlling where your mind goes, of pacifying the monkey and training the elephant. This is an especially important skill to develop early on because without it you can't do many of the other techniques very well.

Think of solving mundane problems. If you can't focus on the broken doorknob, you have no hope of fixing it. If you keep checking your phone every few seconds and can never keep your mind on what your partner is saying, you have no chance of fixing your troubled relationship. Without being able to pay attention properly, many problems become utterly hopeless.

Attending to your breathing in this way can also be very relaxing. The demands and stress of day-to-day living can leave you feeling like a glass of water with sand in it that's constantly getting stirred up. There are so many demands on you, so many things vying for your attention. There are people and events to remember, things you want, thoughts that pop into your head. They can feel like grains of sand bouncing everywhere in your mind. Deliberate and sustained focus on your breath can give the sand a chance to settle and leave you feeling like your mind is calmer, clearer than it was before.

This is the primary reason that this kind of technique has become popular outside of Buddhism. It's often presented without any reference to Buddhism and touted as a remedy for anxiety and stress. This isn't to say that Buddhism owns the idea of developing the ability to concentrate, and of course anything that helps people feel happier and healthier is a good thing. However, when done as a Buddhist practice, this kind of technique is importantly different from simple stress relief.

The most important difference is *why you do it*. In a Buddhist context, the fact that it can reduce stress and make you feel calm is a nice side benefit, but it's not the reason you do it. It would be like telling a dedicated novelist that writing fiction helps prevent dementia. That's a nice benefit to be sure, but that's not the reason they write. Novelists can have a variety of motives. Maybe they write because they have something inside that they want to express, or maybe they were deeply moved by a novel and want to create something of similar value. But whatever the reason, the fact that it helps to prevent dementia is unlikely to be their primary reason for writing. The same is true of the stress-reducing effects of mindfulness for Buddhists.

Buddhists do this kind of practice because they want to solve the problem. Of course, they're aware that there are other benefits.

When traditional sources discuss the benefits of mindfulness practice they talk not only about achieving a tranquil state of mind but also about supernatural benefits like flying through the air and remembering your past lives. Even these benefits, however, are not the aim of the practice and are often described as dangerous distractions.

The reason you need to develop this kind of mental skill is to be able to observe very subtle features of the world and your own mind carefully and accurately. Doing this kind of detailed observation means developing focus and an ability to observe things in detail over a long period of time. Developing this skill is an early step on the long road to actually changing your outlook to match how things really are.

In a Buddhist context, you do this kind of exercise so that you'll be able to see clearly the ways in which everything you experience is composite and impermanent. You do it so that eventually you can see how your perceptions, thoughts, and feelings about life have been insensitive to these facts. Even if you know intellectually that you are a composite lacking any non-relational essence, your patterns of thinking and responses can betray this in ways that are difficult to notice.

Though being calm or relaxed isn't really the goal, it's important to be calm because there are things that are otherwise hard to see. When you're really busy with work or really stressed it's harder to notice that a friend changed their hairstyle or that their tone of voice reveals an inner emotional struggle. You can miss even obvious things because you don't have the mental space to notice what's happening around you. The principle is the same: Without a calm ability to look closely, you won't be able to notice the features of yourself and the world that fuel the problem.

That's part of why this initial technique centers on the breath. There are, of course, some practical reasons for this. Everybody breathes, you don't need to remember to bring it with you, and it doesn't cost anything. More importantly, it helps you to see things not just about your body but your mental life too. Our emotional responses, for example, are also bodily responses. When you feel nervous or angry your palms get sweaty, your heart rate changes, and your breathing changes. As we will see in other techniques, by increasing your awareness of these things you can notice the early signs of these emotions, and this can help you to be more successful in managing them before they carry you away.

Mindfulness of breathing isn't really a self-contained thing. It is *one* step in a longer journey. It's not done simply to relieve stress and be more relaxed, but to be able to focus your mind and see things more clearly. As a Buddhist technique, it is always done in concert with other things—not only with a view of the world and the self in the background, but also while living a certain kind of ethical life and keeping in view the bigger goal of solving the problem. After all, lots of other things can develop your powers of concentration: reading novels, playing chess, or even watching TV.

The ability to focus and sustain your attention is itself a neutral mental skill. It can be put to good or bad uses. An assassin might need intense and sustained focus to successfully kill their target. Part of the Eightfold Path of Buddhism, the traditional treatment for the problem, is "right mindfulness," and the phrase isn't redundant. Right mindfulness implies that there can be *wrong* mindfulness too. Wrong here need not have the moral or theological baggage of a "thou shalt not" kind of commandment. If you want to bake cookies, there is a right and a wrong way to do it. Leaving them in the oven all day or replacing all of the sugar with salt is the wrong way to do it because it won't result in delicious cookies, not because of some divine culinary decree. In the same way, right mindfulness is the kind that allows you to see things in ways that helps you to solve the problem. It also takes *a lot* of practice to be able to do well.

23 | MINDFULNESS OF DEATH

Buddhist practice includes a wide range of reflections on death. Impermanence can be easy to accept as an abstract, intellectual idea, but death makes it personal and tangible. One day each of us will stop breathing and be separated from everyone and everything we care about. As composite things, our bodies will turn cold and decompose.

These reflections can seem pretty grim. That's why it's important to remember their role in the larger context of Buddhist practice. They help us to get used to harsh truths about how the world is and change our habitual responses to accommodate those truths. In this sense, it's a bit like when a therapist helps their patient work through unpleasant realities in order to better deal with them. As with the therapist, the point isn't to just dwell on upsetting or traumatic stuff, but to face such facts responsibly—in the right way and with the right mindset.

Though reflecting on death helps us connect impermanence to our day-to-day lives, many of these techniques do not work well when focused on those we have intense personal relationships with. Thinking about the death of someone you care deeply about will give rise to sadness and grief; thinking about the death of someone you hate might give you a kind of perverse satisfaction. Of course, death is intimately tied up with emotions like this, but cultivating these responses is not the aim. The point is to reflect on the reality of death from a certain frame of mind—a diagnostic one intended to shed light on difficult aspects of reality and how our intuitive responses deny or distort them. In a Buddhist context you reflect on difficult things like death in order to better deal with them, to be able to forge a life in full view of such difficult facts.

The Practices

Some of the most straightforward Buddhist practices around death are simple reminders. Some in the Tibetan tradition will set their cup upside-down before going to bed, acknowledging that they may well die in their sleep and not need the cup anymore. Then when they wake up in the morning, they'll turn it over again, lucky to get another day.

Of course, the practice isn't really about how you store your kitchenware. It's about taking time at the start and end of each day to reflect on the fragility of life and the good fortune to be granted another day. It's nice to have a physical task to make sure you do it, but the point is to internalize the precarious position you're in each and every day and realize there is no guarantee of another day so it's important to use this one well.

Other Buddhist practices are more intense, focusing on the physical realities of death. Many involve close observation of a human corpse. It's important to note that this is typically done by monks under the direct supervision of a qualified teacher, and it is often formalized in many ways—it is determined when you go, what you are to think about and attend to on the way there, and what you do afterward (along with what *other* practices are part of your regular regimen). Needless to say, it is much more than simply going to gawk at a dead body.

Practices that involve observing a corpse often also involve attending to the various ways in which it is repulsive. It assumes a very different experience than that of a typical modern funeral. The modern world has an entire industry full of specialists who are trained to make a dead body appear as a living person who is asleep, typically through the use of chemicals and cosmetics. This is not the experience of a corpse Buddhist texts assume—it is typically assumed that one views a dead body as it is, without intervention.

These meditations involve focusing your attention to different parts of the corpse: the skin, joints, openings, and so on. You look in detail at each part in a set sequence and reflects on how disgusting it is. There is even an extensive taxonomy of the different ways in which things can be gross: They can be bloated, festering, gnawed, rotten, and more. In these reflections you consider how *you*, right now, are the same kind of thing as the corpse in front of you. The dead body in front of you was once a living, breathing, and moving thing. You too will one day decay, decompose, and be eaten by bugs. You're the same kind of thing, just at a slightly earlier stage.

Other reflections on death are broader in nature, focusing on our environment. Our world, for example, can seem like the fixed and permanent setting for the births and deaths of the creatures that live there, but it too will end. A modern version of this might be to think of the sun. It might seem eternal, but eventually it will run out of hydrogen and become a red giant. The Japanese Buddhist writer Kamo no Chomei (pronounced *Kah-mo no chou-may*) gives a famously poetic description of this: "The river flows continuously, and yet the water is never the same. In pools, the shifting foam gathers and is gone, never lasting for long. So it is with people and their homes."

It's not just we who will die, but the places in which we live our lives will end too. Other reflections blur this very distinction. Our bodies are home to millions of tiny creatures: the bacteria in our digestive systems, microscopic mites that live on our eyelashes, and countless microbes that live in our bodies. These tiny creatures far outnumber the actual cells of our bodies, and many are essential for keeping us alive. These creatures live their entire life cycles within our bodies. Our bodies are to them what the Earth is to us, and we are in the exact same position as they are—we will come to an end and so will the place we live.

Still other reflections center on the certainty of death. It's not a matter of *if* you will die, but simply *when*. Birth entails death. All composites decompose eventually. This happens constantly all around us. Leaves turn from green to brown, ants get stepped on, seasons change. Human beings are no different. We might get longer than an ant or a dog, but we get a hundred and twenty or so years at the very most.

Because death is a certainty, none of the various goods of life can help you avoid it. They might help you *delay* it for a bit, but they won't prevent it. Even if you have a strong or attractive body, you're still liable to get sick or have an accident. No matter how famous you are or how many friends you have, none of them will be able to save you from dying. No matter how smart or well read you are, no books or clever arguments can prevent your death.

Death, then, is the certain end of all successes. You can work and fight hard to get money, fame, and power, but one day you *will* lose it all. It's easy to know this intellectually but difficult to internalize this fact. So we end up like passengers on a sinking ship fighting each other for the objects on board—even when we win, it doesn't last long.

Though death is a certainty, its timing is not. It is impossible to know for sure when you will die. Reflections on this emphasize that the conditions that preserve life are rare: food, water, air, and a particular temperature range, among other things. The causes of death, however, are numerous: sickness, radiation, bad food, and viruses, to name just a few. Our bodies are very fragile and even small changes can be deadly. So death often comes without warning. Some die as babies or even in the womb. Many people die while thinking about mundane things like trying to remember the name of an actor or deciding what to have for lunch. Death can happen at any time so there's not even any certainty between this breath and the next.

The Purpose

These may seem like grim and even anxiety-inducing reflections, but the purpose isn't to feel anxious or depressed. Rather, these reflections aim at a visceral recognition of the impermanence of life. They're supposed to loosen your ties to your particular body and the life you currently have. They're supposed to shake into you the deep understanding that the collection of physical and mental events that you call yourself will, like all collections, eventually come apart and is actually constantly in the process of doing so.

The purpose isn't just to point out the obvious fact that everybody will die one day. It's to integrate that abstract knowledge into your moment-to-moment reality. After all, even though we mark certain days on the calendar when the seasons change, in reality they're constantly changing. The same is true of death and the point is to become more comfortable with that.

That's why one needs to do these meditations over and over. Unlike a fact, which you can hear once and remember, getting used to things takes time, particularly when what you're getting used to runs contrary to how you've always related to the world. Often we don't feel any particular rush even though time is running out. You get a vacation and at the start, the days seem to stretch out before you; you've got all the time in the world. But then suddenly you wake up and it's the last day. You didn't do many of the things you planned to do because it never felt urgent enough. There always seemed to be more time.

But time is short. Buddhist texts are full of poetic images to illustrate this. Life is likened to a cat's yawn, the foam on a wave, or a dewdrop on the tip of a blade of grass. We're advised to think of our lives as just like these fleeting and brief things. Part of this is to combat forms of laziness and procrastination: "Yeah it's important to figure this stuff out, but I'm busy. Next year I'll have more time to focus on this kind of stuff." But there's no guarantee you'll be around next week, let alone next year. You have to start solving the problem *now*. You need to practice, as Zen Buddhist teachers sometimes put it, like someone whose head is on fire. When your hair catches fire, you don't put off extinguishing it—you do it immediately.

But there is more to these reflections than "No time! Get to work!" They also aim to bring about deeper changes. Think about the idea of *having stuff*. Not just physical objects, but other things we try to get: health, success, a good reputation, and relationships. These are all things we think we can have. But these reflections highlight how temporary this relationship really is. It's less like ownership and more like renting. In the best case, these things are available to be used for a limited time.

Reflecting on this can help put things like fights, rivalries, successes, and failures into perspective. When you don't get the job, it's not like you missed out on something you'd have forever; it's something you'd have for an indeterminate, but definitely limited, amount of time. Someone might be your rival *right now*, but in the future both of you will change as will the nature of your relationship. Being a rival isn't an unchanging essence they have. It's just a relational feature of the situation you happen to be in—one that will surely change. Since we're all on a sinking ship, is it really worth using the few moments we have left fighting over money and rivalries?

It's not just how you relate to external stuff that changes, but how you think of yourself. Think of the qualities you have that you're most proud of. Maybe you're clever or athletic or charismatic. These too will decay and fade. You will, eventually, lose them. When you start to internalize this, *having* them starts to seem less important than how you *use* them. They're tools that, for now, you have access to. And you can, if you choose, use them to make the world better—to help solve the problem. You, your good and bad qualities, the stuff you have—it's all temporary and in a constant state of flux. So rather than try to hold on to these things, it's better to make good use of them while they're around.

Examining methodically and in detail each of the parts of a corpse prompts reflection on what exactly death means for a composite, especially collections that are constantly changing. Aside from its inevitability, it can come to look pretty different from how it first seemed. Rather than one static thing coming to an end, it feels like a more visible change in what was always a dynamic and composite series of events. It's less like something blinking out into nothing and more like a team or club disbanding. We might say the club or team is dead, but all that happened was the members went their separate ways. There was never a team in the world, it was always just an easy way to talk about a more complex and composite reality. Or recall how "summer" doesn't refer to a thing in the world that disappears when fall arrives. It was always just an easy way to talk about an intricate pattern of meteorological events. If that's all you've ever been, then that's all that death means.

Facing up to this stuff can be scary and unsettling. But you're not alone in this predicament; everyone around you is in the same situation. Rich and poor, famous and unknown, clever and dim, left wing and right wing, all nationalities, all races, all genders— *everyone*. Keeping this in mind can serve as a counterbalance to the ordinary divisions that color our relationships. These distinctions don't seem so important when the ship is going down; the icy water is the same for all of us and we're just trying to make it through. Reflecting on death can serve as a reminder that the situation of everyday life isn't so different.

Impermanence for Buddhists doesn't just mean that things come to an end; rather, they're constantly ending and starting with each moment. Death isn't just some later event but something that is, in a different way, happening right now. It happens as a series of instants, like how a wheel spins but only touches the ground at one point. Since each moment is similar to the last, we mistakenly think it's the same, but it's not. We might talk about a river, but the water is different with each moment. It's impermanent not just because it'll dry up eventually, but because its waters are constantly changing.

This isn't to say there is nothing bad about death or that it can't be sad or depressing. But it is to say that at least some of the very real pain and agony it produces stems from assumptions about what there is, assumptions that can be deeply ingrained in how we experience the world. The point of these practices isn't to stew in anxiety or wallow in grim thoughts. They aim to counter specific obstacles in solving the problem, like vanity or procrastination, and ideally to unsettle these deep-seated assumptions about what we are, what death means, and how we should live.

24 | FLESH AND BONES

Many techniques in Buddhism involve reflecting in detail on physical bodies, both our own and those of others. These techniques typically emphasize the disgusting and repulsive aspects of each part of the human body. They also reveal ways in which we relate to our own bodies and subtle ways we're attracted to or repulsed by those of others. Given how deeply rooted our mistakes about the nature of the world are, a focus on the body makes sense. If you've ever been exhausted or in chronic pain, you know all too well that the way we experience life is intimately intertwined with our bodies.

In traditional sources, women's bodies in particular are singled out for reflection and represented as impure and undesirable. As modern readers, this is one place where we're forced to consider the context of canonical Buddhist texts. Many were written by and for celibate monks in a cultural context where heterosexuality was assumed as the norm and women's status in society was far from equal to men's. There is no denying that for us today, such practices as written reinforce harmful body image norms and sexist attitudes. But rather than pretending that such texts and practices don't exist, we're better off thinking about the underlying purpose of such reflections. This allows us to face up to uncomfortable historical facts while also illuminating how such practices might be adapted to be relevant in our own circumstances.

The Practices

As we've seen, many types of Buddhist meditation involve detailed and systematic reflection on the physical body. There's more to them than just observing the breath or sensations in a neutral way. Like meditations involving corpses, these techniques involve directing your attention slowly and methodically to each part of your body, observing each part in detail. As you do this, you observe the repulsiveness of each part when examined closely.

Consider, for example, your hand. It's covered by skin that might seem nice at a glance but is a patchwork of tiny flakes that are constantly falling off. Underneath are stringy, fibrous muscles soaked in blood. Under that are rubbery tendons and hard bones filled with spongy marrow. The hand at first seemed singular and fairly pleasant, but when looked at closely, it appears as a collection of fairly unpleasant and repulsive things.

You then proceed in this way, slowly and systematically considering each part of your body and analyzing the gory details of each part. In a set order, often moving from the feet to the top of the head, you consider each part in detail: each of your ten toenails, each joint, each tooth, and so on. With each body part, you zoom in and consider the different ways in which the bits and pieces that make it up are revolting and grotesque.

It's not just external body parts you attend to, but what's on the inside too. This includes various fluids contained in your body: blood, pus, phlegm, saliva, sweat, tears, and even the oil on your skin. It also includes the skeletal system: the sinews of your joints, your bones, and the marrow in those bones. The internal organs get the same treatment: your heart, liver, lungs, spleen, and kidneys. It's not just your body itself that gets analyzed in this way but also things in you that aren't strictly speaking part of your body: the food in your stomach, the *piss* in your bladder, and the *shit* in your intestines. These all get carefully considered and analyzed in the highest resolution that your mind allows. The image that emerges is not a flattering one. On closer inspection, what seemed to be something nice, clean, and beautiful is made up of stuff that's gross and repulsive.

As you consider each of these parts, you slowly move through the body and label each one. You focus on the blood and think to yourself, "This is blood," then move on to pus thinking, "This is pus." But as you do this, you're not supposed to focus on the *label* itself, but the physical body part.

As you go through this process you do more than simply think, "This is blood—how gross!" You attend to specific features of the body part you are focused on, things like color, shape, location, and so on. So for blood you notice its deep red color, its runny and slightly slimy texture, and its presence throughout your body. It's important not just to think of it as repulsive, but to picture the specific *ways* in which it is repulsive.

It's not just your own body that's the object of this kind of reflection. Other techniques focus on the body of someone you're attracted to. Traditional texts typically assume this to be a beautiful woman, but it could be anyone you find yourself physically attracted to.

First you think of a person you are attracted to. This could be a real or imagined person. Notice how their body is an object of desire. Then, as before, you reflect in detail about how it is a composite of things that are very undesirable when examined closely. Sometimes this involves close examination of the skin, muscles, organs, bones, and so on. As you mentally analyze each part, you see that what you previously felt to be beautiful is anything but.

This partly works by close examination, putting specific parts under a microscope. It also works by isolation. In a classic example, you might find someone's elegant wavy hair attractive, but when one of those hairs falls out and sticks to your couch or clothes, you are annoyed and throw it in the trash. Reflecting on how each hair seems when taken in isolation is supposed to change how you feel when you see the stylish head of hair on the person you're attracted to.

There is a wide range of other reflections, all of them aimed at undermining physical attraction and the sense of self that underlies it. So you reflect on the fact that this person's body, like yours, will age, die, and decay; then it won't seem attractive at all. After the person dies you're repulsed rather than attracted to the body, but what changed? All that changed, at least at the moment of death, is that the mind is gone. If that's the case, so the reflection goes, what was it that you were attracted to in the first place, their body or their mind?

Other reflections center on the costs of such attraction. Many people buy perfume, makeup, skin cream, and other expensive things to cultivate such attraction. This adds up to a huge cost in time and money—things that, from a Buddhist perspective, could be better put toward solving the problem.

The Purpose

These are rough reflections in many ways. Far from the feel-good positivity of following your bliss, these feel austere and puritanical. The reflections, especially about women's bodies, read like a desperate plea to a teenager by a prudish and over-concerned parent: a shotgun blast of rhetoric against sexual attraction.

Making sense of these practices means thinking about the context they were developed in. These are reflections designed by and for celibate monks to deal with particular problems. Your life and situation are certainly different in many, many ways. Not everyone who experiences sexual desire needs these techniques, but only people for whom lust is an obstacle to their goal of seeing reality clearly. They might be particularly relevant to someone hung up on a person they cannot or should not have sex with (which, of course, for a celibate monk would include everyone).

It's incredibly important to think about this before simply plucking out a practice from a classical Buddhist text and assuming that it will work in your life. Think of a teenage girl in contemporary America who is immersed in a culture that constantly emphasizes the ways her body falls short of a certain ideal of beauty.

Entire industries of cosmetics and advertising depend on creating and maintaining feelings of doubt and insecurity about her physical form. Her entire social circle makes clear, both implicitly and explicitly, the many ways that she should find her own body repulsive. For someone like this, someone struggling to accept their body and to feel comfortable in their own skin, reflecting in detail on the repulsive nature of the body will be destructive and toxic.

The reflections focusing on women's bodies as objects of sexual desire betray a view of women as temptresses and a strong fixation on purity, both of which now seem laughably dated. There's no denying this aspect of many Buddhist texts, and when viewed in their historical context, it's unsurprising. It's possible to both acknowledge the antiquated and sexist assumptions *and* carefully consider the underlying purpose of such practices to see if there is something useful you can adapt for your own life.

It's important to keep in mind that the reflections on the different body parts are done with a particular purpose. Someone studying for an exam in medical school or an especially vain person might also attend to different parts of the body in detail, but they do so for very different reasons. In a Buddhist context, this is done to get used to feeling that your body is a composite thing. It's something with different parts: parts that rely on each other, parts with a particular history, and most importantly, parts that will eventually separate. Like a hurricane or a company or a pile of eggs, it isn't something extra in the world but a temporary collection in constant flux. So worrying about it is a mistake because there's really *nothing* to worry about.

You also attend to the different parts of the body, not in a neutral sense but to counter particular hang-ups you might have regarding your body. Someone who is trying to quit smoking might imagine in detail how gross the black tar in their lungs is *in order to break their habit*. Maybe this is accurate, or maybe their lungs aren't really as blackened as they imagine, but it doesn't really matter for breaking out of the habit. These bodily reflections can work the same way. Maybe the reflections are accurate, or maybe they're just useful for breaking out of the habit of assuming physical bodies to be singular sources of value in themselves.

This is why the reflections proceed by detailed and methodical examination of each part of the body. It's not just for shock value or to indulge some morbid fascination. Things can often look much nicer when viewed at a distance. A battlefield might not look so bad when viewed from an airplane. A hurricane looks almost beautiful from outer space. But zoom in closer and the details tell a different story. These reflections trade on the same thing happening when we ordinarily see our bodies; they appear one way from a distance and another when looked at in detail.

Examining the parts of the body in detail not only helps to emphasize its collective nature but also to extend attitudes from the parts to the body as a whole. The idea is this: If you develop a certain attitude to each of the parts, that attitude can be extended to the whole. If I examine each egg in the pile and see that it's rotten, then I can see that the pile is rotten too. If I examine each part of the body and see it's nothing worth being attached to, then I can see that the whole body is nothing to be attached to either.

Things don't always work this way though. Often this kind of reasoning is bad. If I examine each egg in a pile and see that it weighs forty grams, I cannot conclude that the pile must weigh forty grams. It's sometimes psychologically implausible too.

I might look carefully at each individual ingredient in a hot dog and find it gross, but then see a cooked hot dog on a bun and find it delicious. So this kind of reflection won't always transfer the attitude from the parts to the collection, but it will give you a better sense of what the collection really is, of what exactly you're eating when you pick up the hot dog.

Part of the point is to change how you feel about your own body. It's easy to operate on the assumption that the body is a singular and persistent thing. As you get old it can be a shock to see it changing and decay. It's not as easy to run up the stairs like you used to or to shake off the drinks of the previous night in the morning. It's all too easy to invest your identity and self-worth in your physical appearance, even though that is bound to fade.

Another part of this change in perspective is reflecting on the collective and impermanent nature of the body in detail. Other reflections change your point of view, shifting perspective from seeing your body as a thing that lives in an environment to seeing it *as an environment itself*. Your body is actually a home to millions of tiny living things that live their whole life cycles inside you. Your body is their home and a place for them to live, and their existence is intimately intertwined with your own.

Disgust then functions as a counter to common ways of relating to the world in a self-centered way. Think of how differently you feel when seeing a wart on your own foot and seeing one on someone else's foot. The warts are equally gross, but somehow it can be less repulsive when it's on *your* foot.

Buddhists notice that it's not just how we relate to our own bodies that reinforces a sense of self, but how we relate to others' bodies too. Sexual desire is often singled out here because it's an obvious case and particularly relevant for celibate monks. But there can also be more general insights for us implicit in these reflections. It can be illuminating to stop and think about what happens when you find someone attractive. What are you responding to? Why? Often your concern is less about *them* than about what *you* want. Sometimes it isn't even *the other person* that we're attracted to, but our own mentally constructed image of them.

Perhaps more importantly, we can reflect on the origin of these responses. When thinking of a body that you find attractive or repulsive, why do you feel that way? Is it from a lifetime of advertisements designed to stoke insecurities and reinforce body ideals? A modern version of this kind of reflection might involve taking note of your own attraction or revulsion to a physical body and examining its basis. Is a certain body type attractive as a result of years of beer ads, action movies, or pornography? Insofar as these habits of relating to your own body and those of others reinforce a sense of self, they're getting in the way of seeing things clearly.

This doesn't just happen with sexual attraction. We see people in terms of what they can do for us in other ways too. We see a basketball player in terms of how many points they'll score for the team *we* want to win, the famous person as entertainment for *us*, the cashier as important for getting us the groceries *we* want quickly. We often fashion people into what we want them to be and relate to them in terms of our own desires and goals. Even though these techniques involve seeing yourself and others as mere physical objects, they do so in order to break out of these harmful attitudes. Reflecting on the nature and sources of these habits can help to shake them away, allowing us to relate to others more directly and realistically, fully acknowledging their importance.

At bottom, these reflections are about breaking free from being hung up on things that are impermanent, mistaking them as lasting things that we can keep. From a Buddhist perspective a body is a useful tool for being able to do things in the world and not much more. In this sense, it's a bit like a car. Some people get hung up on their car and are invested in what it says about them; they identify deeply with it. Others hate their car and are ashamed of it, thinking that it reflects poorly on them. Both make a mistake in identifying with what should be a tool for getting places, although the techniques each needs to correct their mistake might be very different.

Many Buddhists point out that our bodies are valuable for what we can *do* with them. They enable us to speak and act. This is a kind of power that can be used for good or ill. Our bodies are like tools that are useful for understanding the world, helping others, and making the world, or at least some small part of it, better. It's bad to obsess about your tools at the expense of the work to be done, but it's important to realize what they enable you to do and take care of them.

It's also important to remember that these reflections are done in concert with other practices and are informed by a particular philosophical outlook. They're done in the service of a specific goal: to move beyond a way of relating to things through the lens of a self in order to see reality clearly and help reduce the suffering in the world.

Again, the context for these reflections is often a celibate monk and not someone in a modern, well-functioning romantic partnership. Such partnerships can also be objects of attachment, but they need not be. After all, other relationships, even for a Buddhist monk, are recognized as beneficial. Most have close relationships with their teachers or fellow monks. These relationships can serve as a place to practice compassion and breaking out of self-centered concerns which can be extended out to strangers and even enemies. These relationships also offer encouragement and support, which are critical for long-term success.

Many of the techniques found in Buddhist texts are dated, but that doesn't mean there is nothing of value in them. The history of Buddhism is one of people rethinking practices to be relevant to their particular situation, and contemporary Buddhists are no different. But it is also important for such Buddhists to be honest about the traditions they draw on and what they're doing. The point isn't to pretend Buddhism has a flawless history or to discredit Buddhism because of bad practices. It's to examine practices in context and try to understand what, if anything, we can adapt and use today.

The general aim of these practices is to confront our own physicality. We are embodied beings, and understanding our place in the world means reflecting carefully on that. The aim isn't to make you feel ashamed; that's a counterproductive response that actually presumes an identification with your body and reinforces a sense of self ("*My* body is so gross, what will they think of *me*?!"). The point is to break out of relating to the world through the lens of a self and counterbalance various forms of attachment to physical bodies.

25 | DEVELOPING AWARENESS

Many Buddhist techniques are directed toward a particular object. You imagine something in detail, you're mindful *of* something, you meditate *on* something. We've seen a few, but there is a huge range: the breath, a corpse, your body, even certain virtues or buddhas. Different objects can be selected for people at different levels of understanding, who have different temperaments, or who face different obstacles.

Other times, however, you're not aiming to be aware *of* anything in particular, but simply aware. You're not focused on any particular thing but instead have a heightened sensitivity to *everything* that's happening. This technique is similar to some of the earlier ones, but it's less like training your eyes to see particular things better and more like improving your sense of vision itself. It helps to develop a kind of discerning awareness of all of the events around you—their origins, duration, and characteristics.

The Practice

As with other meditative techniques, this one is best done in a comfortable and quiet place and begins with closing your eyes and focusing on your breath. You don't count your breaths or think "in" and "out" while you breathe but instead focus carefully on the sensations of the air coming in and going out. Some versions tell you to focus on the area between your nose and mouth, others on the air through your nostrils, and others in your chest. Wherever the focus, as your mind becomes calm and settled, you begin to experience more subtle sensations that you didn't notice before.

You then extend this awareness to the rest of your body, at first by sweeping your attention head to toe and later by extending this sensitivity to your whole body all at once. This step can take a while to achieve. If you think of your mind as a glass of water with sand in it that is all stirred up, when you stop stirring, it can take a while for the sand to settle and the water to get clear. In the same way, when your mind has been agitated for a long time it can take a while for things to clear up—be patient.

When you experience thoughts, perceptions, or feelings, rather than noting them and returning your focus to where it was, allow your observation to turn to them. This doesn't mean you get carried off by them, thinking about all the things you need to get at the grocery store, but you closely and carefully examine the thought or perception itself. You do this with the kind of detached indifference a scientist might have. A scientist studying elephants in the wild might see two elephants fighting. But the scientist doesn't get involved in the fight. They just carefully observe what is happening, how it started, and what it is like.

Here you're like the scientist, but instead of trying to get an understanding of elephant behavior, you're trying to get an understanding of your own mind. So when a thought or feeling occurs, rather than squash it, or note it and turn away, you step back and observe it. Observing your mind in this way is like watching a parade through your window—you're looking closely at it, but you don't get carried away and start marching along with it.

Suppose you feel itchy or hungry. You observe this experience closely and carefully. Where exactly in your body is it? Does it move or stay still? Is its intensity constant or does it flicker like a candle? Does it end suddenly or gradually fade away? What other thoughts and impulses happen around it? Again, you don't respond to it—you don't scratch or eat a snack, you just examine it calmly and carefully without reacting to it.

Though you don't react, there are some aspects to notice. You're not supposed to *think about* these aspects so much as *directly observe* them. These thoughts and feelings are impermanent; they start and end, and even while they're around they are constantly changing. They're a product of many conditions: your body, the environment, and your thoughts. They all influence each other. Any individual thought or feeling is connected with a huge range of mental habits and impulses. Perhaps most importantly, none of this is *you*. It's just stuff that happens.

Of course, at some point you will have to stop your meditation session and go about your day. But this kind of awareness doesn't have to stop when you open your eyes and get up. This technique is more like stretching before a workout. The real practice happens in your everyday life—it's seeing more clearly the nature of your visceral responses and mental habits and making you better able to correct them in real life.

The Purpose

The point of all of this is to see things clearly, to experience reality more accurately. As with seeing or hearing other subtle things, it can be really hard if you're not calm and haven't had much practice. Hearing a faint harmony in a song that's playing is hard if you're rushing because you're late for work. Seeing the way a certain director frames shots in a movie is hard if you're on a first date or just haven't learned much about filmmaking.

By doing this kind of close, calm, neutral observation, you're able to learn much more about your mind and the world than you otherwise would. One way to highlight these things is through philosophical argumentation, but you can also take steps to position yourself to see them directly. By examining your thoughts and feelings in this way you can observe how your responses are rooted in a sense of self, how they're structured by a sense of what is pleasant and unpleasant and what you like and dislike.

You also experience how these thoughts and feelings are episodic. They bubble up to the surface and evaporate. As they do, you see for yourself that they're constantly changing in ways that are difficult to see. It's not just the responses themselves that are impermanent but everything you think of as yourself. As you develop a more acute awareness, you directly experience yourself as a composite, relational, and changing series.

An important part of the technique is examining your thoughts and feelings from a neutral point of view. You remain calm and don't get carried away, not because you're apathetic or don't care, but because that is the best way to see how things really are. If every time you have a certain thought you recoil, if you think to yourself, "Ugh, that's *awful*!" and push it away, you'll never be able to understand it and what caused it. The thought may in fact be awful, but when you're troubleshooting, that's neither here nor there. Many things doctors see are disgusting, but given that they're trying to diagnose and treat an illness, it's not useful for them to respond by being disgusted.

This attitude is sometimes described as a non-judgmental one, but it's better to think of it as being *non-reactive*. This isn't an attitude of radical acceptance, of thinking that no thoughts or feelings are good or bad, but of bracketing your usual reactions so you can bring about certain changes. After all, the whole purpose of the practice is to get past habits of thought and feeling that mislead you about what the world is really like, a task that in fact presupposes that some things are good and others bad.

Another way to see this is to think about times when we maintain awareness in other situations. Someone who is trying be fully aware of what's going on in the kitchen when they're cooking isn't being non-judgmental; they don't just accept anything that happens in the kitchen. Nor are they focused exclusively on a single egg or fork. They're trying to have a clear awareness of the events around them and how those relate to their aims of making a delicious meal and not starting a fire. This will mean ignoring some things, like the exact color of the mixing bowl, and taking an unbiased look at how much sugar they add, not because *any* amount of sugar is okay, but because it matters that *the right* amount gets added to the dish.

So even though this technique involves observing in a non-reactive way, this is done for a very particular purpose. It's not just to relax or be more accepting of what's in your head or heart. It's to see the world and your mind clearly so that you can bring about a change for the better. When the road is hot, you might need to look carefully to see if it really is wet or if it's just an illusion, but you do so in order to be able to drive safely. Even though you observe in a somewhat detached way, you're less like a mechanical camera indifferently accepting everything and more like an experienced doctor calmly and carefully looking for symptoms in order to heal.

These aims are what distinguish this as a Buddhist practice from similar practices aimed at reducing stress and anxiety. When done in a Buddhist context it may well reduce stress, but for Buddhists this isn't the point. It's a nice side benefit that happens when pursuing a more important goal. In a non-Buddhist context, when you non-judgmentally observe thoughts and feelings as they arise and pass away, you accept them all no matter what. As you do this, you become more calm and relaxed, and the technique works.

In a Buddhist context, however, you adopt a non-reactive point of view in order to see clearly the nature of your thoughts and feelings. You do this to see that they aren't singular and independent things, but changing with each moment and the product of a huge web of conditions. You directly observe how they both come from and reinforce mental habits that are rooted in deep mistakes about what the world is like. These habits are, in the long run, bad for everyone. This is why you observe in this special way—to break out of deep-seated ways of relating to the world.

Think about the kind of awareness you need to break a more mundane habit like biting your nails or smoking. You need to be aware of what your hands are doing and what situations make you want to bite your nails or light up a cigarette, but you maintain this awareness because you want to change what you've already acknowledged to be a *bad* habit. You will need to have a subtle awareness of what you're doing, but you do so in order to break the habit.

Understanding the practice in this way makes sense of why you need to closely observe your body. Our mental and emotional responses also have physical aspects. Getting angry means, in part, having sweaty palms and a faster heart rate. By being more sensitive and aware of your body, you can catch impulses earlier and nip them in the bud. If you can notice earlier that you are getting angry or have a desire to smoke, you have a better chance of doing something to head it off. A closer awareness of your body helps you to do this.

There are many teachers, especially in the West, who teach techniques similar to this simply as a counter to anxiety or to increase productivity. Sometimes they emphasize a connection with Buddhism and sometimes they don't. Though these techniques may be Buddhist-inspired, it's worth keeping in mind how things change when this technique is removed from a Buddhist context and the way that many Buddhist practitioners feel when it's held up as *the heart of Buddhism itself.*

Imagine that a trend emerges in China of people doing rosary practice to relieve stress and anxiety. A new generation of Chinese secular rosary teachers emerges. "Sure we learned the technique from Catholics," they say, "but you don't *need* to be Catholic to do it." And they could be right too—saying the prayer and moving the beads between your fingers might reduce stress even if you don't believe in Catholic doctrine or do any other Catholic practices. They start selling their own brands of rosaries and having conferences where they invite Catholic priests to speak, though they ask them to downplay the role of God and faith in the rosary practice. This is because, they say, they've actually discovered the true essence of Catholicism and it doesn't involve any of the other Catholic practices or beliefs at all. Turns out, Catholics have just been mistaken about what their own religion is really about for thousands of years.

If you were a Catholic you'd be understandably annoyed that a bunch of people latched on to one little part of what you do and started telling people *that* is what Catholicism is all about. This is how many Buddhists experience uses of Buddhist-inspired meditation techniques for stress relief. They may well work, but like using a rosary for relaxation, it's pretty different from how it works in its original context.

Again, this isn't to say that using these techniques outside of a Buddhist context is always bad. But you have to be careful when isolating and adapting a single technique from a larger tradition. It's important not to mistake what is relevant for you with what the tradition is really about. It's important to be honest about what you're leaving out and how that changes the *meaning* of what you're doing.

It's important to keep in mind that for Buddhists, this is a technique that's done for a particular purpose. If you're cooking an egg, you should watch the time. This doesn't mean that watching the time is important no matter what you're doing or that time-watching is a critical part of living well. But if you've decided to cook an egg, you should also watch the time to succeed in cooking it well. Similarly, if you're trying to solve a fundamental problem in life by retraining your mental habits, it's important to develop a focused awareness of what's really going on in and around you.

26 | KINDNESS AND JOY

A central part of seeing through the illusion of having a separate and persisting self is changing your intuitive responses to good and bad things in life. We respond quite differently to our own problems and failures than to those of others. This difference both betrays and reinforces the sense that we are separate things with special importance.

Since Buddhist practice aims at breaking out of this mistaken sense of self, changing these responses is an important task. Even praise, admiration, and applause can reinforce our idea of self and so are things that can be obstacles to solving the problem. Thinking that you're great and thinking that you're awful are very different thoughts, but both make things about *you*.

These practices aim to change our feelings about good and bad events in our lives. They involve reflection on ways in which we are similar to others, regardless of the current role these people have in our lives. Such reflections work by extending the goodwill we already have outward, increasing its scope and strength.

The Practices

It's useful to do this practice in a place that is as comfortable and distraction free as possible. It need not be a dedicated meditation space, and you don't have to be seated in a special position or even be sitting at all. All that's required is some uninterrupted time in a calm and comfortable place.

This technique begins by letting your mind go where it often goes on its own anyway—to yourself. First, you think about your hopes and fears. What do you want to happen? What are you afraid will happen? One way to tease this out is to imagine what an amazing day would look like, picturing what you would do, who you'd be with, and what would happen. You can then picture an awful day, considering what kinds of tragic events would affect you the most.

As you think about these things, you next look past the specifics to their more foundational aspects. You want to be happy, safe, and healthy. You want to avoid sorrow, sickness, and loss. Your situation is a fragile one; you're vulnerable to not getting the things you want and running into the things you want to avoid. Sit with these facts a while and let them sink in.

These feelings might be easy to conjure up or they might come slowly. It's important not to rush or force them. Don't get sidetracked thinking about whether or not you *deserve* the good or bad things you imagine. This isn't relevant to the exercise, and for many things, it's neither here nor there anyway. A sunny day or a winning lottery ticket might not be deserved; after all you didn't *earn* either, but they can still be good things that make you happy.

Of course, you might hope for a promotion that you earned, resulting from your hard work rather than from nepotism, but the thing to focus on here is how good achieving this goal would make you feel and how bad you'd feel if you failed.

Next, choose someone you care about very much. Ideally, this is someone you know well and already have a relationship with. It's best not to choose someone you're romantically infatuated with or someone who has died as these can bring up a wide range of feelings like jealousy, resentment, or grief, which would distract from the purpose of the exercise.

With this person clearly in mind, you then think about your hopes and fears for them. You want them to succeed and to have all they need to be happy and healthy. You want them to avoid accidents, illnesses, and setbacks. Again, don't rush, and let yourself fully experience these emotions. Then you consider what you have in common: You both face difficulties, want to be happy and healthy, and try to get through life with a minimum of failure and misery. Your hopes for them are, in a deep way, the same as for yourself.

Next you pick an acquaintance, someone you have minimal contact with and no strong feelings about. This could be someone you see in the course of the day, like a cashier or a mail carrier. You can also generate a contact by simply picking an object around you and considering its source. Odds are, you're near a lightbulb right now. That lightbulb was designed by an engineer and produced in a factory with workers. Think about a newly hired engineer or the janitor at that factory. This person, like you and people you care about, also has aims, goals, hopes, and fears. They too want to be happy and safe, to avoid loss and grief.

Even though you happen to have little or no personal contact with this person, they're similar to you and those you care about in many ways. They have a body like you and also feel shaken during a health scare. They too get frustrated by setbacks and pleased when they finally achieve something they've worked hard for. They too have people they care about that they would be devastated to lose. Let the feelings and wishes you had for yourself and those close to you expand to include this person too. You're all in the same precarious boat in very rough waters.

Finally, you pick someone you dislike or maybe even hate. This could be someone who is hostile to you personally or it could just be someone you think is really awful. Of course, depending on the situation you'll need to be very careful who you pick. Picking someone you're in an abusive or manipulative relationship with can be counterproductive and dangerous. This is one of the places where a qualified teacher can help, but when in doubt pick someone else—life is full of antagonists. It can be helpful to start with someone you mildly dislike, an annoying coworker or neighbor, and over repeated sessions gradually pick those you feel more strongly about.

Initially, you might not even attempt this final stage. Trying it too quickly can cause resentment and fatigue; our minds can resist any suggestion that these people are like the rest. And yet the point is to get yourself to notice how they *are* like you and those you care about. Even if they're annoying or jerks or have done awful things, they too are people with hopes and fears. They too are subject to the changes life brings: happiness, sadness, success, failure, insecurity, and all the rest.

By focusing your attention and imagination in this way, you extend your concern outward from easier to more difficult people. With each step, you maintain the wishes and emotions from the previous one, though you redirect them toward a different object. You want them to be happy, successful, and healthy. You want them to avoid misfortune, loss, and grief.

It can be tempting when doing this to get sidetracked rehashing the particulars of different relationships: remembering events you experienced, wondering what they're doing now, thinking of mutual acquaintances. If that happens, just return to the task and keep at it. As you continue, what you share will be thrown into relief and you'll start to feel a stronger affinity and concern for them.

Another common technique to develop kindness and compassion is to reflect on those who have cared for you. Traditional sources instruct you to reflect on your mother, assuming that everyone has a good mom. But this will not work for everyone. Sadly, some mothers are abusive or neglectful and so won't work for this purpose. Of course, these traditional sources involve an idealized image of motherhood, but reflecting on an ideal that's too far from reality won't work because it will feel too impersonal and won't have the same emotional impact.

You can start simply by thinking of someone who has cared for you, nurtured you, or helped you while you were in need. Someone who was there for you while you were vulnerable and did so not for personal gain, but out of genuine concern. It's often useful to think of those who helped you when you were a baby. Whoever it was, they gave you food and shelter so you wouldn't die. They made sacrifices of time and money to do this. Maybe they had to work hard to do so, but they definitely could have done other things instead. But they didn't and decided to take care of you.

Now think of what a huge difference this made to your life, how much worse off you'd be without their help and support. Now realize that you are in a position to do the same not just for children, but for any of the people you meet during your day. You have the power to, even in some small way, give the same gift that was given to you.

You can play this role not just for friends and family, but for everyone. Traditional accounts appeal to rebirth here. Given how long the cycle of birth and death is, every single person you meet has given you this care. Somewhere in the history of lives, that person has done all of this for you. The person driving the car that took the parking spot you wanted, the annoying coworker, the cashier, they've all cared for you when you were helpless. They did this not out of a sense of duty, but out of real selfless concern. Of course, not everybody thinks rebirth is true. But even if not literally true, this can still be a transformative thought.

The Purpose

These practices aim to change your usual way of relating to others. In particular, they develop a pair of responses called *metta* and *mudita*. *Metta* is often translated as "loving kindness" and is a genuine concern for the happiness of others. *Mudita* is often translated as "sympathetic joy" and means feeling happy when good things happen to others.

Though *metta* is similar to much of what we call love or kindness, it is more specific than either. It's not romantic love and doesn't involve sexual attraction or infatuation. It's not just an intense fondness, as when we say things like "I *love* that movie!" Perhaps most importantly, it's not self-regarding. Sometimes what people call "love" has less to do with caring for someone else and more to do with how that person makes *them* feel. Sometimes what gets called "kindness" is really a kind of trading, concern for others with the implicit expectation that it will be returned to *you* later on. *Metta* is none of these things. It is the opposite of the tendency to look out for you and yours. It's a sincere and selfless concern for others, for their happiness and well-being.

Mudita is a similarly selfless response toward someone, but it's felt in response to a particular event. Something good happens to someone else and you're genuinely happy for them. You don't harbor some secret wish that it happened to you and you're not envious of the attention they get. You're simply glad that something good happened to them. The good things you can be glad about can be of different types. They can be material benefits, like a raise or new car. Or they can be intellectual, like making a scientific discovery or finally becoming conversational in a foreign language. They can even be spiritual, like understanding Buddhist philosophy in a deeper way.

It's critical that this joy is selfless. Sometimes we're happy when something good happens to someone else primarily because of how it benefits *us*. A friend finally lands a job they wanted and you're happy because now *you* won't have to hear them complain about work constantly. A mother feels happy that her son got the top score on his exam because of how it will reflect on *her*. These are ways of feeling happy for others, but they're not *mudita*. *Mudita* is about feeling happy for someone else because you care about them, not because of some way in which their good fortune benefits you.

Metta is a wish for others to be happy, a deep concern for them to do well, and *mudita* is a response when good things happen to them. These responses have a lot in common. It's important to notice that neither makes any reference to what someone deserves (or what you *think* they deserve). This doesn't mean that Buddhists deny that people can be more or less deserving or that they think there's no such thing as justice. But it does mean that the purpose of these exercises isn't served by thinking about what people deserve. If someone wins the lottery, they might not deserve the money in many ways; maybe they don't need it as much as others and they definitely didn't work for it. But you can still feel *mudita* when you hear about their new money. This is because the aim is loosening a particular habit—that of being happy about things that are good for me (and people I like) and being indifferent or annoyed when good things happen to others.

Both *mudita* and *metta* are developed by building on your existing concern. The techniques work by extending the sphere of this concern outward, from easy to more difficult situations. Each step builds on the previous extension, so it's important to bring out the joy and concern at each level. This extension can be done in other ways too. You might do it geographically, starting with people in your house, then extending to those in your town, then your country, then the world, then the universe.

The point is to change how you relate to others. This means not just *thinking* about them differently but feeling and noticing different things too. Part of developing real concern for others means thinking hard about what will actually help them, but it also means having an easier time feeling happy for them and noticing when things make them happy or sad. These responses run counter to other tendencies like jealousy, envy, insecurity, and selfishness. These all involve a strong sense of self, of carving up the world into what is for me and what is for others. For Buddhists, this is a mistake. These responses aren't just obstacles to connecting with others but reinforce a distorted way of seeing reality.

Buddhists often point out that combating this mistaken way of seeing things isn't really a sacrifice you make for others but is actually good for *you* too. Traditional sources emphasize that feeling insecurity, envy, and resentment are unpleasant and often push us to do and say things that we'd rather not. By loosening the grip of these habits, we get out of our own way and participate in the world without a bunch of baggage. Imagine if you just naturally felt happy when something good happened to someone else. Rather than feeling insecure or envious, you're just really happy for them. Not in some grudging or forced way, but because you've become the kind of person who naturally responds like that. This isn't to say it's easy, but it does seem like a really nice way to live. But you can only live that way if you give up the habit of responding to people and events in ways that tie them back to a self—to *your*self.

This can help you to feel less isolated from others. By sharing in their joy and wishing them well, you're more connected with them. This can be daunting, but it's also less lonely. The bus driver is no longer just a thing that gets you to the next stop, but is someone you care about and wish well. It also helps to broaden a myopic focus on your own goals. Being hung up on yourself means you miss out on a potential source of joy in the world: the success and good fortune of others. Focusing less on yourself can allow you to honestly appreciate the goodness in others without comparing yourself to them or wishing that you had what they have.

These reflections can also serve as a useful counterbalance to other more impersonal techniques. Reflecting in detail on death or the physical body can make you callous and indifferent to others. Yes, everyone is impermanent, and yes, they're just composite collections. But they can still experience suffering and, like you, benefit from being treated with love and compassion.

But doesn't starting these reflections by thinking about yourself just reinforce your sense of self? It need not. If you care about all beings, then you care about yourself. You are, after all, a being too. Some people do lack self-concern, and that can cause problems. If you aim to help others, you need to ensure a strong foundation. This is why airplanes tell you to "please secure your own mask before assisting others." You need to have oxygen to breathe in order to help others get it.

For some people, this self-concern doesn't come naturally and they have a hard time focusing on their own goals and happiness. These people might need a different type of technique. Though not a traditional Buddhist technique, someone who naturally puts others ahead of themselves might need to run the extension in reverse, extending the charity and concern they naturally feel for *others* to themselves so they can see things more clearly. Even if it's true that *most of us* get in our own way, for some people it might be putting others center stage that's the problem. Again, this is not a traditional Buddhist technique, but it may be suited for people who really do have a hard time caring about themselves.

When doing this practice, it's critical to imagine particular people in as much detail as possible. Simply repeating "I want them to be happy, I want them to be happy" can become a meaningless slogan with no effect on your outlook. It can also devolve into an abstract thought rather than an engaged way of relating to others. Think of how many people would say they love humanity while being jerks to most of the individual people they meet.

Finally, it's important to keep in mind the Buddhist context of these practices. They're not simply aimed at wanting others to be happy or at feeling glad when good things happen to them. They're aimed at breaking down habits of relating to the world through a sense of self. They're aimed at helping you realize in a deep way that what you really are is composite and relational, to see that it's not just *nice* to care about others, but that failing to do so is based on a fundamental mistake about how things really are.

27 | EXCHANGING SELF AND OTHER

Part of getting past a sense of self is breaking free from your own limited perspective on the world. This technique involves imagining yourself from different points of view and cultivating certain responses from those imagined perspectives. Originating with Shantideva, an important Buddhist thinker from eighth-century India, and later developed in the Tibetan tradition, it aims at changing our fundamental orientation to ourselves and others. In doing so, it attacks feelings of envy, jealousy, and insecurity at their source.

The Practice

As before, this practice is best done in a place where you can focus and won't be disturbed or distracted. Once you're calm and able to focus, you start by thinking of someone who is beneath you in some respect. It might be someone who is poorer, less successful, less well known, physically weaker, or less intelligent than you are. Whatever respect you choose to focus on, it should be a quality that you feel proud of, one that makes you feel satisfied for having. If you're most proud of being well-off, then pick someone you know who is struggling financially. If being well regarded professionally makes you content, then pick someone who is unknown or even a laughingstock in your profession. You can even pick moral or spiritual advancement if that is something you value in yourself.

It's important not to simply have the thought "Some people are worse than me" but to actually try to imagine vividly a particular person and their life. An abstract thought won't do the trick. You need to mentally conjure up the image of a person with their own thoughts and feelings. As long as there are not complicating factors, it helps to pick an actual person in your life, someone you know and have interactions with.

Now step into their shoes and look at yourself through their eyes. Remember, this is a real person. Someone with parents, someone with a favorite food, someone who yawns. Try to see yourself as they see you. Relating to yourself from this new, lower vantage point, let feelings of envy and jealousy come over you. You try and try and try but never get anywhere. Meanwhile, *they* have so much money. *They* are so well known. *They* are so intelligent. But you just can't compete and it feels awful; you feel helpless and discouraged. Sit with these feelings for a while and let them soak in.

Next you pick someone who is more or less your equal, someone with similar gifts, achievements, or skills as you. Now you imagine yourself from *their* point of view. Seeing yourself as a rival, let competitive feelings arise: You want to win, to come out on top. You want to show everyone *their* faults and keep yours hidden. Feel how awful it is when *they* get the awards, the congratulations, the applause. Feel the frustration and anger when they get the recognition and the benefits that you want. Feel the anxiety and the insecurity that comes along with this competition; what if they really are better than you? Along with this, feel the burning drive to work as hard as you can to make sure that won't happen, the fear at the prospect of embarrassment if you fail. Again, give yourself some time to let these feelings sink in fully.

Finally you pick someone who is way ahead of you. Whatever skill you've chosen, they're the best. Whatever goods you've picked, they have the most. Now adopt the position of this person and gaze down at yourself. You would normally not even concern yourself with a person like that; they're simply not worth your attention. Looking down on them now, feel the mix of pity and contempt. They're so much worse than you, it's hard to imagine that they're even trying. But they *are* trying and that's even sadder. You see them stumble over what are to you very minor obstacles. You see them celebrate modest victories, victories that you wouldn't even aim at anymore. Still, your tremendous success alienates you from most people. You feel alone and sometimes worried that your decline will start at any minute. Sure you've done extremely well in the past, but now people *expect* it. The stress to live up to the image other people have of you, and that you increasingly have of yourself, is intense. You're never fully at ease. Spend some time to fully appreciate these feelings.

The Purpose

The central aim of this exercise is a simple one: to make you more compassionate. Imaginatively adopting these different points of view forces you to stop and take other people's experiences seriously. Rather than simply accepting your own take on situations, you start to see more clearly how other people can experience the same situation very differently. This isn't so you will accept their views as authoritative, but so that you will notice that things look and feel very different from a different vantage point.

By adopting these other points of view, you start to see that other people are, in an important way, just like you. They too want to be happy, they too worry about loss, and they too face pressures both internal and external. On this fundamental level, you are the same. You're like different boats on a choppy and dangerous sea, just trying to make it through the storm unscathed. Shifting your point of view, even in a short exercise, starts to shift the focus of your own experience outward. Feelings of jealousy, envy, and insecurity aren't yours alone. They can be felt by others too—and toward *you*, no less!

You see how much it sucks when those above you don't give you any help or encouragement, how their arrogance makes things worse for you. You see how the pressure of success makes even tiny insecurities a source of constant worry. As you do this over time, you start to remember this in your daily life, realizing how harmful these attitudes are to people just like you. This is not a mystical conclusion about how we're all really one. The point is not that there's no difference between your pain and the pain of others; it's that these differences are irrelevant. Your own point of view is one among many and there's no reason to privilege it. Your painful emotions and the painful emotions of others are both painful and deserving of help.

There are, of course, limits to how well you can understand someone else's point of view. Especially in cases of serious trauma or discrimination, simply imagining it won't give you a complete picture. But often it's better than nothing, and making a sincere effort to put yourself in someone else's shoes can go a long way to generating compassion for the difficulties they face. Still, it's important to be aware of your own imaginative limits.

You don't need to be a Buddhist to try to see things from other points of view, but this technique is connected with more distinctively Buddhist ideas. One of these is the idea that there is no independent self. We can sometimes feel like envy, pride, and insecurity illuminate fixed qualities we have. We feel like these emotions show us that *we are* failures or successes in the same way that we are a certain age or have a certain eye color, that this is some kind of independent property of us. But this technique helps us to realize that these things are relational qualities.

When we feel envy or jealousy or selfish pride, we make implicit assumptions about the nature of the self; we feel like a static, persisting entity that has certain inherent good or bad traits. We feel as though the hard work (and good fortune) of the previous years is somehow possessed by the person we are right now. We're like someone bragging about their favorite sports team winning a game by saying, "Did you see how well *we* played?" It's fine if "we" simply means the collection of players that you root for, but one might well respond, "*We*? I didn't see you out there on the field!" If "our" success is just a relational quality of a collection of physical and mental events, it's much less weighty than it seems to be from the usual point of view.

This technique also highlights issues of impermanence. In moving through these points of view, we realize that these comparative relations are fluid and highly variable. You can see this is by doing the practice for an extended period of time. After a few months or years, you'll start to notice that even when you pick the same basis of comparison, you'll select different people for the different roles. Just because someone was in the higher position last year doesn't mean they'll be the best choice for that position today. It might be because they've changed, for better or worse, because you've changed, or perhaps because your *feelings* toward them have changed. It's a reminder that these relations are not fixed but in constant flux.

You'll also notice that if you pick a different basis of comparison, say cleverness rather than wealth, you'll pick different people too. This can be a good reminder that there is a wide range of values in the world, and attitudes like insecurity, arrogance, or envy often operate by focusing on a single, narrow aspect of what's important while excluding everything else. We often feel intense pride or worthlessness because of one small aspect of life, as if professional reputation or the size of your bank account were the only thing of value in the world. It's not, and picking a variety of different domains of comparison can remind us of the wide variety of good qualities people can have.

Most fundamentally, these imaginative exercises are supposed to change our habitual ways of relating to people. We often relate to people in terms of our own goals and desires. Someone is a valuable business contact or an obstacle to getting the promotion. Think of how we relate to other people when driving or when making our way through a large crowd. We know, intellectually, that they are people too, but somehow, we just don't feel that way in the moment. In that moment, they're just slowing us down, preventing us from getting where we want to go.

The aim is not to simply intellectually acknowledge the futility of envy, jealousy, and arrogance but to retrain a wide range of our responses to take this futility into account. This is, of course, incredibly difficult. Our habitual responses run deep and aren't easily changed, certainly not by a couple of minutes of imagination. When feelings of envy or anxiety start to come over you, there might not be time or space to imagine the various roles and go through the entire exercise. But if you've done it regularly, you can in that moment recall what you've imagined. You can remember briefly how others feel these emotions too, and this can help rob these negative emotions of some of their power.

Moving the focus of your experience away from yourself is, perhaps ironically, also better for *you*. There is a peace of mind and a freedom that comes with not being wrapped up in these responses. Life is much happier when you're not confined to your own head and can readily relate to and care about other people. You can do this when you start to see that taking competitive feelings seriously comes at an enormous cost, not just to you but to everyone. Playing such games might give you occasional victories, but that's not enough to justify taking them seriously. Even when you happen to win, there's no peace for anyone.

28 | SENDING AND RECEIVING

Sending and receiving, sometimes also translated as giving and taking, is an imaginative visualization technique developed in the Tibetan Buddhist tradition. It aims at altering how you respond to negativity and helps you to see yourself as a transformational force, one that changes hostility into compassion. In it, you imaginatively receive the badness out in the world and change it into goodwill and compassion, which you send back out.

The Practice

This practice, like others, works best when done in a quiet and comfortable place where you won't be distracted. Before starting the actual technique, it can be helpful to remember why you're doing this. Many of your experiences are filtered through a sense of self, which doesn't really exist. This has distorted your view of the world and, among other things, has reinforced habits that represent others as obstacles and problems. You're doing this exercise in order to break out of these habits and develop genuine concern for others.

You start by focusing on your breathing. Don't count breaths and don't try to make yourself breathe slower or faster. Just pay attention to the feeling of air coming in and going out. If you get distracted with unrelated thoughts, just calmly return to your breathing. Spending a little bit of time here will calm you and help the rest go smoothly.

When starting out with this practice, you first focus on a particular person you know who is in pain or has a bad trait. Maybe it's someone you know dealing with illness or loss. Maybe it is someone who has a lot of destructive rage or hatred. As you progress you can expand what you take on, but it's best to be more focused at first.

Now imagine these bad traits as thick, black smog. Alternate versions of this technique have you picture it as murky, dirty water. What's important is that you picture it as a tangible and polluted substance. A dark cloud of smoke is very common and works particularly well with breathing since it's easy to imagine breathing it in.

As you inhale, picture yourself taking this dark smog into your body. Not just into your mouth and nose, but deep into your core. With each breath you take in more and more until you have it all in you. You imagine this smog eating away at the selfishness in you. Some versions involve picturing this selfishness as a hardened crust around your heart, which the smog dissolves, revealing a bright, white light.

As the smog touches this bright light inside you, it changes. It turns from dark smoke into the same shining and brilliant light. Variations on the imagery are common. The smog might become white, fluffy clouds. If you pictured dirty water, it's changed into delicious nectar. What's important is that you picture the concrete and tangible bad thing changing into a concrete and tangible good thing. Picture the transformation as vividly and clearly as you can. Picture exactly how the bright light looks and imagine in detail how the smog or dirty water looks as it changes.

Finally, as you exhale, picture sending this light or nectar out to the person you chose and to all others with the same difficulties. Your breath carries this healing substance out into the world, going everywhere and helping those in need. Some variations have you picture this light radiating out from each of your pores, lighting up everything. All of these images function as visual representations of the same process: accepting the misery and negativity in others, changing them into happiness and support, and sending this back out to them.

As you get more comfortable with this technique you can start to expand the range of negativity that you take in. You can expand beyond people you know or even those who are nearby. There are real people in Brussels, Sapporo, Boise, and Nairobi experiencing the same kinds of bad things. It's not just humans either. Animals on every farm around the world, all the creatures in the ocean, billions of insects, they all experience pain and suffering. You can also think of the environment in general, all of the pollution and trash that exists. If you're so inclined, you can think of beings in different realms: gods, hungry ghosts, beings in hells. Picture all of this as vividly as you can, in as much detail as you are emotionally and imaginatively able to handle.

You also expand the range of bad things you receive. People are in physical and emotional pain; they're suffering from abuse, loss, sickness, and injury. Some of it is inflicted by others, things like assault and bullying. Some of it just happens—a car accident or chronic back pain. Right now there are people who are hungry, lonely, and deeply miserable. You can also take in people's bad traits: Think of their selfishness, greed, and cruelty. People take things that don't belong to them. People deliberately hurt others, sometimes for their own benefit, other times just for the hell of it. People have hatred, jealousy, and insecurity. This causes misery and pain for both them and others.

In all of these cases, you imagine whatever badness you're focused on in a vivid and visual way as smoke, smog, or sludge. You then picture taking it in and transforming it into clouds, light, or nectar. Finally, you picture sending this newly changed goodness out to everyone.

The Purpose

This technique helps you to start thinking of yourself as a transformational force, one that is able to change harms and negative things into benefits and compassion. As a private visualization it allows you to work at this in a low-stakes environment; if you screw it up, you can just calmly start again.

This technique, like other visualizations, doesn't directly help other people. The smog isn't real and the light or nectar you imagine doesn't actually nourish or heal anyone. But that's not the point. The point is to bring about a change in *you*, in *your* outlook and habitual responses. At first blush this can seem pretty self-involved. Others are suffering and in need, so I'll go off on my own and *imagine* helping them with elaborate visualizations.

Wouldn't the truly selfless thing be to get out there and help them right now?

Of course, Buddhists do think it's important to actually go out and help people. But sometimes the best way to help people is to first turn your focus inward and alter your own selfish and destructive habits. Yes, these techniques are focused on bringing about changes in you, but you do this in order to be less attached to a self-image and better able to help *others* in the long run. And, of course, these are not mutually exclusive options; you can work on both imaginatively changing your outlook *and* helping others.

The transformation of negativity is a common theme in Buddhism. A classic image is that of a peacock. In some Western cultures, because of its huge and colorful feathers, the peacock is a symbol of vanity and pride. In a Buddhist context, however, it represents something very different. The peacock is thought to be able to eat things that are poisonous for other creatures. This makes it an evocative symbol of transformation; it is something able to take nourishment from things that would be harmful to others. It not only consumes things that are usually toxic, but draws strength from them.

This idea also present in another classic Buddhist image: the lotus. The lotus, a beautiful and fragrant flower, is a symbol of enlightenment. But, as countless Buddhist writers have pointed out, it grows out of the mud and shit. This thing of beauty, one of the main symbols of enlightenment, literally grows out of filth. The lotus, and by extension enlightenment itself, involves drawing on dirty and awful things in the world and making something beautiful out of them.

At its heart, this practice is about getting used to the idea of being a transformative force in the world, one with the power to change terrible things in life into goodwill and compassion. You become a factory that takes in negativity and converts it into concern and help. This is very different from how most of us usually respond to harsh and aggressive things that come our way. It runs counter to a common tendency to take what is good and leave bad things for others to deal with. The point here is to flip our usual habits and cultivate the courage to take on these bad things in a secure and productive way—not in a way that is draining, but in a way that actually sustains us and gives us strength.

This is why the visual aspects of the technique can be particularly useful. Talk of bad traits or suffering in general can be very abstract, and it's psychologically more difficult to deal with abstractions. Hunger or injustice *in general* are often harder to get fired up about than a particular starving person or wrongful arrest. So rather than thinking abstractly about changing your responses, it can be helpful to visualize them in concrete and striking ways.

To see why, think about how visualization can change our mental lives in other situations. Someone who constantly stews on a grudge or plays a harsh comment over and over in their mind starts to experience life very differently after a while. This can start a self-perpetuating cycle: You replay the annoying things about someone in your mind, so you start to notice more of their annoying traits, giving you more to replay and then more to notice. Mentally visualizing things can change a lot about how we feel and what we notice.

You can use this psychological fact as a tool to deliberately bring about certain changes. Given that you have a tendency to respond to negativity in unproductive and self-centered ways, visualizing such negativity in a particularly vivid and striking way can help you to retrain your habits. As with other kinds of visualizations, you need to do more than simply conjure up a visual image. You need to evoke details and feelings too. You don't become resentful just by thinking about what someone's annoying traits are; it comes from focusing on details of it and actually *feeling* the annoyance. In the same way, you can't just picture clouds or bright light but need to feel the emotions involved with taking on a burden and giving back relief and compassion in return.

For many of us, our default posture is defensive, one that positions us to block out bad things and fend off aggression with aggression of our own. We see someone coughing on the bus and immediately worry about whether or not *we* will get sick. Someone tells us off and we respond by telling them off right back. This technique flips this and allows you to develop a more open stance, one that allows you to be less fearful and isolated. It also helps you to respond to negativity in more patient and productive ways. Seeing a coughing person will make you want to help and comfort them. Being told off no longer prompts an immediate reflex of anger but a clear-eyed examination of what kind of response will be more beneficial.

You might wonder if you'll actually feel worse by taking in all this negativity. This would definitely be true if you only did the first part of the exercise, but since you also imagine transforming and giving back to others, it shouldn't make you feel worse overall. This technique does have an aspect of toughening up, the way a doctor might need to get over feeling woozy at the sight of blood or injured people in order to help them.

There is a sense in which this technique helps you get used to various kinds of negativity in order to see reality more clearly and better help others.

The real measure of success is whether it actually changes your responses in beneficial ways. If it makes you feel overwhelmed or demoralized, then it might not be the right technique for you, at least not right now. As with many Buddhist techniques, it assumes a natural tendency to over-protect ourselves and an indifference to others. Not everyone has this; some people are too invested in others. If this is true, you might try a variation where you take on *your own future pain* and problems and send compassion to *your future self*. Again, selecting the right technique can be tricky and is one of the reasons that many take supervision by a qualified teacher to be so important.

The point is *not* to load up on the burdens of everyone else, nor is it to make you feel smug and superior about your own altruism. It's for this reason that it can be wise not to tell others that you're doing these techniques. Like someone who boasts about their workout routine, it can be annoying or make people feel bad. As with getting healthier, it's often better to simply let the results speak for themselves.

If this technique works right, it will help to change your relation to others and the negativity we all face every day. It will help you to see past the illusion of a persisting self, fighting the fundamental tendency to take things personally. It will make you more open and connected with others, even those you don't particularly like. Like a sturdier ship, you'll be better able to navigate dangerous waters with minimal damage to all involved in the voyage.

29 | PATIENCE

Some techniques can't be practiced alone in a quiet place but have to be done on the ground in your day-to-day life. Here you work on developing patience not through visualization or imagination but when confronted with real-life people and obstacles. This practice can only be done when confronted with an actual setback or angry person, and it helps you to integrate the progress made with previous techniques into everyday social situations.

The Practice

The best illustration of this practice comes from a classic Tibetan story. One day a traveler sees a monk sitting and doing some kind of meditation. The traveler asks, "Hey, what are you practicing?" and the monk tells him that he's working on developing patience. The traveler immediately sneers, "Pffft—whatever, shithead." The monk gets mad. "You can't talk to me like that!" he shouts. "Who do you think you are? What an asshole!" The traveler then calmly responds, "What was it you were practicing again?"

Patience in a Buddhist context isn't just about calmly waiting for stuff; it's an attitude toward a much wider range of difficulties. In its most basic sense, it means not getting upset when things don't go your way, a calm acceptance of frustrating things. It's this kind of patience we have in mind when we call someone patient because they're calm and understanding when dealing with a screaming child or an annoying person. This is a response they have *in that moment*, when the child is screaming their head off. It's not that they're *waiting* for anything exactly but that they respond calmly and gracefully to difficult things in life.

This kind of patience involves not lashing out, but it's more than that. It involves both inner and outer calm. Someone who holds their tongue while seething on the inside isn't patient in this sense. Of course, keeping your mouth shut is better than lashing out, but to cultivate patience in a Buddhist sense means changing more than just your behavior.

What does it mean to respond with patience when people are aggressive or hostile to you? At the very least, it means not getting angry or aggravated. Ideally, it also involves responding with compassion and understanding. This doesn't mean you have to relent and submit to their abuse. Nor does it mean you smugly respond in a gentle voice with sanctimonious platitudes. That's often just a passive-aggressive way of flaunting that you think you're better than them, that you don't care about what they say or do. Instead, you respond with genuine concern for them and their feelings and have an impulse to help them rather than lash out.

Imaginative techniques like the ones we've seen are important preparation, but exercising patience when sitting alone in a calm space is *very* different from doing so in the real world. The monk in the story might have made some progress through imaginative training, but those improvements must also be deployed in real situations. This can happen when things just aren't going the way you want. The food on the stove has burned, your bus is late, your computer deletes your work. Or it can happen when someone does something rude, inconsiderate, or hurtful to you. The key to this practice is seeing these events as opportunities to retrain your responses.

But *how* do you actually do this? The practice works by using the awareness developed with other techniques to stop, step back, and reflect in ways that curtail frustration and anger. The sharper your awareness, the earlier you can catch it. The earlier you catch it, the easier it is to stop. A roaring blaze is much harder to put out than a single match. Once you've noticed the first signs of anger, you reflect on certain aspects of your situation.

You can reflect on, for example, the underlying source of the other person's behavior. Maybe their aggression comes from a fear of failure or a deep insecurity. Or maybe their behavior comes from being under intense pressure from those around them. Or maybe they just have the kind of brain that compels them to treat others in this way. Sure, it's awful to treat others the way they do, but this can also be an expression of very painful emotions. Reflecting on feelings that you both share can make it easier to respond with compassion rather than anger. Reflecting on the source of their aggression doesn't have to make it acceptable. You can acknowledge their bad behavior *and* feel compassion for them too.

Another set of reflections centers on *you* and what anger does to you. You can reflect on how anger is often unpleasant. It can agitate you and leave you shaken. The insult hurt in the moment, waiting for the bus in the cold was painful, but why let the resulting anger ruin the rest of your day? Perhaps more importantly, anger often gets in the way of an important goal—that of escaping the sense of self that perpetuates the fundamental problem in life.

Not only can anger make it hard to solve complex problems, but it can also reveal much about our outlook. Why, after all, are you angry? We get angry for many reasons. Sometimes it's a moral anger on behalf of others, like when you get angry at an unjust trial or corrupt government. But other times it's more self-centered. If I get angry when someone cracks a joke after I've mispronounced a French word, my anger seems to stem from the fact that a certain image of myself has been threatened. I want to think of myself as a smart and cultured person and now I'm faced with something that undermines that. Here my anger reveals the ways in which I'm still invested in a particular identity.

Think of how this works in ordinary cases of impatience. You're angry because the line at the grocery store is taking so long or because the bus is late. Why? It's likely because deep down you feel that where you're going and what you're doing is important. Of course, maybe what you're doing really *is* important. Maybe you're headed to your shift at the emergency room or on your way to see your long-lost son. But most times, it's not, and this anger can reveal an underlying sense that getting where you want to go is *oh so important*, much more important than *other people* getting where they want to go.

Reflecting in these ways can help not only reduce your anger but also change your attitude toward the people who frustrate you. Despite their intentions, they're helping you to progress. They're showing you things about life and yourself and giving you the chance to retrain your responses in very difficult circumstances.

Traditional texts are explicit here: You should think of these people as your teachers. They hold a mirror up to you and, if you're willing to look, show you ways in which you're still experiencing life through the lens of a self.

The good thing about this practice is that life has no shortage of opportunities. Anything that is irritating or annoying can work. It might be inanimate: a slow computer, an exploded pen, an especially hot day, or an illness. It might be an aggressive or annoying person at work or in the parking lot. They all give you a chance to see your mental habits and hang-ups, and so the world, more clearly.

The Purpose

These reflections serve to direct your mind in ways that combat anger by emphasizing certain aspects of your situation. Think about what happens when you try to cheer up a friend. When you talk to them after something bad has happened, one of the things you do is draw their attention to the silver linings and good aspects of what has happened. This doesn't mean you think that nothing bad has happened to them at all, but given your aim of making them feel better, you emphasize these genuinely good aspects of the situation. In the same way, these reflections direct your attention to certain aspects of the situation in order to help you feel less angry.

Of course, seeing an aggressive or hostile person *as a teacher* is particularly difficult. They are, of course, not like a teacher in every way. They don't tell you about Buddhist philosophy or explain the meaning of Buddhist texts. They don't give you support or encouragement, either. They certainly aren't models to inspire you. But you *can* learn from them, and they can reveal to you your own blocks and hang-ups. Like teachers, they challenge you and test your progress.

This expands the range of who you think you can learn from and who you consider a teacher, which itself involves reducing your self-conceit. We're often too proud to be willing to learn from such people, let alone see them as *teachers*. In fact, they can only function as teachers in this way *by being aggressive and malicious* to you. As traditional texts sometimes point out, those who mean us harm offer us a chance that no buddha ever could. A buddha would never aim to harm you, and so cannot give you the chance to practice responding compassionately to such a difficult person.

It's also important to keep in mind that these are reflections that you engage in for yourself. In many cases, we can say things to ourselves that would take on a very different meaning if we said them to others. When I am working and feel hungry I can tell myself, "No—you need to finish this task, *then* you can have lunch." But it's much worse when a supervisor says the same thing to a hungry employee. These reflections have a similar feature. It's one thing to tell yourself that a hostile person is really a teacher and that this painful situation is a chance to learn, but it's another to say this to *someone else*. It might be okay in a private conversation with a good friend or between a teacher and student, but these aren't generally reflections you're supposed to prompt *other* people to have.

Taken in isolation, this practice can seem like it encourages you to be a doormat. This kind of practice requires care because, if misused, it can reinforce abusive relationships and even promote such abuse. It's important to remember that the technique isn't about being in *denial* about a person's hostility; instead it's about empowering you to respond to it in a more thoughtful and productive way. It's possible to calmly defend your rights, and often the compassionate course of action for everyone involved is for you to remove yourself from a situation or to sever a relationship.

This practice helps you to avoid getting swept away by aggravating situations or malicious people. It involves developing your ability to detect your own responses early and intervene by stopping, stepping back, and reflecting in ways that diminish your anger and replace it with less self-regarding responses. It cannot be done alone in a calm and comfortable place. It must be done with real people in your everyday life. Keep in mind that it's extremely difficult. As the story of the monk implies, even people who have been doing it for a *long time* screw it up. But still, better is better, and even if you only manage to be slightly angry instead of very angry, that's progress.

30 | GIFTS AND OFFERINGS

Giving is a crucial part of Buddhist practice and takes many different forms. There's a wide range of practices that center on offerings and gifts. For Buddhists, generosity is fundamentally about not being attached to things. These things might be material wealth but can also be more abstract things like time, knowledge, or even recognition. A generous person sees clearly that there is no persisting self through time, so rather than holding on to these things lets them go easily.

The Practices

A deceptively simple practice for developing generosity can be done completely on your own. First, you pick up an object of value that belongs to you. Something like a phone or ring would work, but it can be anything of yours that's valuable and small. Start with it in one of your hands and then pass it to the other. Now that the other hand has it, pass it back to the first hand. Repeat a few more times and see how although one hand loses it, the other gains it. This is a kind of simulation of generosity on the smallest scale. One hand gives the object to the other. Even though you don't actually lose the thing, this simulation starts to loosen your attachment to it in a very small way.

Another method is simply extending your natural generosity. It's pretty easy to give to people you know and like. As with other methods, you can gradually extend the sphere of your giving from friends and family out to acquaintances, then strangers, and finally to people you dislike. Here what starts as a generosity that is limited in scope transforms into a more wide-ranging and genuine generosity.

Many of the practices associated with giving in Buddhism involve symbolic gifts. These offerings are often made to an image of a buddha or bodhisattva and are very common in the Buddhist world. Such offerings can take a variety of forms: a candle, incense, water, fruit, flowers, or even liquor. As with other types of giving, different gifts are offered to different buddhas or bodhisattvas. The gifts are typically something that you value, and though there are standard offerings, it's more important to give with the right frame of mind than to give any particular thing.

To pick just one example, a common practice is to make a water offering each day. Doing this involves offering water to an image of a buddha or a bodhisattva in seven clean bowls each morning. There is a particular way to do this, lining them up and filling them left to right, first with a little bit in each, then the rest of the way. As you do this you visualize that you are offering something very precious. This could be easy since in many places clear water *is* quite precious, but you could imagine that it's nectar or even your own good qualities. Since this is a good act, you get merit for having done it. Then in a second act of generosity, you offer this merit to all beings. So you offer not only a gift, but the credit for your generosity too. At the end of the day, you empty the bowls and turn them upside down. In a formalized version you use special bowls specifically for this purpose, but you can also use a single bowl, even the same one you eat from.

Giving in an imaginative way is also a very common form of practice. This is particularly important if you want to cultivate generosity but don't actually have a lot of stuff. There are many variations on these practices but they typically involve vividly imagining all kinds of wonderful and valuable things and then imaginatively offering these things to buddhas or even to all beings. In some cases you use a kind of small model representing the entire universe and offer that. Though just an imaginative act, this exercise helps to break down mental and emotional habits that are obstacles to a generous outlook.

As with other practices, it's critical to imagine these things in as much detail as possible. If not, you run the risk of simply going through a series of ineffective motions. If you simply try to care about "all sentient beings" as an abstraction, it can be ineffective for changing how you relate to any of the particular beings you meet in your life. In the same way, if you simply offer "wonderful things," it's not going to be effective in changing your outlook. It's important to imagine particular things and their details and then picture in detail the act of giving them away. This helps to actually change your relationship to the stuff you have and how you use it.

The Purpose

Cultivating generosity is about developing a lack of attachment to what you have. Once we get things, they psychologically stick to us; we want to keep them around and don't want to let go. It's a relationship between ourselves and the things around us. I find some cash on the ground and within a few minutes it's *mine* and suddenly I'm reluctant to give *my money* away.

Developing generosity means changing this relationship and getting rid of the stickiness. We might think that someone who gives things away but does so reluctantly is a generous person, but from a Buddhist point of view this person still has some work to do. Ideally, a person won't give reluctantly, because that reluctance means there's still some stickiness there. Perfect generosity would mean that you don't feel the thing is yours at all; you were just taking care of it until you found a good use for it in the hands of someone else. And when such a use presents itself, you part with the object smoothly and without hesitation.

That's why the very basic practice of giving an object from one hand to the other can be a way of developing generosity. Even though you don't actually give the object to anyone else, passing it back and forth starts to eat away at the psychological stickiness you have. Of course, you can't become fully generous just by passing things between your own hands, but it can function to chip away very slightly at your attachment to the things you have.

Where does this stickiness come from? As with many of our psychological habits, the source is a mistaken view of the world. When you feel like you own a thing, you're presuming there's both an owner and a thing to be owned, and that both persist through time. But in reality, both you and the thing are conventional abstractions, just names for composites in constant flux. Both the brand-new Porsche and its owner are collections that will eventually come apart and are, in fact, constantly changing. Once you fully internalize this fact, the stickiness—the owner's feeling that they own the Porsche—no longer makes as much sense and won't feel as compelling. And once the stickiness is gone, these transitory things can be put to use toward something that really is important: helping people to see reality better and suffer less.

Since for Buddhists the root of the problem is a psychological tendency, having the right motivation is essential for giving well. Being generous isn't simply about the transfer of goods; your heart must be in the right place. Some texts emphasize this by saying that even a child offering a pile of sand can count as generous as long as the sand is offered with the right frame of mind.

This is why, even though there are standard things to offer to an image of a buddha, it can be more meaningful if you wholeheartedly offer something that *you're* really stuck on. If you really love candy, for example, it can be more meaningful to offer candy than something more traditional like incense. Offering something you're attached to, that you feel to be more valuable, helps to both express your gratitude more strongly and correct your psychological hang-ups in a more effective way.

A way to better understand generosity is to think about what Buddhists call near enemies. Near enemies are things that resemble good qualities but aren't the real thing. Generosity has quite a few near enemies, many of which highlight the importance of having the right motivation. Although we give a gift to someone, sometimes what we're really doing is *trading*. We pick up the check at the restaurant this time, but we do so with the expectation that the other person will pay next time. Giving with an expectation of a later return isn't really generosity. Real generosity is giving without the expectation that the other person will give you something in return or even the sense that they owe you anything. True generosity doesn't involve scorekeeping.

In other cases, gifts can be straightforwardly selfish. Sometimes we give a gift, but it's one that *we* really want to enjoy ("I got you this fine wine. Hey, why don't we open it now and have a taste?"). Sometimes gifts can be not-so-subtle suggestions, or even insults ("I saw this book on time management and thought you could use it"). These aren't real generosity either. Although you're giving someone something, the gift isn't really *for* them, it's *for* you.

Another near enemy is giving in order to get recognition or to look good for others. If you give a gift and then get angry when the recipient doesn't thank you enough (or even at all), your gift was really tainted with the expectation that you'd get something back: thanks and praise. People can even give gifts to humiliate or place a burden on the other person. Think about paying the bill for an entire table at a restaurant. Sometimes this is a way of flaunting how little that amount of money means and so demonstrates how rich you are. Sometimes it's a way of making the person feel bad for being unable to pay. Sometimes it's about making the person admire, respect, or feel indebted to you. Though in these cases you give a gift to others, you do so in a self-regarding way. The stickiness is still there and you're not really being generous.

Selfless giving is strongly emphasized in a practice associated with Japanese Buddhism where you help others secretly, without anyone knowing. This might mean you fix their torn shoes, help with their chores, or buy them something they need. But whatever you do, you do it in secret so that nobody ever knows who did it. This is a way of making sure that the giving is totally free from any hint of desire for praise or recognition. This kind of generosity isn't done to get thanks nor is it done to make others see how virtuous you are. It's done solely to benefit others.

So far, we've focused on giving material objects, but you can give other things too. You can, for example, give your time and attention. This can be easy to undervalue, as people often find large monetary donations more impressive than volunteering one's time. But giving your time is in a way *more* valuable since it's possible to make more money but impossible to make more time.

Many forms of generosity involve using your time and skills in ways that selflessly benefit others. You can give someone your expertise or even just your undivided attention. You can give someone protection, the gift of feeling safe when in danger. Some gifts involve a combination of these. Helping someone move is a gift of your time, work, and often emotional support too.

Buddhists also think of the Buddhist teachings themselves as something you can give to others. By exposing them to Buddhist ideas and practices, you give them the gift of seeing reality more clearly and being able to alter their destructive mental and behavioral habits. Of course, like other gifts, it's a bad idea to force it on people who don't want it. Giving teachings is often assumed to be the domain of educated monks and nuns, and it's true that you have to understand Buddhist teachings well in order to effectively give them to others. But it's also common to support this kind of generosity in more indirect ways, like printing and distributing books or supporting Buddhist institutions. As with other kinds of generosity, it's important that you do it for *them*, not to make yourself feel more important.

Along with the right intentions, effective generosity also requires being perceptive and sensitive. It's a bad idea to give a drug that might be helpful in some contexts to someone addicted to prescription painkillers. Even though they might enjoy the gift in the moment, it's important to consider what will actually benefit them in the long run.

This is a difficult task because many well-meaning actions can turn out to be harmful. In some Buddhist cultures there are people who carry around caged birds that you can buy and set free. This feels like a really nice thing to do since you're giving a bird the gift of freedom. But the more this happens, the more lucrative it is for people to go out and capture birds so they can make more money by selling them to well-meaning Buddhists. It's important to reflect on what is really most helpful to the birds as opposed to what makes you feel like a good person in the moment.

Buddhist generosity is about getting over the psychological attachments to what we think of as *ours*, both our physical stuff and our more abstract possessions. Getting over this means seeing clearly that both you and the stuff you have are impermanent. It's not a question of *whether* you will lose it, but *when*. More importantly, both you and these things are abstractions, convenient fictions. Despite this, such impermanent abstractions can be beneficial.

Cultivating generosity is about helping others but also about changing your experience of the world to better fit with how things really are. This is why many of the practices involve imaginary gifts. Statues can't drink water and imaginary food won't feed anybody, but the point is to bring about a change in your experience. Such practices might seem to be self-centered since they don't directly help others. But it's important to keep in mind that this focus on your experience is in the service of shedding an outlook that prevents you from helping others. Once you get over the stickiness, you don't see things you can own, only ways you can help.

31 | READING, WRITING, AND RECITING

A huge number of Buddhist practices focus on the written word. Though early Buddhist teachings were passed on orally, they eventually took the form of written texts, which began to occupy a special place in Buddhist practice.

Buddhist texts often function as tools to help you reorient your mental life. We interact with books in many ways. They're things we create, use, neglect, admire, destroy, and contemplate. Buddhists in particular spend huge amounts of time and energy reading, reciting, memorizing, studying, interpreting, and translating texts. These are widespread Buddhist practices and can function not only to preserve and spread Buddhist ideas and techniques but also as distinctive practices of their own.

The Practices

The most obvious of these literary practices is one you're already doing *right now*—reading a book about Buddhist teachings. This book is a secondary text—a book that explains other books.

Sometimes this is done to fill in more detail, while other times it's to make the ideas clear and accessible to a general audience.

Other texts are primary texts. These are the original sources or authoritative statements of ideas or practices. In Buddhism, these often claim to chronicle the words of a buddha, bodhisattva, or other teacher who really understood how reality works. The oldest of these were memorized and passed down orally long before they were written down. Primary texts are often, though not always, written in poetic verse. This made them easier to memorize at a time when few people were literate and writing was difficult and expensive.

Like poetry, primary texts in verse can be very dense, packing a lot of ideas into very few words. They also often use specialized words with very specific meanings. They're not usually the kind of book you can just sit down and casually flip through. Often they're only understandable if you *already* know what they say. They sometimes work as a kind of convenient shorthand for remembering a lesson that's already been explained to you by a teacher. In that sense, they're a bit like mnemonic devices—something short and catchy to help you remember what you've already learned in detail.

These texts also often rely on an invisible oral tradition. This happens in other contexts too. Think about classic films and novels. If you just jump into them on your own without any background, they'll be frustrating and confusing. But if you have a well-informed friend or take a class, you can go into the experience knowing why the film or novel is significant and what it's trying to express. Once you know *that*, you have a much easier time appreciating it because you already know what it's getting at. The same is often true of Buddhist texts. They're much more readable if you already know why they're important and what kinds of ideas they contain.

It's not just modern people who face these issues. One of the most popular types of secondary literature is a commentary. There are many classical commentaries that walk you through a primary text, stanza by stanza, and explain what the primary text means. Sometimes they even go *word by word,* explaining in detail what each one means and why it was chosen by the author.

It's natural to want to jump right into the primary texts, to get the teachings directly from the original source. In many traditions, however, the first texts that students read (as opposed to memorize) will *not* be a primary text. You start with something understandable and accessible, something that meets you where you are. Later, after you have the background, you'll be able to interact with the source texts. Most modern universities do something similar. Students in Intro Physics will read a textbook, a secondary source explaining the ideas clearly, rather than Newton's original texts or the latest issue of an academic physics journal. Of course, as students advance, they'll come to be able to read these more difficult source texts, but starting with them would be frustrating and confusing. The same is often true of Buddhist primary texts.

It's also worth keeping in mind that traditionally, reading a text meant reciting it out loud. Reading silently to yourself is a fairly recent convention. Throughout much of history, especially when both books and people who could read them were rare, reciting texts out loud was the norm. The experience of a text was more like singing around a campfire or seeing a play performed than like reading it on your own. This gives reading a more social character; rather than being a solitary activity, it's something you do with others. It's a bit like the difference between watching a movie alone at home and going to the theater to see a movie with friends—going with your friends means a having shared, social experience. Reciting a text is more of an event and helps to highlight the text's shared importance for a group of people.

Traditionally, it's not just reading that's important but *memorizing*. If a beginning student does interact with a primary source, they're more likely to be expected to memorize it than to fully understand its meaning. It's not uncommon to find monks in various traditions who have entire primary texts committed to memory.

Many of the earliest records of the historical Buddha's teachings were passed down in just this way. Ananda (pronounced *Ah-nan-duh*), the Buddha's cousin and right-hand man, was famous for his great memory. A stock opening for Buddhist sutras, texts that claim to record the teachings of the Buddha, is "Thus I have heard. . . ." The "I" here refers to Ananda. He is said to have memorized *all* of the Buddha's teachings and recalled them for others after the Buddha's passing. Even later texts, written hundreds of years after the Buddha's lifetime, appeal to this authority by starting with this phrase.

Memorizing was a way to preserve Buddhist ideas and practices before they were written down. Even today, many Buddhist centers of study emphasize memorization. An important practice is to memorize an important or especially meaningful Buddhist text. Doing this means not only paying close attention to the exact wording but, for most of us, revisiting the text *many* times.

If your memory isn't that good, you might simply copy an important Buddhist text. One way this is beneficial is that it creates another copy of the text—if a text has value, then making another copy puts another thing of value into the world. In this sense, it could be part of the practice to just print out many copies of a text from your computer. Of course, Buddhists don't really do this. They do, however, give money to printing houses that publish and distribute Buddhist texts.

As a practice, though, you typically copy a text, rewriting it by hand, word by word. This can be done even if you don't read the language you're copying—as long as you focus on it and do it with the aim of seeing reality as it is. This serves as an expression of devotion to the text in particular and to Buddhist teachings in general. It can also, like mindfulness of breathing, help increase your ability to sustain your attention for longer periods and so support other practices too. Popular choices for texts to copy include the very short *Heart Sutra* and the much longer *Lotus Sutra*, which itself is actually explicit about the importance of recopying it.

Though not exactly a formal practice, translating itself can also be understood as a Buddhist practice. Buddhism has a long history and has spread to many different cultures. This means there are important Buddhist texts in *many* languages. The earliest recorded Buddhist texts are written in Pali, not the language the Buddha spoke but an important literary language for early Buddhism. Many Buddhist texts are also written in Sanskrit, a very important literary language on the Indian subcontinent. As Buddhism spread, texts were also written in Tibetan, classical Chinese, Japanese, Korean, Thai, Mongolian, and *many* more. Some of these are translations of earlier texts that have been lost; others are new texts, developing and expanding Buddhist philosophical ideas and practical techniques. More recently, both primary and secondary Buddhist texts have been composed in languages like French, German, and English.

Many Buddhists, even those who know several languages, will at some point find themselves relying on a translation to read a Buddhist text or listen to a Buddhist teacher. Translators play a critical role in Buddhism as they directly help countless people to understand Buddhist ideas and techniques. Naturally, the choices translators make have a huge impact on how people understand and respond to Buddhist thought and practice.

Translators have to make difficult choices since words and sentences in different languages often do not line up exactly. So, for example, choosing to use words like "grace" or "heaven" will make people feel like Buddhism is similar to Christianity, while using words like "prosocial" and "atom" will make it seem more scientific. However, leaving terms in Sanskrit or Japanese can make people feel like it's inaccessible or foreign.

As anyone who has studied a new language can attest, it's very difficult—especially if the language has a different script, grammar, and vocabulary from one you already know. Learning a language takes years and years of study and is a task that's never really complete. Learning simple sentences like "This is a pen" can make it seem easy. But explaining how to tie your shoe without gesturing, or comforting a friend after the loss of a loved one is difficult in any language, let alone a new one.

Putting complex Buddhist ideas and techniques into a new language without distorting the meaning *and* while making it accessible to a new audience is incredibly difficult, but it's one that translators are confronted with all the time. Translating, at least ideally, is a selfless act. It's done to help *others* grasp ideas and techniques that will help them better understand reality and navigate the world.

The Purpose

Why do some people have houses filled with shelves and shelves of books? Partly it's because they read them for enjoyment and use them to get information. But it's also because the books themselves, the physical objects, *mean something*. They're a symbol of knowledge itself. You display books because it expresses something about what you value, what you think is important. The shelves of books in a house aren't just storage for tools but also demonstrate that the person who lives there cares not only about learning, literature, or scholarship in general but also specifically about the particular subjects of those books.

Books are tools for communication, but not just through their content. They allow for other kinds of meaningful interaction too. Think about your favorite novel. At some point you had the private experience of reading and enjoying it. But you also might remember particular scenes in detail, or you might have bonded with someone who also enjoyed it (or argued with someone who hated it). You might have a physical copy that is special to you—the first one you read or one that someone special gave to you or one you found on a train while taking a trip. That novel isn't just an inert text; it allows for a huge range of social interactions and personal reflections. Buddhist texts too have a similarly wide range of functions aside from simply preserving and recording ideas.

Of these, memorization can seem the most bewildering to modern sensibilities. Sure it was fine back when few people learned to read and when writing was expensive, but *now*? Now that we have not just books but the entire Buddhist corpus at our fingertips in searchable form, what's the point? This is especially pressing when it's detached from the meaning of the text. You can meet monks who have entire texts memorized, but when asked to explain what those texts *mean*, they are at a complete loss.

This practice grows out of a very different approach to learning, one where you learn the *form* first and the *content* later. This happens in other contexts too. Many Catholics learn prayers like the Our Father or Hail Mary first as a series of sounds, and only later do they come to understand what those sounds mean. Some Americans have a similar experience with the Pledge of Allegiance; it's first chanted at school and understood only later. One benefit of this, as any Catholic or even ex-Catholic can tell you, is that those exact words stay with you for life. They're burned in your brain and soaked into your consciousness.

This is part of the point. If you *really* care about a text, you'll want to carry it with you. This exists in other religions too. In Islam, for example, there's a tradition of memorizing the entire Qur'an. It makes sense that if you think a text holds important answers, you'll want to internalize it. Once you memorize a text, it's *in* you, not just in your bag or saved on your laptop but imprinted on your mind. If you really want to know a text fully and exactly, what could be better than knowing it by heart? Do you *really* know your mom's birthday if you have to look it up in a calendar? Do you *really* know a Buddhist text if you have to look up what it says? Memorization gives you an intimacy with the text that merely reading a book doesn't.

Memorization is also a way of valuing something, an expression of how much it means to you. People often know all the words to their favorite songs. Some people even mouth along to the dialogue in their favorite films—this is because they love it so deeply and have spent so much time with it. Memorization requires spending a good deal of time with a text. That time has to be spent examining it very closely, not just getting the gist of it but looking at *exactly* what it says. This need not be a chore, but can be similar to knowing your favorite song or movie by heart—the natural result of your appreciation, of visiting and revisiting it again and again.

One way to get to know a text well is to recite it. When done with others this can build community and solidarity the way that singing together often does. Think of how stadium chants and karaoke bring people together. For some, listening is easier than reading, and so hearing a text can make it easier to grasp the meaning. The sound itself can be important too. Think about the difference between reading the lyrics to a song you love and actually hearing the song. In the same way, hearing a Buddhist text can make it more moving and more impactful than just looking at the words.

Copying a text can work the same way, except with writing. Writing, even repetitious copying, can be an expressive act. The writing doesn't even have to be intended for *others* to serve this function: Think of a young person in love, writing and rewriting the name of their crush all over their notebook. Even if you can't read it, recopying a text can be a devotional act, one that expresses and reinforces what's important to you. If you can read it, it helps you focus on the meaning in a slow and careful way. It's the opposite of skimming—a focused and deliberate re-creation of each word. For a text that contains the keys to solving an important problem, this can be a moving and worthwhile activity.

Translation aids in the spread of the ideas and practices of Buddhism in order to help others. But translation involves not only a lot of work, studying vocabulary and grammar, but also a lot of time *thinking really hard* about what a text says. This involves thinking about what certain words mean and what certain sentence structures express, as well as the historical and cultural context the text was written in. It also means thinking about your own time and place and how those ideas can be expressed accurately and meaningfully for the people who will read the translation. Doing this means you'll come to understand the ideas much better—how they're precise, how they're fuzzy, and how they fit together.

It's also a daunting and humbling experience. There is enough to learn in Buddhism to fill thousands of human lifetimes. The process of learning a language that's very different from your native tongue changes your outlook. After many years of hard work you might be able to sound like a reasonably smart child. It's something that you can do for twenty years and still feel like you're just beginning. This changes your timescale, giving you a longer view of things.

Some spend most of their lives working out *one single* Buddhist text. Language study in general and translation in particular help you to realize this longer view of things, and once you get it, you can feel at once overwhelmed and humbled. You see that there's way too much to learn to waste time posturing about how smart you are. There's important work to do, work that will help people understand reality. Life is too short for the task, but if you're lucky you might have the chance to make some small contribution.

Here again there are the usual dangers: intelligence, book smarts, scholarship—these can all be identities to get hung up on. You can slip into a smug tone of voice, saying things like,

"Well, *I* memorized that text," or, "If you knew *the Sanskrit* it would be clear that. . . ." Anyone who has spent any time around academics knows that knowledge easily turns into sport: a game of scoring points on others to show how much you know or how many books you've read. Buddhist scholarship is no different. It's all too easy to start off with the best of intentions only to find yourself condescendingly correcting someone when they say something is Sanskrit when it's really Pali. In all of these practices, it's important to keep in view what the point is—to get over a self-involved orientation to the world.

Even the texts themselves can turn into part of the problem. A text is a tool and it's easy to get fixated on tools at the expense of the job they're supposed to do. Some people spend more time talking about different models of guitars than they actually spend playing music. Or they spend more time researching and arguing about what kind of stove is best than they actually spend cooking. In the same way, people can get wrapped up in a text—about how important and brilliant and pure it is—at the expense of actually putting into practice *what it says*.

In Zen Buddhism, there's sometimes an image of a master ripping up a sutra. This striking image is meant to be a counterbalance to just this kind of fixation. Even a Buddhist text can reinforce a sense of self and be part of the problem. Ripping up the sutra means getting past a fixation on quotations and scholarship.

Of course, it's worth keeping in mind when reflecting on this image that the Zen tradition has produced a huge body of literature, one full of technical language and literary Buddhist allusions. Although texts can be part of the problem, they're indispensable tools for solving it too. They contain the message of Buddhism—the ideas and practices that hold the key to understanding how to live in accordance with reality.

32 | SACRED SPEECH

The written word is important, but so is sound. When spoken out loud, words can have a special power. Getting a written message from a loved one just isn't the same as actually hearing their voice. The distinctive timbre, cadence, and phrasing of their speech can make you feel close to them in a way that no written symbols can. Sounds connect and move us in special ways. Many Buddhist practices make use of these special qualities of sound in general and the human voice in particular.

These practices are some of the most popular and widespread in the Buddhist world. They often involve saying a short series of syllables over and over. Sometimes these have linguistic meaning, sometimes not. Other practices involve recalling a particular buddha by saying their name out loud. Though different in many ways, they all rely on the unique power of the human voice.

Traditionally, these practices work because the sounds themselves have a special power. This is often understood supernaturally, the way a magic spell or a prayer might work by invoking some force outside of the natural world, like a deity or spirit. But there are also other, more naturalized ways in which sounds can change the world. A singer hits a certain pitch and a wine glass breaks. A bully says a series of sounds in a certain tone and another child bursts into tears. These are also ways that sound affects the world, but they're usually not thought of as supernatural. Many of these Buddhist practices can be understood in a similar way.

The Practices

In ordinary language, a mantra is just a motto or catchphrase. It's something that companies use to refer to their marketing slogans: "Quality product for a low price is our mantra." As a religious practice, however, mantras are more complex. Mantras aren't exclusive to Buddhism and were used by religions in India long before the Buddha, but they are important and influential practices within the Buddhist world.

Mantras are most fundamentally tools for the mind; they're tools that help to focus and protect your mental life. A particular mantra is a specific series of syllables that you repeat over and over. They might be repeated mentally but are usually repeated out loud, though sometimes quietly, as a barely audible murmur.

Traditionally, the sound itself is supposed to have a special power, so pronouncing it exactly the right way is absolutely critical; otherwise the sound will be wrong and it won't work. In practice, however, pronunciations vary, since people from different places say them with sounds from their native languages. Sometimes, mantras include individual words that are meaningful in a particular language, usually Sanskrit, but they're often not translatable as complete sentences.

Different mantras are supposed to invoke different buddhas, bodhisattvas, or even texts. The mantra is a tool to bring them to mind or call on them. There are many different mantras associated with different figures and texts, so a teacher will often give a student a particular mantra in order to help with a specific obstacle to the student's ability to see reality clearly. Other mantras are just very popular, and repeating them is part of a widespread Buddhist practice.

One of the most famous Buddhist mantras is *Om Mani Padme Hum* (pronunciations vary, but a common one is *ohm mah-nee pahd-may hum*). Some of the individual elements of this mantra are meaningful words (*mani* means "jewel" and *padme* means "lotus" in Sanskrit), but it's not really a complete sentence. Some attribute particular virtues or mental states to each syllable, but it's the sound itself that is most important. It won't work, for example, to say those same words in English or Italian. The mantra has meaning, but not in a linguistic sense. It's closer to the non-linguistic sense of meaning, as when we say that red *means* stop on a traffic light or a sigh *means* someone is bored.

This is the mantra of the bodhisattva of compassion. He is called Avalokiteshvara (pronounced *Ah-vuh-low-key-tesh-vah-ra*) in Sanskrit and Guan Yin in Chinese (though in Chinese Buddhism Avalokiteshvara is female). The mantra invokes compassion. It *means* compassion in the way that a red light means stop. When you say it, you conjure up the image of Avalokiteshvara, compassion incarnate. Some of these images are striking. In one, he has one thousand arms with an eye in the palm of each hand. The eyes represent his ability to notice all of the suffering in the world and the hands are his ability to actually help. So when you say the mantra over and over, you're conjuring up this ideal, one of boundless compassion for all.

Many other buddhas and bodhisattvas have their own mantras, evoking their own character and mood. Texts sometimes have them too. The *Heart Sutra*, a famous text about emptiness, gives a mantra at the end: *Gate Gate Pāragate Pārasaṃgate Bodhi Svāhā* (pronounced *ga-tay ga-tay pa-ruh-ga-tay pa-ruh-sum-ga-tay boe-dhee sva-ha*). Unlike some other mantras, this one can be understood as a meaningful sentence. It's translated in different ways but means "Gone, gone, beyond gone, completely beyond gone—Enlightenment!" It's understood differently by different Buddhists, but it's supposed to contain the entire meaning of Buddhist teachings on emptiness within it. To say the mantra is to bring to mind the empty nature of reality.

It's very common to do physical actions while repeating mantras. Some people use a string of beads, called a *mala*, advancing a bead through their hand between the thumb and index finger for each mantra they say. Tibetan Buddhists often use prayer wheels: a cylinder that's either mounted on a wall or held in your hand. The outside of the cylinder is made of metal and embossed with mantras. Through the center of the cylinder is a small wooden pole with mantras carved into it, and wrapped around that pole is a very long coil of paper itself containing thousands of mantras. The cylinder works like a wheel, and you use it by spinning it clockwise; as it turns, it's as if the mantras are being recited. This is often done while saying mantras verbally and circumambulating a special place.

There are also what are called "self-turning" prayer wheels powered by the wind, the heat of a candle, a stream, or, more recently, solar power. As these turn, they silently "recite" the mantra, sending it out into the world. There are also practices associated with repairing and maintaining prayer wheels; you might repair a broken one, or oil them so they turn more smoothly.

Another oral practice prominent in some types of Buddhism is called *nembutsu* in Japanese or *nianfo* in Chinese. It's practiced in a type of Buddhism called Pure Land Buddhism. A Pure Land is a special realm where a buddha lives, and if you're reborn there, getting enlightened is really easy. There are many depictions of different Pure Lands in art and poetry—they're like a five-star Buddhist resort. Everything is clean and it smells wonderful. When the wind blows through the trees, the rustling of the leaves makes beautiful music that illuminates the nature of reality. It's a place where solving the fundamental problem of life is really easy.

There's a story in the background of this practice and, as usual, it's complicated and has lots of variations. Here's one version: There's a buddha called Amida in Japanese (or Amitabha in Sanskrit). He's the Buddha of Boundless Light (or alternatively, Boundless Life). A long time ago, before he was a buddha, he saw how awful life could be and he made a vow. He vowed that he'd never become a buddha unless he could create a great Pure Land. Not only would it be an amazing place, but it would be open to everyone. Anybody who said his name would, after their death, be reborn there.

This is where the *nembutsu* practice comes in. Amida *did* become a buddha so, according to these Buddhists, in order to be reborn in his Pure Land all you have to do is say his name. Specifically, what you say is *Namu Amida Butsu* (pronounced *nah-moo ah-mi-da boo-tsoo*) or *Namo Amituofo* (pronounced *nah-mo ah-mi-twoh-fo*). The practice is simply saying this over and over. It's understood differently by different schools of Pure Land Buddhism. For some, it's a meditative tool. For others, it is an expression of gratitude to Amida and genuine faith in him. For them, it's this faith that gets you to the Pure Land.

For yet other Pure Land schools, however, all you have to do is *say* it. In fact, some say you only actually have to say it *once* for it to work. So if you happened to have read the previous paragraph out loud, you're already covered. For them, if you say it *right now* then immediately put down this book and never think about Amida or Buddhism again for the rest of your life, you'll *still* be reborn in Amida's Pure Land after you die. There are no conditions on this: You don't have to believe in Pure Lands, buddhas, or even anything remotely Buddhist. You don't even have to be a good person; it works the same regardless of whether you're a saint or a complete asshole. Of course, even these Buddhists typically recommend saying it over and over, but as an expression of gratitude.

This can seem similar to mantra practice, since it involves saying a short, special phrase over and over again. There are, however, some important differences. People often choose different mantras to recite. They might be given a particular mantra by their teacher to combat a particular mental habit or difficult situation they're in. They might recite a particular mantra on a certain holiday or pilgrimage trip. They might just feel a connection with a particular buddha or bodhisattva and so recite that mantra. The *nembutsu*, however, is the same for everyone; linguistic variation and local pronunciation aside, everybody says the same thing.

There are other differences between the practices too. For the *nembutsu*, the sounds themselves aren't particularly powerful or magical. What's important is the vow, the promise that Amida made. Mantras sometimes involve imaginatively embodying a buddha or bodhisattva—in a way *becoming* them. The *nembutsu* doesn't really involve any kind of identification with Amida. It is, unlike a mantra, typically understood as an expression of gratitude and faith.

The Purpose

These practices emphasize how speech, especially when repeated, affects your mind. We sometimes experience this in other ways. Having a constant voice of criticism in your head ("Screwed it up again, dumbass") or affirmation ("I think I can, I think I can . . .") can affect how you feel. Sometimes this might not even rely on linguistic meaning; think about how having an uplifting song or disturbing photo stuck in your head can affect the tone of your entire day.

These practices are very popular, and how they work is understood very differently by different Buddhists. For the vast majority of people who do them, they are understood literally and supernaturally. A Pure Land is a real place that you go after death. Amida is a real being and he directly helps you. This is by far the most common way to understand how these practices work.

Some, however, will emphasize a metaphorical and psychological approach. Here a Pure Land is a special state of *mind*—whenever you're completely at peace and seeing things clearly, you're in a Pure Land. Amida is recast as an ideal or personification of enlightenment. Like all ideas, it is a conceptual projection that isn't part of reality but *can* help you come to see reality more clearly. These two ways of understanding don't rule each other out, but they are very different ways to relate to these practices and how they work.

Talking about the power of speech to change the world can make you think of casting spells or curses, making it seem pretty magical. But it's worth thinking about the ways speech has power in everyday life. I say to a friend, "Don't worry, I promise I'll be there tomorrow," and now both of our plans and expectations have changed. If I don't show up, our relationship and emotional lives will change. A person in a special outfit says the words "I now pronounce you husband and wife" and now two people's lives are legally, spiritually, and socially intertwined. Bomb threats, racial slurs, compliments—these are all things we say, but they have the power to change the world around us—not because they're magical, but because that's just something speech can do.

It's not just words that have this power either; sound itself can do this too. Whistling a favorite tune on your walk to work can help improve your mood. Some people find that humming softly to themselves can keep them calm in very stressful situations. Of course, these aspects often work together. The feeling you get from a song you love is often about both the lyrics *and* the tune. An apology or compliment works best when the words are chosen well *and* when it's said in the right tone of voice.

So although mantras and *nembutsu* practices are often understood supernaturally, you don't need to think that some speech is magical for it to bring about changes in the world. As in these other cases, they can bring about changes in our minds and in our social world through the specific sounds. Mantras can be understood in a similar way—invoking not just a mood but perhaps also the very image and ideals associated with a buddha or bodhisattva.

This can force us to confront what we think is magical or supernatural and why. I might say that a person has a certain vibe. They put people at ease when they're around or maybe they make things awkward wherever they go. Is this a magical power they have? If you quote a movie or song in a conversation, you invoke the mood of that movie or song and so change the feeling of the conversation. Have you cast a magical spell in saying those words? One way to make sense of sacred speech that doesn't appeal to anything magical is to try to understand it as working in ways similar to other speech that changes the world.

An important theme in many of these practices is what you can accomplish with your own effort. Many Buddhists who say the *nembutsu*, for example, think that nowadays it's impossible to know the historical Buddha's teachings. This history of Buddhism, as they see it, is like children playing a game of telephone: Even if people genuinely wanted to preserve what the Buddha said, after thousands of years of translating, copying, and summarizing, Buddhist teachings are too garbled for anyone to make sense of. So, at least in our time, there's nothing we can do to see reality as it is; we can only rely on the compassionate help of Amida. Enlightenment is in a way difficult and easy at the same time. It's impossible to achieve by studying the jumble of Buddhist teachings that have been handed down to us. But thanks to Amida, it's easy because you can simply say the *nembutsu* and take a shortcut to enlightenment through his Pure Land.

Many modern Buddhists feel this cheapens Buddhism. Rather than an intricate and subtle system of philosophy and mental development, it's a rote practice that relies on faith. There's nothing you can do at all to solve the problem, and even for those who think you're supposed to say the *nembutsu* with faith, even that faith isn't something you can decide to have. Part of this reaction is social. People who left religions that place an emphasis on faith and rote recitations are disappointed to find that those things exist in the Buddhist world too.

So even if a faith-based Buddhism isn't to your taste, you can find a practical lesson here. Many goals are achieved through your own deliberate hard work. You go to the gym every day and you start getting stronger. You do a French lesson several times a week and you get better at speaking French. But not all goals work this way. Sometimes trying hard at something makes you *less* likely to succeed. The harder you try to relax, the more tense you become. The more you try to fall asleep, the further restful sleep slips away from you.

Some aspects of seeing reality clearly can be like this. Some things you can only see from a calm and relaxed state of mind. So what do you do when you want to relax? You don't try harder and harder to force yourself into a relaxed state, but instead do things that take your mind off the goal altogether. You read an absorbing book, take a bath, bake a cake. You do something you like that involves no longer thinking about relaxation.

For some, enlightenment works in just this way. If you set your mind on it as a goal and try really hard to work toward it, you're less likely to get there. Like relaxing, it can be so easy that it's hard. If you just put it out of your mind and do something else, you can get there. Like something lost in plain sight, you'll find it easily once you stop looking so intently. So one way to understand how the *nembutsu* works is to think that Amida really helps you. But you might also see it as a tool to help you achieve a special state that you can't aim at directly. Counting sheep might help you fall asleep, not because of anything special about sheep, but because it helps you stop obsessing about getting to sleep. You might think that Amida doesn't help you get enlightened any more than sheep help you fall asleep—they just help you get out of your own way.

This is a broad obstacle in all types of Buddhist practice. The goal can be self-undermining. You start getting hung up on avoiding hang-ups and stuck on not being stuck on things. Seeing enlightenment as a separate, distant goal is like looking all over for your glasses when they're right there on your head. The more you search, the more tense you get and the less able you are to realize they've been with you the entire time. Some people try so hard to have a fun vacation that it spoils their vacation. Their idea of a "fun vacation" is a separate and distant abstraction, one that prevents them from seeing that the fun vacation could be right here if they'd just quit trying so hard.

One family of solutions to this obstacle is to just *stop*. Stop trying so hard to solve the problem. Stop with the philosophy, the texts, the techniques. Just say a phrase over and over. Don't think about what it means or how it works. Don't even try to make up some rationalization of its spiritual relevance. Sometimes trying itself reinforces the problem and doing practices like this can make you stop trying so hard to get where you already are.

33 | CLEARING YOUR MIND

Language and thought can be powerful tools to get things done in the world. They allow us to communicate with each other, predict what will happen, and question things. But like most tools, they're useful for some things and not for others. A wrench is great for tightening bolts but not for pounding in nails.

Many Buddhists have recognized that sometimes language and conceptual thought can be the wrong tool for seeing reality clearly. So, they've developed practices that aim at a direct experience of the world free from concepts and labels. As with other advanced practices, these often presume not only the direct supervision of a qualified teacher but also a solid foundation in other practices.

The Practices

You may have heard of koans before—questions like "What is the sound of one hand clapping?" They're an important practice in some schools of Zen Buddhism. A koan (pronounced *koh-an*) literally means a public record; they're like the casefiles of previous interactions between teachers and students. They're often in the form of vignettes of a back-and-forth with questions like "What is the Buddha?" being answered with "Three pounds of flax."

Koans have many uses and functions, some of which involve moving beyond language and concepts. Koans play an important role as a tool for the teacher to verify that a student has had a certain experience—that they've realized and internalized certain facts about the world. This isn't about whether or not they *know* these things intellectually, but whether they get them on a gut level. Though they might seem like riddles, they're not. Riddles are about wordplay, finding clever words to respond to a question. Koans aren't about being clever, at least not in an intellectual sense. They're more about breaking out of the realm that cleverness operates in.

Some emphasize their role in breaking you out of certain conceptual frameworks. Take, for example, the question "What is the Buddha?" This is a question about something spiritual and abstract. The answer, "Three pounds of flax," is about something material and concrete. In shifting the conversation, it illuminates and undermines an implicit distinction the question makes between Buddhist things and ordinary stuff. The question is a spiritual one, asked expecting a spiritual reply. In giving a reply in terms of ordinary, concrete things it undermines this expectation and the categories that produced it.

Koans can also serve to prompt other reflections. When you try to find an answer, what do you assume it will look like? *Who*, exactly, is doing the trying anyway? So even though there are answers, the real benefit comes from the experiences you have while struggling with them. Struggling to make sense of them can prompt you to other modes of experience, ones that don't rely on concepts and words.

Another practice important in Zen Buddhism is called *zazen*—literally sitting Zen. It's typically done while seated on a special cushion in a particular way, but you can get by with any quiet and calm place where you can sit with an upright posture. You begin by fixing your awareness on your breath, not by counting breaths but simply starting with your awareness there. As you breathe, you let your mind settle and your thoughts melt away. When thoughts occur you just let them go on their own.

As your mind settles, your awareness becomes sharper. Your experience isn't filtered through a constant series of thoughts and your mind isn't crowded by a stream of self-narration. Instead, as you breathe and calm down, you start to experience directly what is happening. This experience isn't one of labeling and categorizing things, but a sensitivity to what's really going on.

A Tibetan tradition called *Dzogchen*, meaning great perfection, involves somewhat similar practices. Here the perfection is Buddha Nature, and realizing it means getting past conceptual thought. Some of these practices are types of seated meditation, but other variations involve staying in complete darkness or gazing at the sky. They all aim at a kind of non-distracted openness, a way of being sensitive and receptive to what is happening. This doesn't always mean being free from *conceptual thought* but rather free from its *distorting effects*. Even when you have a thought, you will immediately get that it's empty. It's less like focusing your attention on a particular object or acknowledging thoughts as they arise and more like a calm, direct awareness of emptiness and Buddha Nature.

In this receptive state you can see Buddha Nature more directly—not as an object of experience, but as the *precondition of any experience at all*. It's less like something you look at, like a cat or a tree, and more like realizing something about your vision itself. In this way, Buddha Nature is a little like a watermark that is impressed upon all of our experiences, though since it too is empty it's a watermark without an intrinsic essence.

Most generally, these techniques aim at getting into a particular calm and receptive state of mind, free from the misleading effects of thought and categorization. In this state you can better realize that *all* experiences are empty. Since they're relational and impermanent, they all contain the key to solving the problem. You can then realize that enlightenment, solving the problem, isn't some separate goal but was right there all along, imprinted on each and every experience you've had. They're all empty of intrinsic nature and so are *you*.

It's important to keep in mind that though these practices aim at getting into a special state of mind, you can't keep that in your head as a goal while you do them. In this sense it's a little like the goal of having fun. We often do things in order to have fun, to be in a special emotional state. But if you keep that goal in mind—if, with every joke and conversation at the party, you have it in your head that you're doing this all *in order to have fun*—you won't have very much fun at all.

These practices can work in a similar way. The point is to have a direct experience of reality, to see intellectual thought and categorizations for what they really are. But to aim at that state as a goal *is* to categorize things; it distinguishes a certain state as a special one, better than the others. Like having fun, even though that might be the goal, having it in mind can spoil your chance of actually experiencing it.

The Purpose

Thinking involves labels and categories. It means classifying things, dividing up the world into this and that. It means making a mental map of things, drawing lines and adding labels. You see a thing on the table and think to yourself, "Hey, there's a pen." In that simple thought you're grouping a bunch of things together. That thing on the table is mentally grouped with a bunch of other things you've seen and used. It's similar to some things (pencils and markers) and different from others (emotions, numbers, and cars). It's part of a category of things and you immediately relate to it as something you can grab or something you can use for certain tasks, like signing your name or drawing a cat.

We project these categories onto the world for a simple reason: It makes it *much* easier to get around. When you go into the store you know which aisle to look for a pen in because you know what kind of thing it is. You can know what to grab from the desk when you need to write something down even without stopping to think, because you've developed this mental habit of sorting the things that are around you. This is incredibly useful and makes getting through life much easier.

This is how thought and language work—they're ways of mapping the world, of drawing lines and adding labels so we can sort things easily and get around more efficiently. As with other maps, they can help us to navigate and coordinate really well. They help us to predict and plan, too. If someone says they'll bring me a pen, I can be pretty sure they won't come back with a boat or a grapefruit.

Even though words and concepts can be useful, they can get in the way too. If you spend a long time looking at maps, you can be startled to see that the world is nowhere near as neat as it seems on paper. It's just dirt and water out there, no stark black lines or labels at all. It's not just the lack of lines and labels—it's that the real boundaries that seemed so clear-cut on the map are murky, vague, and constantly changing.

As with lines on a map, these categories aren't really static, independent features of the world, but reflections of who we are and what our needs are. If we had claws instead of hands or weren't the kinds of beings that needed to write things down, we wouldn't have the idea of a pen at all. If we didn't need to eat we wouldn't have any of the various categories of foods. This by itself isn't a problem. The problem comes when we mistake categories that depend on us for independent features of the world.

Words and ideas can trick us into assuming the world fundamentally has the divisions that we project onto it with our concepts. Having words for colors can be useful, but you might start assuming that there are only as many colors out there as there are names for them. But in reality there's a full spectrum of colors in the world, many more than we could ever name. It's useful to talk about a team, but such talk can make you forget that it's just a collection of players and nothing more. What started as a conventional tool for getting around gets mistaken for the way the world really is.

Buddhists who are most interested in this, particularly the tradition known as Chan in China and Zen in Japan, often tell a certain story about the Buddha. (There's no evidence of this episode in early Buddhist texts, so historians think the story was made up by later Chinese Buddhists. But that doesn't really matter—just because the story might be newer doesn't mean it isn't insightful.) The story goes like this: One day the Buddha was getting ready to teach his students and everyone was gathered, waiting for him to speak. But after arriving, he didn't say anything. Without a word, he picked up a white flower and held it out. Everybody was confused except for one student. He alone smiled because he got what the Buddha was trying to communicate.

What this student understood was that *anything* the Buddha might have said would have involved arbitrary conceptual divisions of the world. That particular white flower, that exact experience of it, couldn't be captured with words. The Buddha didn't want to convey the *idea* of a flower, but a *direct experience*. He understood that words and thinking are conventional—they're a simplification we agree on in order to get by in the world. But if you step out of that convention, you can more directly interact with the world as it really is.

This can sound pretty mysterious, but it's similar to more mundane experiences. Sometimes lacking categories can allow for a more direct interaction. Think about seeing a movie or concert. If you've read a lot of articles and reviews before you see it, they can get in the way of your experience. While you're watching, everything you see and hear gets filtered through all things you've already read. All those ideas and opinions rattling around in your brain get in the way of actually experiencing the movie or the music. For some Buddhists, conceptual thought can work like that—it can get in the way and distract from what is really going on.

A related danger is that we begin to focus on our ideas and words at the expense of the real world. A classic image in Zen Buddhism that illustrates this is that of a finger pointing at the moon. Suppose you're walking with a friend and see a huge full moon in the sky. You try to point it out to your friend, but they turn and look closely at your finger. They've completely missed the point. You were just using your finger to gesture at *the moon*—your finger was just a means to point it out. This is what happens with our concepts. They're meant to point us toward reality, but, like the hapless friend, we get fixated on the concepts themselves instead of what they point at.

This is easiest to see with symbolic things. A diploma is a symbol of the knowledge someone has gained, but people get fixated on having the diploma and forget about the actual knowledge. They focus on getting a piece of paper and showing it off. A wedding ring is a symbol of love but people get fixated on a piece of jewelry while ignoring the love that it's supposed to symbolize. Like the finger, there's nothing wrong with these symbols; they can often be very useful. The problem comes when we forget what they really are and become engrossed in them at the expense of the things they symbolize.

These practices aim to produce and sustain certain kinds of experiences. It's important to distinguish how experiences are different from ideas and conceptions. Think about the difference between liking camping and liking the *idea* of camping. You can like one without really liking the other. One is an abstract idea and the other is something you actually do, an experience you have. These practices try to break you out of seeing enlightenment as an abstract idea and instead force you to embody it as a lived experience.

Think of how this works with emptiness. Emptiness can be an abstract idea: the idea that everything exists only relationally and lacks any independent essence. This is exactly how it was presented earlier in this very book, as a claim made in words that can be evaluated as true or false. The world is either like that or it isn't. But emptiness can also be understood as an experience. It's something you directly perceive, something that can't really be expressed with words or ideas. In the same way that you experience pain or a sunny day, you can experience the relational nature of the world. Both can be important, but knowing the idea and even thinking that it's true doesn't guarantee the experience.

This is why the writing produced in these Buddhist traditions can seem odd. It can be frustrating when the writers don't come out and say directly what they want to say. They use metaphorical language and confusing stories about teachers and students. What the heck does "three pounds of flax" mean? How is *that* the Buddha? The reason that they write in this style is not to give you a certain idea or even defend that idea as true, but to push you toward having a certain *experience*.

We often resort to metaphors when we try to talk about experiences, even mundane ones. Suppose you want to describe the taste of wasabi or hot sauce to someone who has never eaten anything even remotely spicy. You can find yourself saying things like, "It's like a tingle in your nose and then makes your tongue feel like an inflatable raft that's being pricked with tiny pins, but in a good way." This is even more difficult as the experience gets more complicated. Think of what you might say when trying to explain to someone who has never been through a bad breakup *what it feels like* to go through one. There it's even more tempting to say things like, "It felt like my heart was in a vise. It was like there was this black cloud following me everywhere." Things get metaphorical very quickly.

Of course these techniques aren't just trying to *describe* a certain experience; they're trying to *induce* it. This explains why the style can be indirect and enigmatic. Imagine you're with friends and someone cracks a joke but the person standing next to you doesn't get it. A bad thing to do in this situation is to *explain* the joke to them. If you do that, it spoils the joke because it robs them of the experience of getting it. They'll at best understand it in an intellectual way, but they'll miss much of the humor. A better approach is to say things that will nudge them in ways that help them *to see it for themselves*. What you say might be quite cryptic, but the point isn't to *explain* why the joke is funny, it's to get them to have a certain experience of realizing something for themselves. Buddhists in these traditions are often doing the same thing, just with a very different experience. What they say is cryptic and oblique because it's supposed to nudge you toward *having the experience for yourself*.

When thinking about indescribable experiences it's important to be careful about presupposing a universal character that might not be there. When different people talk about something that can't be described, it's tempting to assume that they're all talking about *the same* indescribable thing. But that isn't necessarily so. The taste of a bite of filet mignon is indescribable; it's an experience that can't be fully captured in words. But so is the taste of dogshit. Despite the fact that both experiences are indescribable, dogshit *isn't* filet mignon. They are very different experiences. So when people talk about non-conceptual reality or experiences, don't be too quick to assume that their experience is the same indescribable one that you or others have had.

These practices attempt to go beyond words and ideas and emphasize direct experience, but it would be wrong to assume that this entails a more general anti-intellectualism. Both the *Dzogchen* and Zen traditions have a huge number of important philosophical and literary texts. These texts are often scholastic and rely on a network of specialized philosophical and psychological concepts. They don't hate thinking. They simply point out its limitations: what it's good for and what it's not. We can use words to talk about the limits of what words can do. After all, if I've managed to explain anything at all in this chapter, I did it using words.

34 | GETTING OVER YOURSELF

Buddhism is about solving a problem. A persistent buzz that's sometimes quiet and barely noticeable, sometimes shrill and piercing. But getting rid of it isn't always pleasant and even the buzz itself can be comforting. I once worked the night shift at a grocery store. One night the alarm on the safe malfunctioned and was stuck on. For seven or eight hours, there was a constant high-pitched shriek throughout the store. When the morning manager finally arrived with the key and fixed it, I felt relief but also kind of empty. Over the course of my shift, I got used to the noise and now that it was gone I kind of missed it. Quieting the buzz of suffering can be the same. You're much better off without it, but it can be tough when you're so used to hearing it.

In this book I've tried to explain some of the range and variety of Buddhist thought and practice. In doing so, I've inevitably given my own spin on things. I've emphasized the aspects that I find reasonable and given interpretations that make sense to me. Much of this should be understood as how a modern American philosopher makes sense of Buddhism.

Of course, my take isn't the only one. I've also tried to be honest about ideas and practices in Buddhism that don't fit with this way of understanding it—for example, practices that rely on supernatural forces. I've suggested ways of approaching such ideas and practices that adapt them while staying true to the underlying spirit, but this is just one take and a modern one at that.

Buddhist writing is often full of polemics, people defending their vision of what Buddhism should be. When reading these, rather than police what "real" Buddhism is, it's more rewarding and illuminating to think about *why* a particular writer defends their version of Buddhism. If certain aspects rub you the wrong way, reflect on why that's so. Maybe it's because it really is wrong or mistaken. Or maybe it's a view you never considered, and you need to change your own outlook. Buddhism is a big tent with a lot of ideas—that's what makes it fun and rewarding to explore.

I've explained a lot of different practices, and it's important to keep in mind that *nobody* does *all* of them. There's also a huge variety of medical treatments and exercises, but nobody does *all* of those either. Which treatments someone does depends on where and when they live, their particular medical issues, and what actually works for them. That doesn't mean that it's a free-for-all when it comes to medical treatments, but it does mean that you have to be thoughtful and careful about selecting a course of treatment. The same is true of Buddhist practice. There are lots of options and what works for you will depend on a lot of variables.

It can be tough, especially when *reading* about Buddhist practice, to remember that practice is *practical*. It can be easy to get sucked into fine distinctions between the special states of mind you can achieve, various technical terms, and the long histories of particular Buddhist techniques. Learning that stuff can be illuminating and worthwhile, but it's not the same as doing it. Learning about how running shoes are made isn't running. Sorting through recipes isn't cooking. Studying ideas about Buddhist practice isn't practicing.

Practices sometimes work the same way as philosophy—they help you see something about the world that you couldn't see before. But much of the time practice is less about learning and more about absorbing, internalizing, and getting comfortable with what you've already learned. Practicing the piano might illuminate some features of music theory, but it's mostly about getting your hands used to making the right sounds. Knowing some music theory might help, but if you already know how the song goes, you practice it so that playing it becomes second nature.

For Dogen, a famous Japanese Buddhist philosopher, *anything* you do can be a form of Buddhist practice as long as you do it with the right mindset. He wrote about things like brushing your teeth and bathing not just as advice on personal hygiene but also to demonstrate how even these everyday actions can help change your orientation to the world. You can reflect on the body's composite nature as you wash it or on how ideas of clean and dirty are relational qualities and so are empty of intrinsic nature. Or you can take it as an opportunity to experience the feel of the water without any conceptualization, noticing how it appears and fades away.

This counters a temptation to think of practice as something formal, something that happens *only* at a meditation center, temple, or at least a special cushion in your house. But ideally, Buddhist practice isn't limited to these sacred domains; it's everything you do in your life. It's not just about how you meditate or prostrate to a statue, but how you talk to a waiter, how you treat a cat you meet, how you take a shower.

This can sound overwhelming, but Dogen's insight is that practice isn't something you do in order to reach enlightenment—it *is* enlightenment. Think about someone dancing, not formally as a ballerina or in a tango class, but just having a good time while listening to music they love. Their dancing isn't a means to reaching some separate state of having fun—the dancing *is* the fun. Like dancing and fun, you can understand practice and enlightenment as being deeply intertwined. This can make it feel less overwhelming when *anything* you do can be Buddhist practice.

In addition to different ideas and practices, Buddhism attracts a lot of different personality types. Some are hard-nosed and philosophical, saying things like, "All you are is a heap of mental and physical events." Others are warm and fuzzy and are more apt to say stuff like, "May the Dharma nourish you and bring you bliss." For others it's familial: "Grandma wants us to stop by the temple on the way to the wedding." And, of course, others are bookish scholars, who are much more long-winded and often say technical stuff that's inaccessible to all but the most studious Buddhists, stuff like, "Though not prominent in Vasubandhu's *Abhidharmakośakārikā*, his later treatment of *aṣṭa vijñānakāyāḥ*, particularly *ālāyavijñāna*, prefigures how it's taken up by subsequent Yogācāra thinkers." These are all Buddhists, even though they each relate to Buddhism in *very* different ways.

In exploring Buddhism there are plenty of mistakes to make; I know because I've made most of them. In the interest of saving you time and energy, please be careful. Be careful of keeping Buddhism weird, strange, or distant. People come to Buddhism in different ways, sometimes because it's different from what they're used to, sometimes because of family heritage. But understanding it means coming to see that it's a normal and meaningful way for people to relate to the world.

Be careful of dismissing what some people do as an unimportant ritual. Especially if you're new or an outsider, it can be tempting to call whatever you don't understand a ritual. It's easy to think that just because something isn't meaningful to *you*, it's therefore devoid of meaning. Part of understanding Buddhism means coming to see how what didn't make sense to you at the start, what seemed strange and merely ceremonial, can be an important and meaningful act.

Also be careful of thinking that you know more than you do. It's all too easy to read a few books, find a practice that works for you, and then feel like you've discovered the *true essence* of Buddhism. It's absurd to think that in a few short years, by reading only translations, you've discovered what others have missed for thousands of years. There's a lot to learn and discover in the Buddhist world, and the more you know the more it starts to feel like there is no such essence.

Finally, be careful of projecting your hopes and ideals onto Buddhism. The Buddhist world, like any world, contains a lot. Some of it is bad: There's sexism, abuse, and dogmatism. Some of it is good: There's understanding, compassion, and help. Part of what Buddhism illuminates is our tendency to inject ourselves in subtle ways into what happens around us. Our sense of self colors our experiences, thoughts, and feelings. We make things about ourselves even when we don't realize it consciously. It's all too easy to make this same mistake with Buddhism itself.

Nevertheless, the heart of Buddhism, if there is such a thing, is recalibrating how we relate to ourselves and to the world. It's about confronting unpleasant realities directly, with an attitude of problem solving. It's about acknowledging these things and, rather than living in denial, forging a way of life in light of them. Yes, our thoughts, feelings, habits, and perceptions are fundamentally mistaken, but they can be fixed.

There are lots of different takes in Buddhism about what exactly the world is like and how exactly to go about recalibrating our experience of it. But there is widespread agreement that our intuitive way of relating to life is broken. We get in our own way, in large part because we think of ourselves as persisting, separate entities. Recalibration in this sense means not just changing your self-image but getting past the idea of a self-image altogether.

It's about getting over yourself. This means losing the habit of seeing the world through the lens of a self. This habit can appear in different ways. One is through pride or arrogance. This leads you to separate others into losers and rivals, preventing you from connecting with them. You're so worried about coming out on top that you can't appreciate the goodness in others.

A self-centered outlook can also come in the form of insecurity. Someone constantly stewing in their own shortcomings or the opportunities they missed out on is also experiencing life as primarily about themselves. Some people hate going to museums because they constantly worry about how they appear to others, about whether they linger too long on the wrong paintings or move too fast past brilliant ones. The reality is that most people don't care at all about how other people look at the paintings in a museum. In assuming that everyone in the museum cares about how *you* look at the paintings, you actually miss out on a valuable experience. Here you are in a building full of wonderful art and you can't really enjoy it because you're too wrapped up in your self-image.

Understanding, not just intellectually but viscerally, that you are a composite, relational, and impermanent thing can help to dissolve these barriers and allow you to more fully engage with the world. Sure it makes the applause you get feel less thrilling, but it cuts the roots of a lot of mental habits that are painful and isolating: insecurity, failure, ideas about how "your life" is supposed to go—these all get exposed as deeply mistaken.

There are a bunch of games we play in life. For the most part, you'll still have to play them. You still have all the roles you had before, you still do the jobs you did before. But when you start taking on the root of the problem, you start relating to them very differently. You don't fall under their spell and mistake them for what's really happening; you don't take them as seriously as you used to. You still play the games, but you see them for what they really are.

Solving the problem makes life feel different, but also the same. You still wait in line, brush your teeth, catch up with an old friend, but these things take on a different tone. You see that so much about how you felt about yourself and the world was built on a mistake. Getting over this mistake means interacting with others and facing obstacles without being haunted by the ghost of a self. It means living without the selfishness, insecurity, and fear that this ghost brings with it. You still succeed and fail, but these things mean something different now. It means getting out of your own way and finally quieting that damn buzz.

FURTHER READING

If you're interested in reading more about Buddhism, here are some suggestions about where to start. For classic texts, I've recommended particular translations and secondary sources that are useful starting places. For particular techniques, I've suggested prominent books that explain them in detail. Foreign terms, especially from Indian languages, often use special diacritical marks. I did not use them in the book, but I've included them here to make it easier to find what you're looking for.

IMPORTANT BUDDHIST TEXTS

The Pāli Canon

This isn't a single text but a huge collection of the earliest Buddhist teachings. Written in an Indian literary language called Pāli, it's divided into three sections: the *vinaya* (rules of monks and nuns), the *sūttas* (recorded teachings of the Buddha), and the *abhidhamma* (scholastic work in philosophy and psychology). It's a huge collection of texts but you can find many free English translations at www.accesstoinsight.org. The *suttas*, the recorded teachings of the Buddha, are divided into five collections called *nikayas*. The best translations to get are those published by Wisdom Publications.

The Dhammapada

This is part of the Pāli Canon but is a concise and poetic text covering a wide range of Buddhist teachings. It's one of the most famous Buddhist texts and very accessible to beginners. It's been translated many times. Translations by Ananda Maitreya (2001, Parallax Press) and Valerie Roebuck (2010, Penguin) are good places to start.

Path of Purification (Visuddhimagga) by Buddhaghosa

Written by the famous fifth-century Sri Lankan scholar Buddhaghosa, this is one of the most important sources for theory and practice in Theravada Buddhism. Very long and systematic, it includes many meditative practice and philosophical ideas; this is a systematic manual for coming to see reality as it is. It is freely available at accesstoinsight.org. The translation by Bhikkhu Ñanamoli (Pariyatti, 2003) is very detailed, though at over 900 pages, it isn't for the faint of heart.

Words of My Perfect Teacher (Kun bzang bla ma'i zhal lung) by Patrul Rinpoche

A very popular overview of the Buddhist path by a famous Tibetan teacher. Written in Tibet in the 1800s it is full of stories, anecdotes, and analogies to illustrate the ideas and practices it explains. The translation by the Padmakara Translation Group (Yale, 2010) is clear and accurate. For those who are very interested, Khenpo Ngawang Pelzang's *A Guide to the Words of My Perfect Teacher* (Shambhala, 2004) provides a chapter-by-chapter commentary. It's helpful but not necessary in order to read the original.

Questions of King Milinda (Milinda Pañha)

Written around 100 or 200 CE, this text is a dialogue between a Greek king (known in Greek as Menander and in Pāli as Milinda) and a Buddhist monk named Nāgasena. The back-and-forth is an interesting read and includes discussion of various philosophical topics often explained with easy-to-follow analogies. Existing English translations are a bit dated but still worth reading: There is one done by Rhys Davids in the late 1800s and one by I. B. Horner done in the 1960s. Both are available from various publishers.

The Way of the Bodhisattva (Bodhicaryāvatāra) by Śāntideva

This text, written in India in the 700s, is widely studied in the Tibetan tradition. It is a classic guide to becoming a bodhisattva and touches on ethics, psychology, and metaphysics. It has many good translations, though with different titles. The Padmakara Translation Group's *The Way of the Bodhisattva* (Shambhala, 1997) is clear and very accessible. Vesna Wallace and B. Alan Wallace's *A Guide to the Bodhisattva Way of Life* (Snow Lion, 1997) includes footnotes comparing the Sanskrit and Tibetan version. Kate Crosby and

Andrew Skilton's *The Bodhicaryāvatāra* (Oxford, 1995) gives more historical context. Whatever translation you read, the Tibetan commentary *The Nectar of Manjushri's Speech* (Shambhala, 2010) will help you to better understand what the text means.

Heart Sutra (*Prajñāpāramitāhṛdaya Sūtra*)

The full title is *The Heart of the Perfection of Wisdom*, but it's most commonly known simply as the *Heart Sutra*. This text is not only one of the most famous Buddhist texts in the world, but it's also one of the shortest. Dealing with emptiness, the entire text can easily fit on a single page and is often memorized and recited. Since it is so terse, it's important to read it with a commentary. Fortunately many are available: Donald Lopez's *Elaborations on Emptiness* (Princeton, 1998) includes various Indian and Tibetan commentaries. The 14th Dalai Lama's *Essence of the Heart Sutra* (Wisdom, 2005) and Sonam Rinchen's *The Heart Sutra* (Snow Lion, 2003) are both very good contemporary Tibetan commentaries. Doosun Yoo's *Thunderous Silence* (Wisdom, 2013) is a commentary from a Korean Buddhist perspective.

Fundamental Verses on the Middle Way (*Mūlamadhyamakakārikā*) by Nāgārjuna

A difficult, dense classic on emptiness and the two truths. Written by one of the most famous Buddhist philosophers, this text is important in the Tibetan, Chinese, and Japanese traditions. It's impossible to understand without a guide: Jay Garfield's *The Fundamental Wisdom of the Middle Way* (Oxford, 1995) gives a translation and philosophical commentary that makes it much more accessible. Though not limited to this particular text, Jan Westerhoff's *Nāgārjuna's Madhyamaka* (Oxford, 2009) presents a clear explanation of the key ideas.

The Platform Sutra (*Liùzŭ Tánjīng*)

The full title is *Sutra from the High Seat of the Dharma Treasure*, but it's more often known as the *Sutra of Hui Neng* or *The Platform Sutra*. It tells the life story of an important early Zen Buddhist master named Hui Neng and contains main insights about Buddhist philosophy and practice. Philip B. Yampolsky's translation (Columbia, 2012) is the most scholarly. The translation by Red Pine (Counterpoint, 2008) is more poetic and includes an explanatory commentary. Shodo Harada's *Not One Single Thing* (Wisdom, 2018) also provides a very clear translation and explanation of the text.

The Lotus Sutra (Saddharma Puṇḍarīka Sūtra)

The full title is *The Discourse on the White Lotus of the True Dharma*, but it's most commonly known simply as the *Lotus Sutra*. One of the most famous and revered Buddhist texts in East Asia, this text is full of interesting parables and striking poetic imagery. The translation by Burton Watson (Columbia, 1993) is the best place to start, and Donald Lopez's *The Lotus Sūtra: A Biography* (Princeton, 2016) gives a clear and entertaining introduction to this famous text.

Shōbōgenzō by Dōgen

The title means *The Treasury of the True Dharma Eye*, but it's more commonly referred to by its untranslated Japanese title. Written by the famous thirteenth-century Buddhist Dōgen, it is one of the most important texts in Japanese Buddhism. A large collection of shorter essays, it offers both interesting philosophical ideas while maintaining a focus on concrete practice. The size of the collection can make it hard to approach so it's best to start with an edited translation. Waddell and Abe's *The Heart of Dōgen's Shōbōgenzō* (State University of New York Press, 2002) and Thomas Cleary's *Shōbōgenzō: Zen Essays by Dōgen* (Hawaii, 1986) are good places to start.

THE LIFE OF THE BUDDHA

The Life of the Buddha by Bhikkhu Ñāṇamoli (Buddhist Publication Society, 2001)

This version of the Buddha's life takes descriptions of events from various texts and places them in chronological order to form a scholarly, responsible, but readable telling of the historical Buddha's life.

Buddha by Osamu Tezuka (Vertical, 2017)

Originally published in the 1970s and '80s, this is an epic story inspired by the life of the Buddha in comic form. By the master of Japanese comics, it spans eight volumes, and though it often takes liberties with the story, it's a moving and warm reinterpretation.

Sugata Saurabha by Chittadhar Hṛdaya (Oxford University Press, 2010)

The title in English would be *The Sweet Fragrance of the Buddha*; this wonderful epic poem was written in Nepal in the 1940s and translated by Todd T. Lewis and Subarna Man Tuladhar. It is a telling of the Buddha's life that is at once both modern and classical.

Jātaka-Mālā

Usually translated as *The Jataka Tales*, this is a collection of several hundred fables of the previous lives of the Buddha. A complete translation takes up many volumes, but many editions of selected stories are available. Sara Janet Shaw's translation (Penguin, 2007) is a good place to start.

PARTICULAR BUDDHIST TECHNIQUES

Mindfulness and Vipassana

A great starting place for mindfulness meditation is Thich Nhat Hanh's modern classic *The Miracle of Mindfulness* (Beacon, 1999). A less Buddhist and more secular version of mindfulness techniques is presented in Jon Kabat-Zinn's *Wherever You Go There You Are* (Hachette, 2005). William Hart's *The Art of Living* (HarperOne, 2009) gives a clear introduction to the vipassana style of Buddhist meditation as taught by the modern teacher S. N. Goenka.

Lojong/Mind Training

These Tibetan texts offer a huge range of imaginative techniques to change your outlook. *Mind Training: The Great Collection* (Wisdom, 2006) edited by Thubten Jinpa is a very complete collection of primary texts and commentaries. Traleg Kyabgon's *The Practice of Lojong* (Shambhala, 2007) and Gomo Tulku's *Becoming a Child of the Buddhas* (Wisdom, 1998) both offer more digestible introductions.

Zen/Chan

Thich Thien-An's *Zen Philosophy, Zen Practice* (Dharma, 1975) gives a good introduction to Zen ideas and practice. Katsuki Sekida's *Zen Training*

(Shambhala, 2005) is an accessible handbook for Zazen or sitting Zen practice. Isshū Miura and Ruth Fuller Sasaki's *The Zen Koan* (Mariner, 1966) gives a good overview of the history and purpose of koan practice.

Pure Land

Taitetsu Unno's *River of Fire, River of Water* (Image, 1998) is a good introduction to Japanese Pure Land Buddhist practice. Kaspalita Thompson and Satya Robyn's *Just as You Are* (Woodsmoke, 2015) also offers an accessible introduction to Pure Land Buddhist practice.

CONTEMPORARY WORK ABOUT BUDDHISM

Land of No Buddha by Richard Hayes (Windhorse, 1998)

A collection of moving and reflective essays by an American Buddhist philosopher written in a straightforward and direct style.

Indian Buddhist Philosophy by Amber Carpenter (Routledge, 2014)

A very clear introduction to Indian Buddhism presenting Buddhist arguments for and against various philosophical positions and places them in the broader cultural context.

Buddhism as Philosophy by Mark Siderits (Hackett, 2007)

A clear explanation of arguments from Buddhist philosophy, often including passages from the primary texts where they're found.

The Making of Buddhist Modernism by David McMahon (Oxford, 2008)

An insightful analysis of the rise of modern, scientific forms of Buddhism and their interactions with previously existing Buddhist traditions. An essential read if you want to understand a range of debates within Buddhism.

Mindful America by Jeff Wilson (Oxford, 2014)

An interesting and insightful history of the reception and development of mindfulness in America. Essential to read if you are interested in mindfulness practices.

Seeing through Zen by John McRae (California, 2003)

A very clear introduction to the history of Zen and Chan Buddhism.

INDEX

For the benefit of digital users, indexed terms that span two pages (e.g., 52–53) may, on occasion, appear on only one of those pages.